World War II in Global
Perspective, 1931–1953

WILEY SHORT HISTORIES

General Editor: Catherine A. Epstein

This series provides concise, lively introductions to key topics in history. Designed to encourage critical thinking and an engagement in debate, the books demonstrate the dynamic process through which history is constructed, in both popular imagination and scholarship. The volumes are written in an accessible style, offering the ideal entry point to the field.

Published

World War II in Global Perspective, 1931–1953: A Short History
Andrew N. Buchanan

A History of the Cuban Revolution, 2nd Edition
Aviva Chomsky

Vietnam: Explaining America's Lost War, 2nd Edition
Gary R. Hess

A History of Modern Europe: From 1815 to the Present
Albert S. Lindemann

Perspectives on Modern South Asia: A Reader in Culture, History, and Representation
Kamala Visweswaran

Nazi Germany: Confronting the Myths
Catherine Epstein

World War I: A Short History
Tammy M. Proctor

World War II in Global Perspective, 1931–1953

A Short History

Andrew N. Buchanan

WILEY Blackwell

This edition first published 2019
© 2019 John Wiley & Sons, Inc.

The right of Andrew N. Buchanan to be identified as the author of this work has been asserted in accordance with law.

Registered Office
John Wiley & Sons, Inc., 111 River Street, Hoboken, NJ 07030, USA
John Wiley & Sons Ltd, The Atrium, Southern Gate, Chichester, West Sussex, PO19 8SQ, UK

Editorial Office
350 Main Street, Malden, MA 02148-5020, USA

For details of our global editorial offices, customer services, and more information about Wiley products visit us at www.wiley.com.

Wiley also publishes its books in a variety of electronic formats and by print-on-demand. Some content that appears in standard print versions of this book may not be available in other formats.

Library of Congress Cataloging-in-Publication Data
Names: Buchanan, Andrew, N., 1958- author.
Title: World War II in global perspective, 1931–1953: A Short History / Andrew N. Buchanan.
Description: First edition. | Hoboken, NJ : Wiley-Blackwell, 2019. |
   Series: Wiley short histories | Includes bibliographical references and index. |
   Identifiers: LCCN 2018042186 (print) | LCCN 2018043500 (ebook) |
   ISBN 9781119366119 (Adobe PDF) | ISBN 9781119366089 (ePub) |
   ISBN 9781119366072 (hardback) | ISBN 9781119366096 (paperback)
Subjects: LCSH: World War, 1939-1945. | BISAC: HISTORY / Military / General.
Classification: LCC D743 (ebook) | LCC D743 .B74 2019 (print) | DDC 940.53–dc23
LC record available at https://lccn.loc.gov/2018042186

Cover Design: Wiley
Cover Image: © Imperial War Museum (SE 3640)
The British commander and Indian crew of a Sherman tank of the 9th Royal Deccan Horse, 255th Indian Tank Brigade, encounter an elephant on the road to Meiktila, 29 March 1945

Set in 10/12.5pt Bembo by SPi Global, Pondicherry, India

Printed in Singapore by C.O.S. Printers Pte Ltd

10 9 8 7 6 5 4 3 2 1

To Mary Nell

Young Alexander conquered India.
Was he alone?
Caesar defeated the Gauls.
Did he not have so much as a cook with him?
Philip of Spain wept when his armada
Went down. Did no one else weep?
Frederick the Second was victorious in the Seven Years' War.
Who else
Prevailed?

from "Questions of a Worker Who Reads"
by Bertolt Brecht

Contents

List of Illustrations

Maps

Figures

Acknowledgments

This book was made possible by the contributions of numerous students, colleagues, and friends. It benefited – whether they know it or not – from the collective participation of hundreds of students who have taken my class on World War II at the University of Vermont over the last 10 years. In particular, I would like to thank the students who took part in an informal seminar on the first few chapters: they include Alex Ellis, Colby Fisher, Sarah Jauris, Oliver Moore, and Jacob Reich. These undergraduates were joined by Bill Ryan and Richard Piliero, lifelong students who have audited my classes more times than they care to remember. A draft was discussed at an informal seminar held at the Grange Hall in my hometown of Whallonsburg over a long upstate New York winter: participants included: Andrea Barret, Mary-Nell Bockman, Ted Cornell, Barry Goldstein, Rev. Craig Hacker, Adam Reed, David Reuther, Margie Reuther, Bethany Teitelbaum, Richard Teitelbaum, and Colin Wells. I also thank Mike Baumann for his constructive criticism.

My colleagues in the History Department at the University of Vermont heard a paper on this project soon after I started writing, and their enthusiasm convinced me that I was on the right track. In particular my thanks go to Paul Deslandes, Erik Esselstrom, Melanie Gustafson, Jonathan Huener, Abby McGowan, Sarah Osten, Nicole Phelps, and Amani Whitfield for supplying all kinds of useful idea, insights, and information. I am also grateful to other scholars and friends who read and commented on all or part of the manuscript, including Tom Buchanan and Peter Wilson in Oxford, Marco Maria Aterrano in Naples, Pablo del Hierro in Maastricht, and Scott Waterman in Vermont. My thanks go to Ann Pfau for tracking down the image of the GI protests, to Capt. James C. Hare and the 57th Fighter Group Association for the picture of the Italian partisans in Verona, and Andrew Stewart for the Indian soldiers in Asmara. The maps are based on the orthoapsidal projection created by Erwin Raisz, and the base map was the work of Carlos Furuti; UVM student Max Muller added all the details. I thank them for their work. I am also indebted to series editor Catherine Epstein for her constant encouragement; to the three unknown scholars who reviewed and improved the manuscript; and to the production team at Wiley for their timely and accurate work: they include Janani Govindankutty and Shyamala Venkateswaran in India, Brigitte Lee Messenger in the UK, and Jennifer Manias in the United States.

Introduction

Matsushita Kazutoshi fought a very long war. Born in a fishing village on the Japanese island of Kyushu in 1923, Matsushita was conscripted into Japan's Kwantung Army in 1944. He took part in Operation *Ichigō*, the last and largest Japanese land offensive of the war in China. *Ichigō* dealt harsh blows to Chiang Kai-shek's Guomindang (Nationalist) army, but it also exhausted the Japanese. Matsushita deserted, only to be captured by the Guomindang, who enlisted him in their army. When civil war flared between the Guomindang and the Chinese Communist Party in 1946, Matsushita was captured again. This time, he joined the Communist-led People's Liberation Army (PLA). Matsushita was impressed by the way Communist fighters treated civilians, and he fought with the PLA until it defeated the Guomindang in 1949. Even then his war was not over. In 1950, Matsushita joined the Chinese People's Volunteer Force that crossed the frozen Yalu River to join North Korea in its war against the American-backed South. He fought in the brutal winter battles around the Changjin (Chosin) Reservoir and was eventually captured by the Americans in August 1951. He was a prisoner of war until the 1953 armistice. He finally returned home the following year, by which time his family had given him up for dead.

Matsushita's odyssey was truly remarkable. He was away for 10 years and served in three different armies before surrendering to a fourth. He fought in desperate battles, witnessed devastation on a vast scale, and participated in a world-changing revolution. Matsushita's journey was unique, but it also offers a concentrated reflection of the experiences of millions of people around the world. During the interlocking series of conflicts we know as World War II, "Burma Boys" from British-ruled West Africa fought with the British-Imperial

World War II in Global Perspective, 1931–1953: A Short History, First Edition. Andrew N. Buchanan.
© 2019 John Wiley & Sons, Inc. Published 2019 by John Wiley & Sons, Inc.

Army in Southeast Asia, some of them led by Polish officers. Punjabis from British-ruled India served in North Africa and Italy. Spanish volunteers crossed Europe to join Germany's war against the Soviet Union, where they joined tens of thousands of Romanians, Hungarians, and Italians. Brazilians fought alongside Americans in Italy, and a Mexican fighter squadron flew with the US Army Air Force in the Philippines. Farm girls from the American Midwest served with the Women's Army Corps from Berlin to Tokyo. Africans, Arabs, and Berbers from France's North and West African colonies spearheaded Allied campaigns in southern France, only to be unceremoniously pushed aside as the French Army was "whitened" by the inclusion of Resistance fighters. Poles captured by the Soviets in 1939 ended up fighting with the British in Italy and with the Red Army in the final attack on Berlin; some settled in Palestine and many made homes in Britain. One American soldier – Joe Beyrle – was captured by the Germans and then rescued from prison by the Soviet Red Army. He joined a Soviet tank unit and fought his way into Germany from the east under the command of a woman he knew simply as "Major."[1]

The fabric of this global conflict was woven from extended and entangled personal histories like these. Around the world, boys like my father imagined the interconnected story of which they were a part, studying the movement of armies by poring over maps in newspapers. Even under conditions of terrible persecution in the ghettos of German-occupied Poland, Jews like 18-year-old Dawid Sierakowiak followed the course of the war as best they could, piecing together scraps of information from clandestine British Broadcasting Corporation (BBC) radio broadcasts, scrounged newspapers, and overheard conversations among German soldiers. They studied the morale of soldiers heading for the front and they counted the wounded returning. Within days of the Allied victories at Stalingrad and Alamein, the news reached Sierakowiak's ghetto in Łódź, prompting secret celebrations. In August 1942, Sierakowiak reported "an incredible uplifting of spirits" as news of Partisan advances in Yugoslavia arrived, but he also reported his fear that Germany would "finish off the Jews in Europe before losing the war."[2] Intimately *connected* to the wider war, ghettoized Jews calculated what these faraway Allied victories meant for their own chances of survival.

These narratives challenge us to think about interconnection over space and about the meaning of events in one place for distant and seemingly unconnected people. But Matsushita's odyssey also prompts us to think about time. When he joined Japan's war of conquest in China in 1944, that struggle had been raging since Tokyo's conquest of Manchuria in 1931. And, as Matsushita discovered, the formal end of World War II brought no peace to much of Asia. National liberation movements in India, the Dutch East Indies, Burma (Myanmar), Vietnam, and elsewhere battled for political power, while in China a short-lived coalition government gave way to civil war, revolution, and renewed fighting on the Korean peninsula. Some stability was finally established after an armistice suspended hostilities in

Korea in July 1953, but some parts of East Asia had suffered continuous war from 1931 to 1953. In Indochina, Vietnamese nationalists battled a succession of Japanese, French, and American occupiers: their war did not end until 1975.

Timeframes are equally elastic in Europe. Here the outbreak of World War II is conventionally pegged to the Anglo-French declarations of war on Germany on September 3, 1939. But this is a very Allied-centric perception. German armed forces had reoccupied the Rhineland in March 1936 and had been in action in Austria and the Czech Sudetenland in 1938. Fascist Italy invaded Ethiopia in 1935 and Albania in 1939, while in Spain civil war between the elected Republican government and conservative army officers backed by Germany and Italy raged from July 1936 to April 1939. The surrender of Germany in spring 1945 ended major combat operations in Europe, but political stability was only consolidated with the solidification of the Cold War partition of the continent in the early 1950s. In North Africa, war loosened France's grip on its colonial empire, prompting wars for national independence that ended in Algeria in 1962.

This brief survey suggests that "World War II" was both a site of global interconnection *and* an event – or an intersecting series of events – that sprawled messily over more than two decades of the mid-twentieth century. It was not a unitary war with clearly delineated sides, and it resists being forced into the conventional 1939–1945 timeframe. Even the widely accepted title "World War II" was itself a carefully crafted product, fashioned by American leaders keen to impose their own narrative in the context of claiming global leadership in the postwar world. Nazi leaders also had a vision of *Weltkrieg*, or world war, but only the United States had the economic might, military muscle, and political vision to make it a reality. But alternative narratives exist, and the war continues to have different names reflecting different realities. In Russia, it is the "Great Patriotic War," while China fought the "War of Resistance to Japanese Aggression." Japan began fighting the Manchurian and China "Incidents," moved on to the "Greater East Asian War," and ended up losing the "Pacific War." The British toyed with a number of names before following America's lead in 1948: control of the naming rights, as British civil servant Llewellyn Woodward noted sourly, was yet "another American victory."[3]

Woodward had a point. Viewed from a global perspective, the single most significant consequence of the war was the establishment of American predominance within the capitalist world. The US helped destroy German, Italian and Japanese bids for regional hegemony and as it did so it eclipsed Britain as a global power. When the United States entered the war, it had long been the world's leading manufacturing power, and Wall Street was challenging "The City" (of London) as the world's premier financial center. But its army was small – the 18th largest in the world – and its navy, although nominally on a par with the British Royal Navy, was limited by its lack of overseas bases. By 1945, the United States was the world's predominant military power, and its global reach rested on over 2000 overseas bases.

America briefly enjoyed a monopoly of nuclear weapons, refusing in the short term to share them even with Britain, its closest ally. This unprecedented military might, buttressed by the tremendous productive capacity of America's wartime economy, allowed Washington to restructure the global capitalist economy, unleashing a protracted economic boom that continued into the late 1960s.

The story of this transformation in America's world position is central to a global history of this long World War II. It is a story that unfolds through an overlapping series of wars that eventually culminated in the defeat of America's enemies in Germany, Italy, and Japan; in the marginalization of its British ally; and in the "containment" of its Soviet rival. It is the story of the establishment of what magazine publisher Henry Luce referred to in 1941 as the "American Century," a project envisioned as an unprecedented surge of US-led economic growth wrapped in an ideology of American liberal internationalism. In the context of the entangled and transnational narratives touched on above, it is the story at the heart of this global history. There is, of course, much more to it than that. A global history must also include the efforts of radical nationalist regimes in Berlin, Tokyo, and Rome to establish their own colonial empires, with all their brutal and genocidal consequences. It includes the efforts of the old-school imperialists in London, Paris, and Den Haag to hold onto their empires – empires that had structured global politics and economics. It incorporates the successful war waged by the Soviet Union, a state founded in anti-capitalist revolution, against German invasion. And it highlights a building wave of anti-colonial resistance that brought decolonization and national independence to vast swaths of the world long ruled from the capitals of Europe.

Finally, a word to American readers. Young Americans, most of them men, participated in large numbers in the transnational travel that was part of the global experience of war. Americans fought in the Atlantic and the Pacific, in Europe and in Asia. They witnessed the ruin of Japanese and German cities, they gazed at tourist sites in Italy, and they drank warm beer in Britain. But in many ways the American experience of war was radically different from that of people in other countries. As a 10-year-old girl, my mother hunkered down in an Anderson shelter – a flimsy piece of corrugated steel covered with garden dirt – as German bombs fell on the industrial city of Sheffield in Britain. She escaped injury, but her house was destroyed. Over 600 people were killed in Sheffield in just two nights of bombing in December 1940, and thousands more died in other British cities. Her childhood experience was shaped by the terrible certainty that young men in unseen – but clearly heard – bomber aircraft were trying to kill her. Hers was an experience shared by millions in cities from Hamburg to Tokyo and from Leningrad to Nanjing. In France, people faced the additional horror that it was their "liberators" who were doing the bombing, and more than 53 000 of them were killed by *Allied* bombs. Yet, while the scale of the slaughter expanded as the war went on, none of the millions of civilian casualties – with the sad exception of the six people killed by a Japanese balloon bomb while picnicking in Oregon – were Americans.

For many Americans, as Pulitzer Prize-winning author Studs Terkel noted, World War II was the "Good War." For those not in uniform, war work was easy to come by and paid well. Millions of women entered the workforce for the first time, and many African Americans set out on a second "Great Migration" from the rural South to the booming war plants of California and the North. No American cities were bombed. No infrastructure was destroyed. Food was plentiful, and no one starved as a result of enemy action. These things all became foundational elements of the postwar American Dream. In the context of America's overwhelming military victory, they shaped – and continue to shape – a very specific and American-centric view of the global World War II. It is a view of a war in which two clearly defined sides faced off against each other in a struggle defined by unambiguous moral clarity, and it is a war that takes place within a precisely defined timeframe. This is not a view that is widely shared in other parts of the world. Approaching World War II as a *global* event therefore demands a conscious effort to step outside of traditional American- (and Western-) centric frameworks. It does *not* require abandoning deeply held moral convictions, but it does ask that we view them in the context of comparative experiences that begin with the world as a whole and not with *any* particular country.

Notes

1. Taylor, T.H. (2002). *The Simple Sounds of Freedom: The True Story of the Only Soldier to Fight for Both America and the Soviet Union in World War II*, 256. New York: Random House.
2. Diary entry, August 17, 1942, in Sierakowiak, D. (ed. Alan Adelson, trans. Kamil Turowski) (1996). *The Diary of Dawid Sierakowiak*, 208. New York: Oxford University Press.
3. Quoted in Reynolds (January 2003), 38.

Reference

Reynolds, D. (January 2003). The origins of the two 'world wars': historical discourse and international politics. *Journal of Contemporary History* 38 (1): 29–44.

Further Reading

Cesarani, D. (2014). "The Second World War and the fate of the Jews." Raul Hilberg Memorial Lecture, October 27. Available at: https://www.uvm.edu/~uvmchs/?Page= HilbergLectures.html&SM=submenunews.html.
Morris-Suzuki, T. (May 2015). Prisoner number 600,001: rethinking Japan, China, and the Korean War, 1950–1953. *Journal of Asian Studies* 74 (2): 1–22.

Bibliographic Note

The short reference and further reading lists at the end of each chapter are *not* designed to be an exhaustive guide to the literature on the events covered in that chapter; that would be a book-length project in itself. Instead, they list books that are particularly insightful, thought-provoking, or informative, and that will help to open up whole subject areas to interested readers.

The following two books provide an overview of World War II, primarily from the standpoint of military campaigns:

Mawdsley, E. (2009). *World War II: A New History*. New York: Cambridge University Press.
Millet, A.R. and Murray, W. (2000). *A War to Be Won: Fighting the Second World War*. Cambridge, MA: Harvard University Press.

1

The Crisis of the Old World Order

Before World War II, much of the world was still dominated by the imperial powers of Europe, with Britain and France foremost among them. World War I had ended with the overthrow of vast territorial empires of the Hohenzollerns (Germany), Habsburgs (Austria-Hungary), Romanovs (Russia), and Ottomans (Turkey), but both Britain and France had expanded their overseas empires, especially in the oil-rich Middle East. The British had consolidated their leading place in the world-system after the Napoleonic Wars in the early 1800s. It was based on the dynamism of Britain's industrial economy – the first in the world – and on the worldwide collection of semi-independent dominions, directly ruled colonies, protectorates, and island outposts that formed the British Empire. Britain's global trade networks and the wealth, resources, and markets of its empire were protected by the Royal Navy, by far the most powerful navy in the world.

Britain did not have a large land army, relying on soldiers recruited in India to police much of its empire, and on its diplomats and politicians to ensure that no single rival could dominate Europe. This combination of economic and military power enabled the City of London to function as the preeminent world center of banking, finance, and insurance. Its global hegemony rested not only on the "hard power" of economic and military might, but also on its ability to use "soft power" – free trade, liberal democracy, and a claim to be benefiting its colonial subjects – to assert moral leadership. And, while the military and diplomatic arrangements of this *Pax Britannica*, or "British Peace," maintained Britain's global hegemony for over a century, there were few years in which its military was not in action to uphold its rule in some part of the empire.

World War II in Global Perspective, 1931–1953: A Short History, First Edition. Andrew N. Buchanan.
© 2019 John Wiley & Sons, Inc. Published 2019 by John Wiley & Sons, Inc.

Other European powers established sprawling colonial empires, although none rivaled the global scope of the British. The Dutch ruled the Netherlands East Indies (modern Indonesia), a legacy of its seventeenth-century reign as the world's leading commercial power. During the last decades of the nineteenth century, several European nations engaged in a frenzied "scramble" to establish colonies in sub-Saharan Africa, carving up almost the entire continent without regard for pre-existing boundaries and co-opting local elites into systems of "indirect rule." In Southeast Asia, France grabbed Indochina (today Vietnam, Cambodia, and Laos) in the 1880s, while London ruled a vast crescent of territory running from northern Borneo and Malaya to Burma (modern Myanmar) and India, the "Jewel in the Crown" of the British Empire. Only Latin America escaped this pattern of direct colonial rule. Here anti-colonial revolutions had freed much of the continent in the early 1800s, although independent but relatively weak nation-states remained locked in circuits of trade dominated primarily by Britain and, increasingly, the United States, exporting raw materials and importing manufactured goods.

In the last quarter of the nineteenth century, this British-dominated world order was challenged by the newly unified nation-states in Germany, Italy, Japan, and the United States. These new states were the product of wars of national unification – including the US Civil War and the Meiji Restoration in Japan – and in all of them, with the partial exception of Italy, unification triggered sustained economic growth. By the end of the nineteenth century, America had become the world's top manufacturing power, and Germany had also surpassed Britain in key economic sectors. In Asia, Japan emerged as the major regional power after successful wars against China (1894–1895) and Russia (1904–1905). These states jumped into the scramble for overseas colonies in Africa and the Pacific, and they joined British and French efforts to open up new markets and spheres of imperial domination in China, where the Qing Dynasty was weakened by economic stagnation, peasant revolt, and regional fragmentation. Intensified international competition for empire destabilized Europe, where Franco-Russian concerns about the rise of Germany intersected with conflicts between Russia, Austria-Hungary, and the Ottoman Empire in the Balkans. In August 1914 these overlapping European and imperial conflicts led to the outbreak of World War I.

World War I and the Postwar Settlement

These multilayered causes of World War I shaped the character of the war. Much of the fighting and most of the 10 million battlefield deaths took place in three European war zones, including a protracted attritional struggle between Anglo-French and German armies in the trenches of the Western Front; an equally savage but more mobile war between Russia and the Central Powers (Germany and Austria-Hungary) on a front stretching from the Baltic to the Black Sea; and an Alpine front between Italy and Austria-Hungary. These European war zones were connected to critical conflicts in other parts of the world. While far fewer troops were involved, fighting in colonial spaces was often fluid, fast-moving, and decisive. In Africa, Allied armies of Indian and African soldiers overturned German colonial rule in the modern-day states of Cameroon, Namibia, and Tanzania. In the Middle East, Arab rebels and Allied armies fought the Ottoman Empire for control of Iraq, Syria, and Palestine, and then from 1919 to 1923 the new nation-state in Turkey fought to defend its independence against Allied attempts to dismember it. Meanwhile Japan, then a British ally, rolled up German colonial outposts in the Marshall, Marianas, and Caroline islands and on China's Shandong Peninsula.

The mobilization of colonial labor, food, and raw materials enabled Britain and France to fight a long attritional war. French colonial troops from West and North Africa fought on the Western Front, while the Indian Army and other colonial forces sustained British-led campaigns in the Middle East and Africa. These imperial mobilizations drew colonized peoples into the maelstrom of world politics, and overseas military service exposed them to new experiences and ideas. These factors contributed to a mounting tide of anti-colonial agitation. When Mahatma Gandhi and the Indian National Congress stepped up their campaign for Home Rule, the colonial authorities responded with harsh repression, shooting over 1000 unarmed protestors in Amritsar in 1919. In Ireland, the forceful suppression of an armed uprising against British rule at Easter 1916 boosted support for the nationalist cause, leading to a war for national independence and the establishment in 1922 of the Irish Free State in the southern part of the country. In other colonies the impact of war was less dramatic, but it nevertheless spurred the emergence of anti-colonial movements that became increasingly important over the following decades.

During World War I, the major combatants mobilized the totality of their national resources for war. Governments directed workers into military service or into key industrial jobs, reorganizing industry to maximize the output of weapons and munitions. Denied access to overseas trade by the British naval blockade, the strain of this effort was particularly acute in Germany. Berlin managed to produce the military matériel necessary to sustain a long two-front war, but by the winter of 1916–1917 Germany's civilian population was going hungry. With its slender industrial base, the Russian Empire was also hard hit, and as the war progressed economic breakdown and military defeat combined to produce a deep political crisis. Britain and France, with their economies sustained by their empires and by massive inflows of American funds, food, and military supplies, were better placed to meet the demands of total war. Nevertheless, for three years, and despite the commitment of millions of men and massive quantities of matériel – including tanks, airplanes, and poison gas – neither side achieved a decisive military breakthrough.

The first cracks in this military deadlock emerged in 1917 as the grinding social consequences of total war produced political crises in Russia and then in Germany and Austria-Hungary. In 1917, the Tsarist regime in Russia was toppled by two popular revolutions, the first led by liberal democrats in February and the second in October led by Vladimir Lenin's Bolshevik Party. Acting on their slogan of "Bread, Peace, and Land," the Bolshevik government took Russia out of the war. In the short term, Russia's exit benefited Germany, which quickly annexed a broad swath of former Imperial Russian territory in Poland, Ukraine, and the Baltic States. German conquests were formalized at the Treaty of Brest-Litovsk in March 1918, where the Bolsheviks traded land for the time they needed to consolidate their socialist state. Germany's victory in the East allowed Berlin to redeploy troops to the Western Front in preparation for a major offensive in spring 1918. After three years of deadlock, a German military victory suddenly seemed possible.

These events overlapped with the second major political development of 1917, the formal entry of the United States into the war. American money and matériel had sustained the Allied war effort since 1915, but under President Woodrow Wilson the United States remained neutral. Wilson's decision to join the war in April 1917 was triggered by the resumption of German submarine attacks on neutral shipping in the Atlantic, but it was fundamentally driven by the desire to block the emergence of a German-dominated Europe – a development that was rightly seen as a threat to the rise of American power. America joined Britain and France as an "associate power" (rather than a formal ally), and US troops began arriving in France in time to come to support Allied armies reeling in the face of Germany's 1918 spring offensive. By the fall, there were one million American soldiers at the front, poised for an advance into Germany.

As it turned out, revolution arrived in Germany before the Allied armies. The German government was overthrown in November 1918 by a popular insurrection that began with a naval mutiny and spread to working-class districts in Berlin and throughout Germany's industrial heartlands. As in Russia, workers and soldiers formed revolutionary councils that functioned as organs of popular political power. Kaiser Wilhelm II abdicated, and an alliance of moderate socialists and military leaders signed an armistice with the Allies on November 11.

The armistice ended the war, but it did not stop all the fighting. Civil war raged in Russia until 1922, as military expeditions from Britain, France, Japan, and the United States boosted counter-revolutionary efforts to overthrow the new Union of Soviet Socialist Republics. In Turkey, nationalists led by Mustafa Kemal Atatürk fought until 1923 to prevent the new Turkish nation-state from being carved up by the victorious allies. Revolutionary uprisings shattered the Habsburg Empire in 1918, establishing short-lived socialist regimes and laying the basis for the creation of new nation-states in Austria, Hungary, and Czechoslovakia. In Germany, the moderate socialist leaders of the new Weimar Republic – named for the city where the constitutional assembly met – used gangs of nationalist *Freikorps* to crush waves of communist-led working-class rebellion that rolled through Berlin, Bavaria (the Munich Soviet Republic), and the Ruhr industrial region between 1918 and 1923. In 1920 strikes and popular protests derailed the Kapp Putsch, an attempted right-wing military coup.

These events showed that great modern wars bring with them the possibility of economic and social collapse and, particularly for the losers, popular insurrection. As in Russia, popular revolutions could lead to the formation of governments determined to overturn the economic foundations of capitalism. For ruling elites everywhere, this terrifying prospect would weigh heavily on their political thinking in the years after World War I. The postwar revolutionary wave in Germany and Central Europe was finally contained, but the existence of large communist parties in many countries meant that the possibility of a working-class challenge for power had not gone away. It is impossible to understand either the post–World War I settlement or the course of World War II without understanding how large this issue loomed in the minds of contemporary policymakers.

The Rise of American Power

Britain and France won World War I, but at a crippling cost: an entire generation of young men had been slaughtered, their economies were exhausted, and their governments had gone deeply into debt to fund the war. The United States, on the other hand, had only entered the war in 1917, and while its military presence on the Western Front had established it as a major player in European politics, its military ranked behind that of Britain and France. At the same time, American industrialists and financiers supported the Allied war effort from the beginning, generating an economic boom at home and transforming the United States from a debtor nation into a global financial superpower. To some British observers the United States appeared as a new type of "super-state," and they were acutely aware that while American aid had allowed them to prevail over Germany, the price tag was a dramatic shift in economic power westwards across the Atlantic.[1] Nevertheless, America's late entry into the war meant that its economic predominance did not translate directly into overwhelming military power and political influence. As a result, while World War I shattered the old world order, it did not immediately produce a new one.

Allied leaders approached the 1919 Paris Peace Conference in Versailles with different and contradictory goals. Woodrow Wilson hoped to establish a new US-led world order based on free trade, national self-determination for selected

European countries, and a League of Nations capable of settling international disputes by negotiation. In contrast to this liberal internationalist vision, British and French leaders were intent on punishing Germany by dismantling its military, imposing huge reparations payments, and redrawing its borders in favor of new or expanded states in Eastern Europe. Given the relationship of forces on the ground in Europe, the Anglo-French approach won out, and at Versailles Germany was saddled with a massive reparations bill and the loss of 25 000 square miles of territory, much of it given to newly independent Poland. France was assigned the coal production of Germany's Saar Basin for 15 years, during which time the region would be administered by the League of Nations.

These punitive measures were offset to some degree by the Allies' desire to contain the Soviet Union. Although deprived of tanks and heavy artillery, the Allies wanted the German army to be strong enough to resist both domestic insurrection and Soviet expansionism. For similar reasons, Wilson's principle of self-determination was applied primarily to the creation of a chain of new nation-states stretching from Finland through Poland to the Balkans in an extended buffer zone or *cordon sanitaire* designed to contain Germany and to isolate the Soviet Union. The Allies' contradictory goals at Versailles thus produced a contradictory treaty. The punitive aspects of the Versailles Treaty – not least the loss of seven million citizens – angered all shades of German opinion, but the settlement was not *so* harsh as to preclude the possibility of German recovery.

After Versailles, the United States Congress voted against joining the new League of Nations. Many lawmakers feared that League membership would take critical foreign policy decisions out of their hands. Nevertheless, while their rejection of the League indicated that American elites were not yet willing to embrace fully the political consequences of their new global standing, it did *not* reflect a generalized American retreat into "isolationism." During the 1920s the United States remained deeply engaged in international politics, trade, and finance, functioning as the world's major economic power but not, as yet, as its fully fledged hegemon.

This contradictory relationship was underscored by the 1921 Washington Naval Conference. Often described as a disarmament conference because it led to a 10-year moratorium on battleship construction, its key accomplishment was to regulate the relative sizes of the world's major navies by fixing the battleship tonnage of the United States, Britain, Japan, Italy, and France in the ratio of 5:5:3:2:2. This formula recognized America's claim to parity with Britain. The Royal Navy had been the world's dominant navy for over two centuries, but London accepted this tectonic shift in global power out of fear that America's shipbuilding capacity would allow it to surge ahead in a naval arms race. The conference also registered the rise of Japanese power. Tokyo was rewarded for its wartime services to the Allies by securing approval for a navy capable of significant power projection in Asian and Pacific waters. In addition, the Four- and Nine-Power treaties signed during the conference consolidated postwar relations in Asia, acknowledging the rise of Japan while reaffirming China's sovereignty and territorial integrity. For many in Japan, British and American recognition of Japan's status as the third global naval power vindicated Tokyo's cooperation with the West and, in exchange, Japan handed the former German colony on the Shandong Peninsula back to China.

Europe in the 1920s

The continued dislocation of the German economy undermined the fragile stability of the Weimar Republic. In 1923, hyperinflation brought economic crisis and rising unemployment, undercutting Germany's ability to make reparations payments to Britain and France. Paris responded by occupying the Ruhr industrial region, where their troops faced a campaign of widespread civil disobedience. In October, the German Communist Party (KPD) led working-class uprisings in Hamburg and in Saxony that were eventually crushed by the Weimar army after fierce street fighting. The following month radical nationalist Adolf Hitler and his newly formed National Socialist German Workers (NSDAP, Nazi) Party attempted to seize power in Bavaria in the "Beer Hall Putsch." This attempted coup was defeated by the army, and Hitler and other Nazi leaders were imprisoned. By the end of the year the Weimar Republic had weathered challenges from the communist left and the nationalist right, but it was clear that unless economic stability was restored further crises would inevitably follow.

Germany's economic crisis was addressed in 1924 by an international committee of experts led by two Americans, banker Charles Dawes and industrialist Owen Young. Their report, adopted in summer 1924 and known as the Dawes Plan, reduced the burden of Germany's reparations payments by rescheduling them to end in the 1980s. At the same time, the Dawes Plan boosted Germany's ability to make regular reparations payments by guaranteeing it loans from a group of Wall Street financiers led by J.P. Morgan. More Morgan money secured French approval, and Paris withdrew its troops from the Ruhr. American loans, combined with deep cuts in social spending, tamed Germany's hyperinflation and restarted economic growth. With renewed German reparations payments enabling Britain and France to service their wartime debts to the United States, the Dawes Plan helped to restore stability in Germany while generating profit for Wall Street.

Despite the defeat of the postwar revolutionary upsurge and the inflows of American capital, Europe's recovery remained fragile. This fragility was particularly apparent in Italy. One of the weakest of the European powers, Italy joined the war in 1915 on the basis of Allied promises that it would be rewarded with territory carved out of the Austro-Hungarian Empire. Instead, the Italian army suffered a string of humiliating defeats that culminated in a complete collapse at the Battle of Caporetto in November 1917. The war cost Italy over 600 000 lives, failed to deliver any significant territorial gains, and left a battered economy dependent on American loans. Italian leaders secured some modest territorial gains at Versailles, but they fell well short of Allied promises made in the secret 1915 Treaty of London – now embarrassingly made public by the Communist government in Moscow.

Many Italians felt cheated by this "mutilated victory," and in September 1919 poet Gabriele D'Annunzio led a band of ultra-nationalist activists to seize the city of Fiume (Rijeka) on the coast of the Adriatic. Fiume/Rijeka was claimed by the new Kingdom of Yugoslavia as well as by Italy, and its garrison of British and French troops was quickly ejected by D'Annunzio's militiamen. D'Annunzio's coup signaled the emergence of a radical nationalist – soon to be termed "Fascist" – movement in Italy. At the same time, socialist-minded workers and peasants launched a series of strikes, factory occupations, and land seizures. During the *Biennio Rosso* – the Two Red Years – of working-class militancy in 1919–1920, the Italian Socialist Party (PSI) voted to join the new Moscow-based Communist International.

Alarmed by this working-class militancy, Italian factory owners and landlords turned to Benito Mussolini's new National Fascist Party for help. Fascist "Blackshirts" carried out a campaign of street violence and bombings against communist, trade union, and peasant activists, and in October 1922 Mussolini launched a bid for power by sending 30 000 Blackshirts on a well-publicized March on Rome. The force of this attempted coup convinced King Victor Emmanuel III to invite Mussolini to become prime minister, a position he then legitimized with a rigged electoral victory in April 1924. When socialist leader Giacomo Matteotti complained that the election was fixed, the Blackshirts assassinated him.

Mussolini quickly consolidated his dictatorship, restricting democratic rights and strengthening the powers of the Fascist state. The regime's "corporatist" ideology promised to overcome class divisions between workers and bosses by promoting national unity, cultural rejuvenation, and the creation of a new Roman Empire on the shores of the Mediterranean. Business leaders admired Mussolini's fervent anti-communism and quickly aligned themselves with the new regime, particularly after it imposed a 20% wage cut on Italian workers. A similar accommodation unfolded internationally. European and American politicians were alarmed by Mussolini's expansionist rhetoric, but they appreciated his anti-communism and accorded him remarkable prestige. Britain and France defused a League of Nations protest against Italy's assault on the Greek island of Corfu in 1923, and throughout the decade they worked to draw Fascist Italy into the framework of European diplomacy.

The inflows of American credit initiated by the Dawes Plan helped to stimulate a period of economic growth in Western Europe. Britain rejoined the gold standard in 1925, and others followed suit. This return to "gold" – the convertibility of national currencies into gold at fixed rates – registered the growing stability of international markets and signaled the end of the postwar economic crisis. Increased political stability followed, registered in 1925 by the Locarno Treaties. The most important of these agreements was signed by France, Britain, Italy, and Germany. It normalized Germany's international position by confirming the country's western borders as determined at Versailles, paving the way for Berlin to join the League of Nations the following year. With its border secured by agreement with Germany, France deemphasized its anti-German alliances with the countries of the *cordon sanitaire*, implying the possibility of territorial adjustments in Eastern Europe in Germany's favor. France and Britain seemed to be willing to satisfy Germany at the expense of their allies in Eastern Europe, and to many Poles and Czechs the much vaunted "spirit of Locarno" appeared as a betrayal of their national interests.

The new mood of optimism produced by economic prosperity and political stability was expressed in 1928 in a remarkable multilateral renunciation of war. The Kellogg-Briand Pact rejecting war as an instrument of foreign policy was signed by 28 countries, and although American pressure kept the Union of Soviet Socialist Republics (USSR) out of the signing ceremony in Paris, Moscow also embraced the accord. The agreement had no regulatory mechanism, and in the light of the worldwide slaughter that followed it seems utterly naïve. Nevertheless, it did reflect the widely held hope of elites in Europe, Japan, and the United States that the twin threats of war and revolution had been vanquished and that open-ended capitalist prosperity had returned.

Revolution and Counter-Revolution in Russia

The October 1917 revolution in Russia resulted in the formation of the USSR. This supranational union consisted of Russia and the new socialist republics in Ukraine, Byelorussia, and the Caucasus, and it promised to replace the Tsarist Empire's "prison-house of nations" with a voluntary association of independent states. In the early years of the revolution, Soviet leaders were committed to the international extension of the socialist revolution. They recognized that Russia was the most economically backward of the great powers, and they argued that if the new socialist state was to survive it had to be joined by workers' republics in the industrial heartlands of Western Europe. In the years of economic crisis and working-class insurgency in Germany, Austria-Hungary, and Eastern Europe that followed World War I, this seemed a realistic prospect. The Russian Revolution also won broad working-class support in France and Britain, and it inspired two years of strikes and factory occupations in Italy.

The Russian Revolution transformed working-class political parties around the world. In Europe and the United States, the moderate socialist parties that had supported their own national governments during the war split apart as revolutionary-minded workers sought to follow the Bolsheviks' lead. In France and Italy, the old socialist parties went over to the revolutionaries. In the European colonies and semi-colonies of the Middle East and Asia, groups of workers, peasants, and intellectuals formed new communist parties dedicated to interlinked struggles for national independence and socialism, and in 1921 radical students met in Shanghai to set up the Chinese Communist Party (CCP). Soviet leaders encouraged these developments by forming the Communist International (or Comintern) in Moscow in March 1919 and by dispatching tested leaders to work with inexperienced new parties around the world. Unlike the moderate and eurocentric Socialist International, the Comintern acted on the idea that world revolution would combine working-class insurrections in the old imperialist heartlands with anti-colonial struggles for national liberation.

With the triumph of Fascism in Italy in 1922 and defeat of the revolutionary upsurge in Germany the following year it became clear that socialist revolution was not about to triumph in Western Europe, while the Dawes Plan restabilized European capitalism and stimulated a new period of economic growth. Within the Soviet Union, the consequences of war, civil war, and foreign intervention hampered economic recovery, and Western hostility made it difficult to secure the investment necessary to rebuild the economy. Continued economic dislocation and isolation in a world of reinvigorated capitalist states underpinned a transformation of Soviet politics. After Lenin's death in 1924, a faction of Soviet leaders led by Joseph Stalin and based in the new administrative bureaucracy seized power. In place of socialist internationalism, Stalin was narrowly focused on building up the strength of the USSR; he also overturned the equality of the republics within the USSR, replacing it with a forceful assertion of Russian domination. Tens of thousands of "Old Bolsheviks" were removed from office, imprisoned, or executed in a campaign of terror that culminated in a purge of the Red Army's officer corps in 1937 and in the murder of exiled opposition leader Leon Trotsky in Mexico in 1940. At the same time, the Comintern was transformed into an instrument of Soviet foreign policy, and Soviet operatives – and Soviet money – ensured that communist parties around the world followed the twists and turns of Stalin's political line.

Stalin's political counter-revolution did *not* restore private capitalism in the USSR. In 1928 Moscow launched a Five-Year Plan designed to industrialize the USSR at breakneck speed. State-owned industries grew rapidly as the government used coercive and bureaucratic measures to mobilize human and physical resources. At the same time, Soviet workers were initially inspired by the great leap into modernity promised by this drive to "build socialism" in the USSR, and many participated enthusiastically. The Five-Year Plan produced untold human suffering, but it also fashioned the coal mines, steel mills, and manufacturing plants of a modern industrial economy. Much of the plant necessary for this great leap forward came from the United States, and the USSR became the top overseas consumer of American industrial and agricultural machinery. On the land, Stalin sought to boost agricultural productivity by forcing peasants into large collective farms mechanized using imported Ford tractors. Many peasants resisted forced collectivization, and thousands were killed in clashes with Soviet authorities. Many more died as a result of the famines caused by this massive dislocation of rural life; in Ukraine, where collec-tivization was accompanied by an assault on national independence, nearly four million starved in 1932–1933.

Given the police-state bureaucratism of the USSR under Stalin, it cannot be regarded as "communist" in any meaningful sense. But neither was it a capitalist state, and Western governments never lost sight of the fact that they were dealing with a state that had come to power through an anti-capitalist revolution and in which there was no large-scale private property, no free market, and no openings for foreign investment except under tight state control. This contradiction is critical to understanding the evolution of the relationship between the USSR and various Western states before, during, and after World War II.

Japan, China, and the Deepening Conflict in Asia

During World War I Japan seized Germany's colonial outposts in the Pacific and on China's Shandong Peninsula. These territorial gains were legitimized at Versailles, and although Japan was forced to give up Shandong at the 1921 Washington Conference, many viewed Japan's recognition as a great power as adequate compensation. During the postwar period of "Taishō democracy" (named after the Taishō emperor, r. 1912–1926), Japan's recognition as a great power was linked to a period of parliamentary democracy at home and to a weakening of direct military control over Japanese politics. Advocates of aggressive army-led expansionism into Manchuria were eclipsed by politicians who favored integration into the Western-dominated world order. A long and unpopular campaign in Siberia against the Russian Revolution lowered the prestige of the army, as did its violent repression of nationwide protests against high rice prices in 1918. The advocates of continental expansionism in the army's "Imperial Way" faction and in other military cliques remained influential, but for much of the postwar decade they did not dominate political life.

Economically, Japan benefited from the absence of European competition dur-ing the war, running a trade surplus with the Allied powers and even making loans to them. Postwar deflation, a stock market crash, and the devastating 1923 Tokyo earthquake made for a more difficult postwar situation. Economic hardship prompted the growth of militant labor unions and of the underground Japanese Communist Party, founded in 1922. Wall Street floated emergency loans to get Japan through the crisis, but by 1927 Prime Minister Tanaka Giichi's Seiyukai Party government was more interested in relaunching Japanese expansionism in Manchuria than in pursuing integration into Western-dominated markets. With rightist cliques in the Kwantung Army based in the Japanese colony of Korea making the running, Japanese forces plunged into a series of violent confrontations with Chiang Kai-shek's Chinese Nationalists and with Manchurian warlord Zhang Zuolin. By the late 1920s Japan's window of liberal democracy was closing as military expansionism on the Asian mainland again came to the fore.

China was itself a site of political and military turmoil during the 1920s. The revolutionary overthrow of the Qing Dynasty in 1911, carried out in the face of mounting intervention in China by imperialist powers in Europe, the United States, and Japan, produced a weak central government besieged by numerous well-armed regional warlords. Sun Yat-sen, the Guomindang (Nationalist Party) leader who inspired the revolution and served briefly as the first president of the Republic of China, was forced into exile in Japan, and his successor Yuan Shikhai ruled as would-be emperor. Like Japan, China supported the Allies during World War I, sending over 100 000 laborers to work on the Western Front (Figure 1.1).

Figure 1.1 A British officer giving instructions to workers of the Chinese Labor Corps at the Tank Corps' Central Workshops in Teneur, France, spring 1918. Over 100 000 Chinese laborers supported Allied armies on the Western Front. (*Source*: © Imperial War Museum, Image 9902.)

Their common support for the Allies did not prevent Tokyo from demanding a long list of economic and political concessions from the Chinese government in Nanjing, and at Versailles Germany's Shandong colony was awarded to Japan. China's unfair treatment at Versailles sparked a wave of student-led protests in 1919 organized by the May Fourth Movement. Protestors campaigned against foreign imperialism and domestic warlordism, and many went on to help form the CCP in 1921.

Sun Yat-sen returned from exile in 1921 and set up a provisional revolutionary government in Guangzhou. Rebuffed by Western governments wary of his leftist nationalism, Sun turned to the USSR for help. Moscow responded by sending military advisers to train the National Revolutionary Army, and it advised the CCP to form a united front with the Guomindang. Widespread outrage against the repression of workers' protests by British authorities in Shanghai and Guangzhou in 1925 gave the Guomindang the popular support it needed to renew the struggle for a unified Chinese nation-state. Led by Sun's successor Chiang Kai-shek and supported by the CCP, the 1926–1928 Northern Expedition established Guomindang control over much of China.

Building on these advances, Chiang became president of a unified Chinese state with its capital in Nanjing. Chiang's victory marked the beginning of a period of relative political stability and economic progress known as the Nanjing Decade. Despite the success of the Northern Expedition, however, much of the country remained under the control of local warlords who pledged allegiance to the new government without abandoning their own regional power bases. Meanwhile, Chiang's fear of the growth of communist influence within the Guomindang prompted the launch of a violent assault on CCP members in 1927, and tens of thousands of communists were slaughtered by Chiang's soldiers in Shanghai and other industrial cities. Led by Mao Zedong, many surviving CCP members responded to this disaster by rejecting Marxist orthodoxy and setting out to base their party on rural peasants instead of on urban industrial workers.

The new unity of the Chinese Republic and Chiang's ferocious anti-communism led Britain and the United States to reevaluate their attitude to the Guomindang. Both countries maintained enclaves in Shanghai and elsewhere in China, but neither was interested in further territorial annexation. In the name of the "Open Door," they sought unrestricted access to the vast Chinese market, and they hoped that a stable, pro-business, and pro-Western government in Nanjing could provide the best conditions for achieving it. Influenced by a long tradition of missionary work in China, some American elites also hoped that the Guomindang might eventually become America's junior partner in Asia. During the 1920s, Japan also sought markets in China, but Japanese policymakers viewed the consolidation of a unified Chinese nation-state with concern. Unlike Britain and the United States, Japan had territorial interests in the region, and Tokyo saw the extension of Guomindang control into Manchuria as a direct threat to its own colonial ambitions. By 1930, Japan and China were on a collision course.

Note

1. British Chancellor of the Exchequer Austen Chamberlain in 1924, quoted in Tooze (2014), 516.

Reference

Tooze, A. (2014). *The Deluge: The Great War, America and the Remaking of the Global Order, 1916–1931*. New York: Viking.

Further Reading

Clark, C. (2012). *The Sleepwalkers: How Europe Went to War in 1914*. New York: Harper.

Gerwarth, R. and Manela, E. (2014). The Great War as a global war: imperial conflict and the reconfiguration of the world order, 1911–1923. *Diplomatic History* 38 (4): 786–800.

Gerwarth, R. (2016). *The Vanquished: Why the First World War Failed to End*. New York: Farrar, Straus and Giroux.

Kennedy, P. (1989). *The Rise and Fall of the Great Powers: Economic Change and Military Conflict 1500–2000*. New York: Fontana.

Osterhammel, J. (2014). *The Transformation of the World: A Global History of the Nineteenth Century*. Princeton: Princeton University Press.

Paine, S.C.M. (2017). *The Japanese Empire: Grand Strategy from the Meiji Empire to the Pacific War*. New York: Cambridge University Press.

2

The Great Depression and the Opening Guns of World War II

In the last week of October 1929, the New York Stock Market went into free fall. In just two days, $30 billion was wiped off share prices. The crash was quickly followed by a sharp downturn in economic output and a steep rise in unemployment, signaling the start of the decade-long Great Depression. The effects of the crash rippled out from Wall Street, choking off international trade and plunging economies around the world into crisis. World trade tumbled from a benchmark 100 in 1929 to just 28 in 1935. The Depression shattered the fragile political order of the postwar world, prompting ultra-nationalist coups, revolutionary upheavals, and intense regional wars in both Europe and Asia; together, these events sounded the opening guns of the global conflagration that would become World War II.

By the time share prices finally bottomed out in July 1932, the market had lost nearly 90% of its value. As such crises always do, the meltdown in financial markets – the most volatile sector of the capitalist economy – reflected an accelerating accumulation of difficulties in other economic sectors. In the late 1920s, industrial profits began to fall as glutted domestic markets in the United States depressed prices, prompting investors to turn towards stock market speculation. The result was the inflation of a speculative bubble that then inevitably burst. The circuits of war debt, reparations payments, and speculative investment created during World War I and bolstered by the Dawes Plan now ensured that Europe was quickly drawn into the financial meltdown on Wall Street. The structures of European colonial rule spread the crisis worldwide, channeling the effects of the banking collapse down farm roads in rural Tasmania and into village marketplaces across India. In the United States, the

World War II in Global Perspective, 1931–1953: A Short History, First Edition. Andrew N. Buchanan.
© 2019 John Wiley & Sons, Inc. Published 2019 by John Wiley & Sons, Inc.

crash brought the Roaring Twenties to a sudden end: by 1933, over 25% of the workforce was unemployed and 5000 banks were shuttered, creating a liquidity crisis that devastated family farmers already struggling with a worldwide fall in commodity prices.

The Wall Street crash ruptured the circuits of American credit, German reparations, and Anglo-French debt repayment established by the Dawes Plan. This breakdown had severe consequences in Germany, where postwar recovery remained fragile, but it also tipped Britain, France, and Italy into depression. In all the major capitalist countries, elites responded to the Great Depression by turning inwards to focus on domestic economic recovery. Notions of autarky – economic self-sufficiency – became commonplace, and they were linked, with varying degrees of virulence, to nationalist rhetoric. In the United States, the 1930 Smoot-Hawley Tariff raised import duties, provoking retaliatory responses from America's trading partners. Leaders of the British Empire meeting in Ottawa in 1932 adopted a policy of Imperial Preference in an effort to protect intra-imperial trade from foreign competition. This cycle of tariff and counter-tariff ended the relatively free trade of the 1920s, effectively shutting down world trade. Trade in agricultural commodities was particularly hard hit, and the various autarkic schemes included plans for food self-sufficiency, achieved through the intensified exploitation of existing colonies or the acquisition of new ones.

The collapse of trade led to a breakdown of the gold standard. This regulatory mechanism was viewed as a marker of economic health, and its restoration in the 1920s indicated the return of capitalist prosperity. In 1931, speculative pressure forced the pound sterling off the gold standard. This was a painful decision for the City of London, which viewed itself as the world's financial center, and it triggered a broader retreat from gold. Japan, which had rejoined the gold standard in 1930, left again in 1931. Italy quit in 1934, while France hung on until 1935–1936. Newly elected president Franklin D. Roosevelt took America off gold in April 1933, explaining in a dramatic telegram to the London World Economic Conference that the United States would not stabilize the dollar to promote global recovery. Roosevelt's statement torpedoed the conference, and in underscoring his administration's autarkic priorities it reinforced the general climate of economic nationalism. In October 1933, Adolf Hitler's new government announced that Germany would no longer be bound by debt and reparations obligations.

The New Deal

Franklin Roosevelt took office in 1933 pledged to alleviate the devastating domestic effects of the Great Depression. In a flurry of activity during its first months, the new administration acted to end the banking crisis, stimulate industrial demand, and create jobs by initiating public works programs; in the following years, similar schemes promoted conservation efforts, developed rural electrification, and built new bridges and highways. This disorganized raft of measures became known as the New Deal. A modest economic upturn in the mid-1930s prompted a revival of trade union militancy, prompting hard-fought struggles that unionized auto, steel, and other basic industries. Responding to this development, the government gave trade unions new legal protections and enacted far-reaching social reforms, including state-funded old-age pensions. The New Deal did not end the Depression: unemployment spiked again in 1937, and there was no sustained industrial recovery until rearmament began in 1939. But New Deal programs did ameliorate the social effects of mass unemployment, buffering the political crises that might otherwise have occurred. In this sense, the New Deal saved American capitalism, and in doing so it legitimized large-scale government intervention in the economy.

The domestic New Deal dovetailed with efforts to promote American trade in Latin America. Here, the Good Neighbor policy proclaimed at the 1933 Pan-American Conference signaled a move away from the military interventions typical of American policy in the early twentieth century. Secretary of State Cordell Hull negotiated bilateral trade agreements with several Latin American countries, while a new Export-Import Bank extended credit for overseas trade and Congress lowered tariffs on imports from "most favored" Latin American countries. American trade with Latin America tripled between 1934 and 1941 as the Good Neighbor policy extended the realm of New Deal autarky by creating an American-led trade bloc in the Western Hemisphere. While reinforcing American political influence in the region, these measures also provoked clashes with Argentina, whose meat exports tied it to Britain. Argentinian elites saw themselves as regional leaders, and during the 1930s they promoted domestic industrial development, much of it funded by British investors. Washington, meanwhile, forged relations with dictatorial governments in Guatemala, Honduras, and the Dominican Republic, and established military ties with the rightist regime of Getúlio Vargas in Brazil.

Depression and Military Expansionism in Japan

The 1929 financial crisis and the collapse in world trade hit Japan hard. Exports fell sharply, unemployment rose, and pressure on the yen forced Japan off the gold standard. The crisis convinced many Japanese leaders that the policy of openness to the West and of integration into world markets was mistaken, and, as elsewhere, their response to the Depression was marked by economic and political nationalism. The same large-scale autarkic impulses that turned Washington towards regional predominance in Latin America and led London to adopt Imperial Preference riveted Tokyo's attention on Manchuria. Bordering its existing colony in Korea and long the site of Japanese imperial ambition, Manchuria's rich resources, fertile farmland, and potentially huge market seemed to offer Tokyo what army leader Yamagata Aritomo described as an "absolute lifeline."[1] Ultra-nationalist factions in the leadership of both branches of the military championed this expansionist course and, after a bewildering series of political assassinations and failed military coups, liberal democracy was shouldered aside in the early 1930s as military leaders assumed direct control of Japanese politics.

On September 18, 1931, a bomb planted by members of Japan's Korea-based Kwantung Army damaged the Japanese-owned South Manchuria Railway near the city of Shenyang (Mukden). Army leaders blamed the bombing on Chinese terrorists and invaded Manchuria in the name of defending Japanese interests, quickly defeating regional warlord Zhang Xueliang and occupying a vast area with a population of 30 million. Launched without Tokyo's approval, the invasion stimulated a wave of popular nationalism that helped to turn Japanese politics decisively towards continental expansionism. Responding to the Kwantung Army's victory, Tokyo set up the new state of Manchukuo with the last Qing emperor at its head. In reality, Puyi was a Japanese puppet and the Kwantung Army controlled Manchukuo, leading an industrialization effort based on abundant reserves of coal and iron ore. Inspired by the state-directed industrialization of the Soviet Union, the Kwantung Army set up the Shōwa steelworks in Anshan in 1932. Employing super-exploited Chinese workers, the sprawling complex quickly became a world-class center of steel production. Tokyo also promoted the emigration of Japanese farmers to the "new paradise" of Manchukuo with the twin goals of relieving perceived overpopulation at home and consolidating control of its new colonial space.

As it secured control of Manchuria, Japan probed Chiang Kai-shek's Chinese state. In early 1932, Tokyo used an attack on Japanese monks in Shanghai as a pretext to launch a violent assault on Chinese military forces in the city. Fighting raged for several weeks, and Japanese bombers launched from aircraft carriers lying offshore attacked Chinese residential districts. The League of Nations-brokered peace settlement was supposed to demilitarize Shanghai, but in fact it forced the withdrawal of Chinese troops while allowing Japan to maintain a military presence.

To Italian Fascists and German Nazis, Tokyo's conquest of Manchuria offered an inspiring example of a new form of "total empire," combining military conquest of contiguous colonial territory with industrialization and large-scale settlement in a way that promised to generate vast new resources. The League of Nations criticized the annexation of Manchuria but took no action, and to many Western leaders Japanese rule seemed preferable to an expansion of Soviet influence into this critical borderland. Nevertheless, League criticism did prompt Tokyo to withdraw from the organization in 1933, and when the 1935 London Naval Conference declined to give Japan naval parity with Britain and the United States, it walked out of that, too. No longer bound by international treaty, Tokyo put its new steel mills to work building two gigantic *Yamato*-class battleships and several large aircraft carriers. Shipbuilding was part of a broader rearmament program that boosted economic recovery and ended the Depression in Japan.

Japan's conquest of Manchuria was accomplished without direct fighting between the Kwantung Army and Chinese Nationalists. Nevertheless, the establishment of Manchukuo was a humiliating setback for Chiang's project of uniting China under his rule, and the 1933 Tanggu Truce extended Tokyo's influence deep into northern China and Mongolia. Chiang's initial response to this reversal was to buttress his own position by launching a renewed offensive against the communists. Driven from the cities by the 1927 Shanghai Incident, the Chinese Communist Party (CCP) was based primarily in the rural south, where it won support from peasant farmers through its militant opposition to rapacious "landlordism." During this time Mao Zedong, the central advocate of a new communist strategy based on rural peasants, advanced his claim to party leadership through a series of Stalin-style purges. In 1934, Guomindang attacks forced the CCP to abandon its southern base areas and set off on a desperate 5000-mile retreat to the northeastern province of Shaanxi. Of 80 000 CCP supporters who set out on the fabled "Long March," only 7000 arrived in Shaanxi. The survivors quickly built a base of support among the local peasants, but as war with Japan loomed the party and its peasant supporters found themselves right on the frontline.

The Rise of Nazi Germany

In Germany, the breakdown of international trade combined with a domestic banking crisis to halt the precarious postwar recovery. In 1930, industrial production fell by over 40%, while the stock market lost two-thirds of its value and 6.2 million Germans (30% of the workforce) were unemployed. Economic breakdown unhinged Germany's fragile democracy. Divided over funding for unemployment benefits, the Social Democratic Party (SPD)–People's Party coalition fell in March 1930, and the new chancellor (prime minister), conservative politician Heinrich Brüning, failed to secure a parliamentary majority. Instead, Brüning began governing by executive decree. Brüning's deflationary policies cut government spending, deepening the economic hardship facing many Germans. Politics became increasingly polarized, with many workers turning to the Communist Party (KPD) while the Nazis' nationalist and anti-Semitic message got a hearing among the crisis-ridden middle classes and the unemployed.

25

Nazi rhetoric had a radical edge, blaming capitalists and bankers for the crisis as well as communists. In Nazi ideology, "cosmopolitan" Jews were either communists or "plutocratic" capitalists, and the two merged together into a Judeo-Bolshevik conspiracy against the German people. The National Socialists secured 18.3% of the vote in the September 1930 elections (up from 2.6% in 1928), while the KPD won 13.1% (up from 10.6%).

Hitler's anti-communism, radical nationalism, and his vision of an expansionist "Eastern Orientation" designed to secure colonial *Lebensraum* (living space) in Eastern Europe began to interest top German industrialists.[2] Germany's old-school business and military elites never particularly *liked* Hitler. They found him coarse and uncultured, and they laughed at his lowly wartime rank of corporal. But the Nazi Party (NSDAP) offered both a firm bulwark against the communist challenge and a road out of the economic crisis that promised territorial expansion, economic recovery, and military glory. German elites believed that they could control Hitler, but the NSDAP was not a traditional political party. Instead, the Nazis were building a mass movement that promised its supporters *action*, including election campaigns, mass rallies, and violent attacks on their opponents organized by paramilitary *Sturmabteilung* (SA) stormtroopers. By 1932 SA membership had grown to around 400 000 as working-class men, many of them unemployed, joined the organization's original student and middle-class cadre. In return for their loyalty and commitment, the SA offered its members a sense of belonging and empowerment, male sociability bonded by violence, and – not unimportantly in the context of the Depression – jobs with Nazi-owned businesses.

Intense street violence unfolded as SA "Brownshirts" attacked Jews and Jewish businesses and battled the paramilitary defense forces of the Communist and Socialist parties. One hundred and forty-three stormtroopers were killed in street battles between 1930 and 1932, and over 8000 paramilitaries from all parties were seriously injured during 1931 alone. In the context of this violent assault, divisions between the Nazis' main opponents facilitated Hitler's rapid rise. Under orders from the Stalinist-dominated Comintern, the KPD insisted that the greatest danger facing German workers was not the Nazis but the moderate socialists of the SPD. Communist hostility to the "social fascist" SDP led to violent confrontations between the rival working-class organizations, and during the 1932 Berlin tramway workers' strike, Communist and Nazi paramilitaries joined forces against SPD officials. Even at the height of NSDAP electoral success in July 1932 they barely had more votes that the combined KPD/SPD total, but divisions between the working-class parties blocked effective opposition and smoothed Hitler's path to power.

Chancellor Brüning's government by executive decree raised state power above parliamentary control and signaled the breakdown of Weimar democracy. Brüning was unable to solve the economic crisis, and in summer 1932 German president and veteran war leader Field-Marshal Paul von Hindenburg replaced him with right-wing conservatives Franz von Papen and then General Kurt von Schleicher. Both followed Brüning's example and ruled by executive decree, which von Papen used to oust the SPD-led Prussian state government. Meanwhile, the Nazi vote rose to 37.4% in the July 1932 Reichstag elections, only to slump to 33.1% in November – less than the KPD/SPD total. NSDAP votes in provincial elections declined even more sharply. Many Germans, including some Nazi leaders, thought that their challenge had peaked. Then, in a maneuver against Schleicher, Papen persuaded Hindenburg to appoint Hitler as chancellor. He took office on January 30, 1933.

Hitler's rise to power was not inevitable. Hindenburg's decision to make Hitler chancellor was the product of political intrigue, not unstoppable force, and united Socialist and Communist Party action might have stopped the Nazis in their tracks. At the same time, the growth of the NSDAP was the product of the economic and social crisis unleashed by the Depression, and the party's radical nationalism appealed to the dispossessed middle classes *and* to key sections of the elite. The NSDAP only held a minority of seats in Hitler's first cabinet, and an attempt to secure electoral legitimacy in early March failed to deliver a clear Nazi majority. Nevertheless, Hitler moved quickly to consolidate power. Blaming a mysterious fire in the parliament (Reichstag) building on the Communists, Hitler seized dictatorial power with the passage of the Enabling Act on March 23. With that vote, the Reichstag put itself out of business, and after President Hindenburg's death in August 1934 Hitler consolidated his dictatorship by creating the new office of *Führer*, or "Leader."

As the Nazis seized control of state and local government, thousands of SA paramilitaries were made auxiliary policemen, giving official cover for their violent campaign against socialists, communists – the KPD was already effectively banned – and trade union activists. In 1933, 80 000 opponents of the new Nazi government were detained, first in makeshift jails and then in concentration camps. Many were beaten or tortured, and many more were frightened into abandoning political activism. Leftist newspapers were banned, and by summer 1933 the Socialist and Communist parties had been neutralized and their affiliated trade unions destroyed. The dissolution of bourgeois political parties followed next, leaving the NSDAP as the only legal party in Germany. These moves were accompanied by a powerful upsurge of anti-Semitism. Violent street attacks on Jews and on Jewish stores and synagogues intensified, and the civil service, universities, and professional associations all began to purge Jews from their ranks. Jewish emigration from Germany increased rapidly, and under the 1935 Haavara Agreement between the government and German Zionists, 60 000 German Jews emigrated to British-ruled Palestine.

As these attacks unfolded, the "coordination" of political, social, and artistic life gave the Nazis control over all aspects of German society. Local and state governments were replaced by Nazi *Gauleiters*, distinctions between party and state organizations dissolved, and all manner of sports and recreational clubs and associations were replaced by Nazi-run organizations. Despite its outward appearance of decisive top-down decision making, however, the Nazi regime was riven by factionalism, overlapping jurisdictions, and blurred lines of command as various Nazi leaders and the organizations under their command competed for Hitler's approval. This fractious, polycentric, and often inefficient power structure remained in place during the entire period of Nazi rule.

Hitler was particularly concerned by the growth of the radical wing of the movement based in the SA and composed of men – many of them from the industrial heartlands – who had taken the Nazis' anti-capitalist rhetoric seriously. On the "Night of the Long Knives" in June 1934 Hitler conducted a bloody purge of the SA that killed its central leader, Ernst Röhm. Having tamed the unruly Brownshirts, domestic security became the province of disciplined organizations that combined party and state functions, including Heinrich Himmler's *Schutzstaffel* (SS, or Protection Squadron), Reinhard Heydrich's SD (Security Service), and the various police agencies under their control. Brownshirts continued to play an important role in German society, offering millions of men a direct link to the Nazi state and managing social welfare projects, but the locus of political power moved firmly into the hands of top Nazi leaders and their key allies in big business and the military. The murder of the openly gay Röhm also triggered an intensification of anti-gay persecution; between 1934 and 1945, 50 000 men were found guilty of homosexual behavior, and thousands of them died in Nazi concentration camps.

Public support for the Nazi regime was buttressed by a large-scale public works program centered on the construction of the *autobahn* (highway) network. Begun in fall 1933, highway construction created a sense that the government was acting to alleviate the Depression: in fact, as with similar New Deal programs in the United States, a flurry of activity concealed the fact that the actual economic impact was modest. In Germany, as elsewhere, recovery from the Great Depression rested on large-scale rearmament. The Nazis' goal of *Lebensraum* required large armed forces, and from his first days in power Hitler declared "everything must cede preponderance to the task of rearmament."[3] However, while many German industrialists were enthusiastic supporters of rearmament, they lacked the raw materials and finance necessary for a rapid increase in production. Financial difficulties were solved when the Reichsbank began funding rearmament using "Mefo Bills" drawn on a shell company. Export subsidies and state control over the import of raw materials reoriented German trade away from Britain and the United States and towards Central Europe, and by 1936 this package of measures allowed rearmament to get underway.

In January 1935 the people of Saarland, a region separated from Germany under the Versailles Treaty, voted overwhelmingly to rejoin the country.

Emboldened, German leaders reintroduced conscription and announced the creation of an air force, both banned at Versailles. Impressed by the results of state planning in the USSR, Berlin launched its own Four-Year Plan in 1936, establishing a sprawling state bureaucracy headed by Hitler's key ally Hermann Göring to oversee the rearmament effort. Initial market-based measures to boost German exports were now replaced by a drive to strengthen German self-reliance by promoting the development of synthetic rubber, textiles, and fuel oil. Under this autarkic scheme, Germany would be fed by Romanian and Hungarian grain as these countries were drawn into a German-led regional bloc.

Germany's accelerating rearmament drive overlapped with an increasingly assertive foreign policy. Under the Versailles Treaty, Germany was barred from stationing troops in the Rhineland, a swath of German territory bordering France. This violation of German sovereignty rankled with most Germans, and many applauded when Hitler sent the army marching into the Rhineland on March 7, 1936. The move was a tremendous gamble. French troops had only withdrawn in 1930, and Paris was reluctant to see the region reoccupied by German troops. London was less concerned, and many British politicians openly sympathized with Germany's move. Lacking British backing, France did not resist the German advance, and the Nazi gamble paid off. Berlin's growing political confidence was signaled in November 1936 by the signing of the Anti-Comintern Pact with Japan. Berlin was impressed with Tokyo's conquest of its own version of *Lebensraum* in Manchuria, and the pact expressed their common hostility to the Soviet Union.

Towards the "Axis" Alliance

The Great Depression also propelled the rise of an authoritarian dictatorship in Austria, where Engelbert Dollfuss's conservative Fatherland Front seized power in 1934. Dollfuss assumed dictatorial power over a paralyzed parliament, and he consolidated the new *Ständestaat* (or corporate state) by launching army attacks on Social Democratic Party strongholds throughout the country in a four-day civil war. Other opposition parties, including the Communists and the Austrian Nazis, had already been banned; while Austrian Nazis advocated a unified Germany under Hitler's leadership, the Fatherland Front emphasized Austrian nationalism, and their corporatist outlook echoed Italian Fascism.

Mussolini was initially ambivalent about Hitler's rise to power, partly because Italian leaders were concerned that Nazi Germany would annex Austria, creating an expansionist state on Italy's long-disputed northern border. In April 1935, Italy joined Britain and France in the Stresa Front, a diplomatic bloc pledged to uphold Austrian independence and to obstruct German attempts to nullify the Treaty of Versailles. At the same time, however, the emergence of the Nazi dictatorship emboldened Fascist plans for Italian expansionism in North Africa and the Balkans. In a step towards the establishment of a new Roman Empire, 200 000 Italian troops invaded Ethiopia in October 1935. By the following May well-equipped Italian ground troops, backed by airplanes dropping poison gas on soldiers and civilians alike, had crushed Ethiopian resistance and forced Emperor Haile Selassie into exile. In 1938, Rome expanded its colonial project by settling 20 000 Italian farmers in Libya in a move designed to relieve alleged overpopulation in Italy while providing the homeland with new sources of food.

Rome hoped that the Stresa Front would provide diplomatic cover for its aggression in North Africa, and initially Paris endorsed Mussolini's Ethiopian adventure in the hope that it would keep Rome and Berlin apart. Nevertheless, public opinion in the West was appalled by the brutality of the Italian invasion, and following London's lead the League of Nations criticized Rome's actions and voted to impose limited economic sanctions on Italy. In practice, however, the reluctance of the democracies to take action against Italy made the sanctions ineffective, particularly as the United States – which was not in the League of Nations – continued to trade with Italy. At the same time, Nazi Germany made its support for Italy clear by boosting coal exports. The Ethiopian crisis thus pushed Rome and Berlin together, and Mussolini endorsed Germany's remilitarization of the Rhineland in March 1936 before announcing in November that European politics would in future revolve around a "Rome–Berlin axis." The "Axis" alliance was starting to take shape.

Britain, France, and the United States continued their efforts to peel Mussolini away from Hitler, but events were moving in the opposite direction. Italian leaders admired Tokyo's conquest of Manchuria, and Rome's victory in Ethiopia was applauded in Japan and Germany. Japanese and Italian leaders both saw their conquests as a new form of "proletarian" imperialism in which long-suppressed underdogs challenged the old imperial order, and Nazi leaders viewed their plans for *Lebensraum* in the East in much the same light. Given their ultimate failure, it is hard today to take these imperial projects seriously. But it is important to do so. Axis plans all featured the creation of large, contiguous territorial spaces integrated into the imperial homeland by rail or by short sea crossings, and in this sense they differed from earlier forms of overseas colonialism. All were intended to create massive autarkic blocs that could, in collaboration with each other, marshal the necessary resources to challenge the rising power of the United States. The Italian conquest of Ethiopia brought the three future Axis allies closer together, a convergence registered in November 1937 when Rome joined Berlin and Tokyo in the Anti-Comintern Pact.

Moscow and the Search for Collective Security

Soviet leaders were naturally alarmed by the advance of fascism and Japanese militarism. In 1932, Moscow launched a second Five-Year Plan focused on heavy industry and armaments production, and by the time Germany began to rearm the Soviet effort was already well underway. During the 1930s, the Soviet economy grew at around 10% per year, and the Great Depression had little direct impact within the USSR. Given the economic catastrophe in the capitalist world, these economic advances reinforced the USSR's appeal to workers and progressive-minded intellectuals worldwide. Less well known was the fact that Stalin was simultaneously consolidating the power of the administrative bureaucracy through a series of purges and show trials. Tens of thousands of real or imagined opponents were executed or dispatched to the extensive archipelago of penal labor camps known as the *Gulag*. In 1937, Stalin's paranoid fear of political opposition prompted a ferocious purge of the Red Army's officer corps that disrupted military preparedness and negated the gains of the rearmament effort.

Internationally, Moscow responded to the Nazi threat by seeking anti-fascist alliances with the democratic capitalist states. Spearheaded by People's Commissar for Foreign Affairs Maxim Litvinov, this pursuit of "collective security" marked a further retreat from the revolutionary internationalism of the early Russian Revolution. The campaign scored some notable successes. In 1933, the new Roosevelt administration in Washington granted the Soviet Union diplomatic recognition. This move went against the grain of the isolationism characteristic of Roosevelt's first term, and it may be that the president was already thinking about an alliance capable of containing German expansionism. Two years later, Litvinov secured a Franco-Soviet treaty promising mutual assistance in the event of foreign aggression; signed just after the formation of the Stresa Front, the signatories hoped that the pact would complete the diplomatic isolation of Nazi Germany. The USSR was admitted to the League of Nations in 1934, giving Moscow an international platform from which to advocate collective security. Nevertheless, the League's failure to respond to the Italian invasion of Ethiopia undermined its credibility and weakened Moscow's effort to build an international anti-fascist front.

Despite these difficulties, Moscow had other levers to hand. Under Stalin, the Comintern functioned as an instrument of Soviet foreign policy, and national Communist parties were ruthlessly subordinated to Moscow. As the consequences of the Nazi seizure of power became clear, the Soviet leadership instructed Communist parties around the world to end the kind of bitter sectarian attacks that had divided German workers in the early 1930s and to work instead for "popular front" alliances with anyone – including "bourgeois" parties – willing to resist fascism. The new policy appealed to the concerns of workers and of middle-class radicals, and it registered significant successes. In 1936, Communist Party activists in both France and Spain helped to assemble Popular Front coalitions that won national elections, countering the rightist advances in Italy and Germany with liberal-leftist electoral victories.

Popular Front in France and Civil War in Spain

The French government's refusal to abandon the gold standard prolonged the depression, and its effects fell heavily on peasants, artisans, and small businessmen. These classes provided fertile ground for the growth of ultra-nationalism, and in the early 1930s several fascist organizations emerged in France. The most prominent was the Croix de Feu (CF or Cross of Fire), led by former army officer François de La Rocque. In February 1934, La Rocque led 2000 CF members in an attack on parliament, provoking a crisis that toppled the Radical Party government. The CF grew rapidly following the February events, claiming 300 000 members by 1935. Beyond the openly fascistic CF there was a substantial bloc of leading politicians known as the *mous*, or "softs," who favored accommodation with Germany and tough anti-working-class policies within France. With a new conservative government following Brüning's example and ruling by executive order, it was clear that the parliamentary democracy of the French Third Republic was in deep trouble.

The French Communist Party (PCF) responded to these developments by intensifying its effort to create an anti-fascist bloc, and it joined the Socialist and Radical parties in the Popular Front alliance. In May 1936, the Popular Front won a narrow majority in the general election, and Socialist Party leader Léon Blum became premier. The PCF doubled its vote, reflecting an upsurge in working-class militancy that produced a great wave of strikes and factory occupations in summer 1936. Trade union membership leapt from 785 000 in 1935 to over four million the following year, with autoworkers and other industrial workers joining in large numbers. Under working-class pressure, the Popular Front government granted workers a 40-hour workweek, paid annual vacations, legal protection for trade union activity, and sweeping wage increases. Blum and his PCF allies ensured that working-class militancy did not develop into a generalized challenge to capitalism, but French elites remained deeply hostile to the PCF and the unions. Working-class radicalism also alarmed the Radicals, who quit the Popular Front and ended Blum's premiership after just one year. In this polarized atmosphere fascist organizations thrived, and in 1940 La Rocque turned the CF into the populist French Social Party (PSF) with a membership of 700 000.

Deepening social polarization with its accompanying waves of left- and right-wing radicalism also found expression in Spain, the most economically underdeveloped state in Western Europe. King Alfonso XIII was deeply unpopular due to his association with the military dictatorship of the 1920s, and after his abdication in 1931 there was an outpouring of popular protest as peasants and workers responded to long-standing social oppression and to the economic impact of the Depression. Caught between popular militancy and mounting right-wing reaction, liberal prime minister Manuel Azaña was pushed aside in 1933 by a series of conservative regimes that crushed strikes and popular protests. Under Moscow's guidance, the small Communist Party of Spain (PCE) helped to form a Popular Front alliance that included liberals, socialists, and some of Spain's many anarchists. Led by Azaña, the Popular Front won a narrow electoral victory in 1936.

The election of the Popular Front encouraged many workers and peasant farmers to step up their fight for revolutionary social change, but it also provoked senior army officers to launch a coup against the Azaña government. Nationalist forces led by General Francisco Franco and backed by a coalition of monarchists, the Catholic hierarchy, and the fascist Falange party advanced quickly but failed to seize Madrid. Supporters of the Republic rallied to its defense, and a bitter and protracted civil war followed. Franco appealed to the fascist regimes in Berlin and Rome, which responded by sending military contingents to Spain and by funneling arms to the Nationalists. Fifty thousand Italian soldiers fought in Spain, along with the 7000 men and aircraft of the German Condor Legion. The Soviet Union was concerned not to disrupt its search for collective security by alienating the European democracies, but it did send some military equipment – including tanks and airplanes – to the Republican government. The Comintern also organized an outpouring of international solidarity, with 40 000 volunteers from 50 countries traveling to Spain to fight as members of the International Brigades.

Léon Blum initially wanted the French Popular Front government to support its Spanish neighbor, but French and British elites both feared that a Republican victory in Spain might lead to a socialist revolution, and they pushed for a Non-Intervention Committee to prevent foreign military aid from reaching Spain. Given that committee members Italy and Germany were already helping the Nationalists, non-intervention was always an exercise in hypocrisy. Backed by the United States, the arms embargo choked off the supply of weapons to the Republican government but did nothing to prevent men and equipment reaching the Nationalists. The Republic was further undermined by the authoritarian behavior of the PCE and its Comintern advisers, who sought to centralize political and military power in their own hands while repressing revolutionary-minded Republican forces that included anarchists and Trotskyists. While Moscow supported the Republic against its Nationalist and fascist opponents, it had no interest in a socialist revolution that might escape its control and endanger its diplomatic relations with Britain and France. Not for the last time, Stalin's government acted to derail a radical revolutionary movement.

These circumstances forced the Republican government to fight a long defensive war under increasingly unfavorable conditions. It was finally battered into submission in April 1939, by which time the war had claimed over 500 000 lives. In the aftermath of his military victory, Franco consolidated a conservative dictatorship that looked to the fascist powers as allies. The rightist victory in Spain occurred at a critical point in the development of Berlin and Rome's own expansionist plans, and both Mussolini and Hitler were emboldened by the evident fact that the democracies were more concerned with the threat of socialist revolution than they were with fascist expansionism.

Anschluss, **Appeasement, and Rearmament**

As we have seen, foreign policy in Berlin, Tokyo, and Rome during the 1930s was increasingly driven by racialized visions of colonial conquest. The practical business of expansionism, however, did not proceed according to preconceived master plans, but by opportunistic lurches as new openings were probed and exploited. Emboldened by its unopposed remilitarization of the Rhineland and with its Condor Legion gaining combat experience in Spain, Berlin turned its attention to Austria. Although explicitly prohibited at Versailles, the *Anschluss* (unification) of Germany and Austria was popular in both countries. Elsewhere, *Anschluss* was widely viewed as a legitimate expression of self-determination by a people who shared the German language and a great deal of culture. Moreover, the accelerated convergence between Rome and Berlin undercut Italian support for Austrian independence under the "Austrofascist" Fatherland Front government.

The withdrawal of Italian support left the Austrian government under Dollfuss's successor Kurt Schuschnigg dangerously exposed in the face of German demands for unity. Berlin used a political crisis provoked by Austrian Nazis in March 1938 as an excuse to invade the country, derailing Schuschnigg's plan for a referendum on Austrian independence. German troops faced no opposition. Hitler followed his soldiers, making a triumphant procession through his homeland to Vienna, where he was welcomed by enthusiastic crowds. In April, a plebiscite delivered a 99.7% majority in favor of *Anschluss*. Jews were barred from voting and many opponents of the regime were already in detention, but the merger with Germany clearly enjoyed the support of most Austrians. From 1938 until 1945 Austria was incorporated into the Reich as the *Ostmark* or "eastern march," and its eight provinces became *Reichsgaue* under Nazi officials who were both civil governors and Party heads, or *Gauleiters*. Men in the *Ostmark* were liable to military service on the same basis as those in other parts of Germany: 1.3 million of them were conscripted into the *Wehrmacht* and 250 000 were killed.

Berlin followed the *Anschluss* by asserting its claim to the Sudetenland, the German-speaking borderland of the Czechoslovak state created at Versailles. Eager to avoid war in Central Europe, the prime ministers of Britain and France met with Hitler and Mussolini in Munich in September 1938. Czechoslovakia was not represented. Intimidated by Hitler's threats, Neville Chamberlain and Édouard Daladier agreed to a German annexation of the Sudetenland, while Poland and Hungary were also awarded chunks of Czech territory. Abandoned by its Western allies, Prague did not resist the German occupation, which cost Czechoslovakia its defensive frontier and much of its industry. Chamberlain returned to London to announce that the Munich meeting had secured "peace in our time!"

Today, Chamberlain's proclamation seems laughable, and Munich appears as the hopeless conclusion of a doomed policy of trying to avoid war by appeasing Germany. At the time, however, people fearful of a new European war greeted the Munich settlement with enthusiasm. From Washington, President Roosevelt encouraged Hitler and Mussolini to hold the conference, and he endorsed the "universal sense of relief" that peace had been preserved.[4] In the United States, appeasement was intertwined with a desire to avoid foreign entanglements that was reflected in the four Neutrality Acts passed between 1935 and 1939 prohibiting the sale of arms to warring countries. In Britain, appeasement also reflected a belief that German demands for a revision of Versailles were justified and that a strong Germany could provide a welcome bulwark against communism. Leading figures in the British political establishment and in the royal family expressed admiration for Hitler, and in the 1935 Anglo-German Naval Treaty London gave its approval to Berlin's warship building program.

Appeasement is often presented as a softheaded refusal to confront Nazi aggression, but many appeasers simply hoped to accommodate the growth of a reinvigorated Germany without disrupting the overall balance of power in Europe. This did not seem entirely far-fetched; after all, Mussolini's Italy had been successfully integrated into European politics in the 1920s. What the appeasers misunderstood was that Nazi Germany was the product of profound economic and political crisis that, so its leaders believed, could *only* be resolved through the creation of colonial *Lebensraum*. German expansionism necessarily pointed towards war, and Hitler was entirely ready to use force against Czechoslovakia in 1938.

When the Munich agreement failed to stop German expansionism – German armies occupied the remainder of Czechoslovakia in early 1939 – London and Paris finally and reluctantly recognized that appeasement could not stop Hitler. In Paris, the *mous* were temporarily silenced. Anglo-French leaders still hoped to avoid a European war, but both countries now launched major rearmament programs. France had already begun constructing a massive series of fortifications known as the Maginot Line and the Popular Front government had stepped up military spending, but Paris now launched an astonishing rearmament drive that gave it parity with Germany in tanks by late 1940. France also began talks on purchasing large numbers of American-made aircraft, while Britain ramped up the production of fighter aircraft and other war matériel. In January 1939, Anglo-French staff talks mapped out joint war plans. These measures were accompanied by Anglo-French treaties with Poland, Romania, and Greece. These pledges of military support in the event of a German invasion did not stem from moral opposition to fascism, but from a long-delayed recognition that Germany's march towards hegemony in Central Europe could not be halted peacefully.

Towards an Asian War

The USSR's pursuit of popular front alliances extended to Asia, where Moscow pressed for the formation of a Second United Front between the Chinese Communist Party and the Guomindang. Negotiations began in summer of 1936, and in the Xi'an Incident Manchurian warlord Zhang Xueliang and other northern generals kidnaped Chiang to force him into the alliance. As this new sense of unity developed in China, an unplanned clash between Chinese and Japanese troops precipitated all-out war. On July 7, 1937, Japanese soldiers based in Beijing under the 1901 agreement ending the Boxer Rebellion got into a firefight with Chinese troops near the Marco Polo Bridge. Bolstered by the new united front, Chiang did not back down, and Prince Konoe Fumimaro's government responded by launching Japan's Kwantung Army into Northern China. Chiang rallied Nationalists, Communists, and local warlords for a war of resistance, and he quickly opened a second front by committing his crack German-trained units against Japanese troops in Shanghai. The Imperial Japanese Navy ferried reinforcements into the city, and by August China and Japan were locked into a two-front war.

Shanghai fell to Japan on November 8, 1937 – although the city's International Settlement escaped Tokyo's control until 1941 – and Japanese troops pursued the retreating Nationalists up the Yangtze to Nanjing, which they stormed in December (Figure 2.1). The capture of the Nationalist capital was followed by the Rape of Nanjing, an orgy of violence, destruction, and sexual predation during which Japanese soldiers slaughtered as many as 200 000 Chinese civilians. It was one of the worst atrocities of the entire war. Japanese advances in Central China were matched in the North, where Japanese troops occupied Beijing and other major cities. Despite these dramatic military successes, however, a worrying pattern soon became clear to Japanese officers. China was a vast country, and although Japanese troops almost invariably won in battle, they only had sufficient forces to secure the urban centers and the railroads connecting them. Beyond these "points and lines," civil society simply collapsed in large areas of the country,

Figure 2.1 Japanese troops advance quickly through Wuxi on the railroad from Shanghai to Nanjing, December 1937. (*Source*: Bundesarchiv, Bild 183-S34828.)

with power often passing to local warlords loyal to neither side. In Shaanxi and other northern provinces, these chaotic conditions favored the Communists. Their forces were organized for guerrilla war, and their political appeal to the peasants allowed them to fill the political vacuum with resilient new power structures built from the village level upwards.

In May 1938, Japanese troops won a hard-fought battle for the city of Xuzhou, securing the north–south rail link and joining the two war fronts. Retreating Nationalists tried to delay the Japanese advance on the key industrial city of Wuhan by destroying dikes on the Yellow River and inundating a vast area. The flooding killed an estimated 900 000 Chinese civilians and displaced nearly four million more; as historian Rana Mitter points out, it would have been considered a "prime atrocity of the war" if it been committed by the invading Japanese.[5] Japanese forces avoided the worst of the flooding by deploying naval vessels on the Yangtze, and in October they captured Wuhan. Chiang and the Nationalist government retreated further up the river to the provincial center of Chongqing. With Japanese naval landings sealing off the coast by capturing Guangzhou and other coastal cities, Nationalist China was pushed into the interior of south-central China, and by summer 1938, 21 of China's 29 provinces were fully or partially occupied by the Japanese.

In Chongqing, the Nationalists worked to rebuild a functioning state, providing assistance for refugees and raising a two-million-man conscript army. As the Japanese approached Wuhan, the city's munitions factories were evacuated to Sichuan. Despite intense state-directed efforts, however, relocation and a narrowing resource base meant that arms production fell to 40% of prewar levels. At the same time, tax revenues collapsed, inflation and government borrowing soared, and Chongqing turned to the opium trade for funds. The Nationalist government also reached out for Soviet aid, and between September 1937 and April 1941 Moscow supplied 1,235 airplanes, tens of thousands of guns, and numerous military advisers, pilots, engineers, and truck drivers. Soviet-crewed airplanes provided Nationalist forces with a degree of air support, and over 200 Soviet pilots died in China.

At first, Nationalist China received little support from the Western democracies. The British government was preoccupied with the crisis in Europe, while the United States was so keen to avoid a conflict with Tokyo that when Japanese aircraft sank the US Navy gunboat *Panay* on the Yangtze in December 1937, Washington accepted Tokyo's tepid apology without complaint. As the Japanese advance continued Western attitudes began to change, and in early 1939 the US Treasury brokered a $25 million loan to Chongqing. At the same time, British forces began building the Burma Road, a tortuous trail from the railhead at Lashio in British-ruled Burma to Kunming in Guomindang-ruled Yunnan province. This overland route ensured that a trickle of Western aid could reach Chiang's beleaguered forces.

Unable to win a quick and decisive victory in China, Japanese leaders began to look for other lines of advance that could unlock the resources necessary for a protracted war. Hostility to the Soviet Union had long been central to Japanese thinking, signified by Tokyo's signing of the Anti-Comintern Pact in 1936, and the recently purged Red Army seemed unlikely to offer much opposition. There had been a long series of small-scale clashes between Japanese and Soviet forces on the border of Manchukuo during the 1930s, and in May 1939 Kwantung Army probes into the Mongolian People's Republic around the Khalkhyn Gol River escalated into a full-scale conflict. Both sides rushed in reinforcements, and in a series of battles over the next four months Soviet armored forces led by General Georgy Zhukov achieved a stunning victory over the Kwantung Army. The fighting on the Khalkhyn Gol had far-reaching consequences, convincing Tokyo to avoid war with the USSR and leading to the April 1941 Soviet–Japanese Non-Aggression Pact. With their hopes of moving against the Soviet Union stymied, Japanese leaders turned instead towards the rich resources of Southeast Asia. At the same time, peace with Japan forced Moscow to end its military support for Nationalist China, leaving Chongqing dependent on a trickle of British and American aid arriving overland from Burma.

Towards a European War

In March 1939, Berlin invaded the remainder of Czechoslovakia, partitioning the country to create the Reich Protectorate of Bohemia and Moravia and the client state of Slovakia. Hitler's bold action quietened military leaders wary of a premature war, and the occupation secured control of the Czech arms industry. Italy also stepped up its expansionist efforts, making claims on French colonial territory in North Africa in late 1938 and then invading Albania in April 1939. Albania offered an entry into the Balkans and had long been under Italian influence, and it was now annexed to the newly proclaimed Italian Empire. King Zog was easily toppled despite popular calls for armed resistance, and King Victor Emmanuel III added "King of Albania" to his many titles. France and Britain kept silent in the hope of keeping Germany and Italy apart, but in May Berlin and Rome signed the Pact of Steel, a formal alliance whose secret protocols called for closer economic and military integration.

In the light of the rapidly growing Axis threat and of British and French reluctance to confront it, Moscow made an abrupt change of course. Soviet leaders still believed that a clash with Nazi Germany was inevitable, but they wanted to delay it for as long as possible to buy time for rearmament. As a result, Moscow abandoned the fruitless search for collective security and instead sought accommodation with Berlin. On August 23, 1939, the new Commissar for Foreign Affairs Vyacheslav Molotov and German Foreign Minister Joachim von Ribbentrop met in Moscow to sign a non-aggression pact. Secret protocols divided Poland between the two states and recognized Soviet predominance in Finland and the Baltic States. The pact was accompanied by a trade agreement that facilitated the export of German capital goods to the USSR in exchange for oil, wheat, and other raw materials. Not surprisingly, the Molotov–Ribbentrop Pact threw Communist parties around the world into confusion as Comintern orders arrived instructing them to abandon anti-fascist popular fronts in favor of propaganda campaigns against Anglo-French imperialism.

The Molotov–Ribbentrop Pact allowed Berlin to move ahead with its planned invasion of Poland. Although ruled by a conservative military dictatorship and protected by a 1934 non-aggression pact with Germany, Poland had long been central to Nazi expansionist designs. Poland had received big slices of German territory at Versailles, which also made Danzig a "free city" under League of Nations oversight, and Berlin's demands for the restitution of these territories justified its war preparations. But Nazi aggression had a bigger goal in mind. Poland's fertile soils offered the ideal space for colonial *Lebensraum*, and its Slavic and Jewish populations were deemed suitable for dispossession, liquidation, or reduction to semi-slavery. German invasion plans moved ahead in the knowledge that Anglo-French pledges of support for Poland made European war a possibility. For Berlin, this gamble was justified by the belief that accelerating rearmament programs in Britain, France, and the United States would soon nullify Germany's military advantage, and that therefore there was nothing to gain by waiting. And, with Germany's eastern flank secured by the Molotov–Ribbentrop Pact, a war with the European democracies was a manageable proposition.

The German invasion of Poland began on September 1, 1939 and was successfully concluded in just six weeks. The Polish army deployed along the frontier, where it offered an inviting target for the large-scale envelopment operations favored by German military planners. German attacks were backed by the use of tactical airstrikes and by tanks and mobile artillery, all of which put the experience gained in Spain to good use. Nevertheless, while the elements of blitzkrieg – or lightning war – began to coalesce in Poland, most German soldiers still marched into action on foot and moved their supplies in horse-drawn carts. The Poles were not defeated by a new way of war; instead, they were outnumbered and outfought by what was still a rather conventional army. The Poles fought fiercely, inflicting unexpectedly heavy casualties and destroying significant numbers of German tanks and airplanes, but their fate was sealed by the intervention of the Red Army. The Soviet invasion began as soon as Moscow received the news of the victory on the Khalkhyn Gol, and in late September Soviet and German forces met to complete the partition of Poland.

On September 3, 1939, Britain and France declared war on Germany. Distance – and lack of preparation – made it impossible to participate in the defense of Poland, and the German–Soviet invasion was over before British troops could arrive in France in large numbers. In September, the French launched a half-hearted offensive into the Saarland, but over the following months the European war was characterized by such widespread inactivity that it became popularly known as the Phony War or "sitzkrieg." In Britain, fear of German bombing led to the evacuation of nearly 1.5 million people – mostly schoolchildren and mothers with infants – from major cities, but when German raids failed to materialize many soon returned home. But if the war looked phony, the global crisis underpinning it was far from fake, and as the decade of the Great Depression came to an end, full-scale – but as yet quite separate – wars were underway in both Asia and Europe.

Notes

1. Paine, S.C.M. (2017). *The Japanese Empire: Grand Strategy from the Meiji Restoration to the Pacific War*, 103. New York: Cambridge University Press.
2. Hitler, A. (1971 [1924]). *Mein Kampf*, 641–668. Boston: Houghton Mifflin.
3. Hitler, February 9, 1933, quoted in Epstein (2015), 99.
4. Roosevelt, quoted in Dallek, R. (1995). *Franklin D. Roosevelt and American Foreign Policy, 1932–1945*, 171. New York: Oxford University Press.
5. Mitter (2013), 161.

References

Epstein, C. (2015). *Nazi Germany: Confronting the Myths*. Chichester: Wiley Blackwell.

Mitter, R. (2013). *China's War with Japan, 1937–1945: The Struggle for Survival*. New York: Penguin.

Further Reading

Hedinger, D. (2017). The imperial nexus: the Second World War and the Axis in global perspective. *Journal of Global History* 12: 184–285.

Hobsbawm, E. (1996). *The Age of Extremes, 1914–1991*. New York: Vintage.

Jackson, J. (2001). *France: The Dark Years, 1940–1944*. New York: Oxford University Press.

Kershaw, I. (1993). Working towards the Führer: reflections on the nature of the Hitler dictatorship. *Contemporary European History* 2 ((2)): 103–118.

Kotin, S. (1995). *Magnetic Mountain: Stalinism as Civilization*. Berkeley: University of California Press.

Mahnken, T., Maiolo, J., and Stevenson, D. (eds.) (2016). *Arms Races in International Politics: From the Nineteenth to the Twenty-First Century*. New York: Oxford University Press.

Patel, K.K. (2016). *The New Deal: A Global History*. Princeton: Princeton University Press.

Siemens, D. (2017). *Stormtroopers: A New History of Hitler's Brownshirts*. New Haven: Yale University Press.

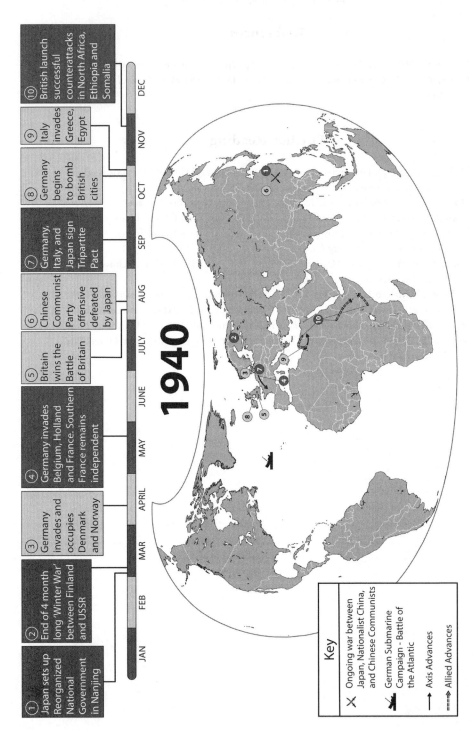

1 Japan sets up Reorganized National Government in Nanjing

2 End of 4 month long 'Winter War' between Finland and USSR

3 Germany invades and occupies Denmark and Norway

4 Germany invades Belgium, Holland and France. Southern France remains independent

5 Britain wins the Battle of Britain

6 Chinese Communist Party offensive defeated by Japan

7 Germany, Italy, and Japan sign Tripartite Pact

8 Germany begins to bomb British cities

9 Italy invades Greece, Egypt

10 British launch successful counterattacks in North Africa, Ethiopia and Somalia

JAN FEB MAR APRIL MAY JUNE JULY AUG SEP OCT NOV DEC

1940

Key

✕ Ongoing war between Japan, Nationalist China, and Chinese Communists

✈ German Submarine Campaign - Battle of the Atlantic

→ Axis Advances

═══▶ Allied Advances

Map: 1940. (*Source:* © Andrew Buchanan. Map drawn by Max Muller.)

3

1940: Axis Victories and New Strategic Choices

In the opening weeks of 1940, the wars in both Europe and Asia seemed deadlocked. Hitler had hoped to maintain the momentum of the victory in Poland by moving quickly to invade France but, to the relief of many senior *Wehrmacht* officers, the capture of German operational plans when a staff aircraft crashed in Belgium forced a postponement of the invasion. This extension of the Phony War was welcomed in London and Paris, where politicians still hoped to avoid an all-out European conflict, but it also gave the *Wehrmacht* time to make good its losses and to redraft its plans in the light of lessons learned in Poland.

In China, the deadlock had a broader character. Major military operations continued, and a renewed Japanese advance up the Yangtze in the spring of 1940 captured the rice-rich Hunan province and brought the Guomindang capital of Chongqing within range of Japanese aircraft, but these operational successes failed to secure victory. Japanese forces and their local allies gained nominal control of huge swaths of territory, but they lacked the manpower to pacify the vast Chinese countryside, while the establishment of client governments based on regional warlords and Guomindang defectors failed to create political stability. In March 1940, Tokyo installed former Guomindang leader Wang Jingwei as head of the Reorganized National Government in Nanjing. Wang claimed to be Sun Yat-sen's true successor, and his regime used Guomindang flags and symbols. Reorganized National Government troops joined Japanese attacks on Communist Party forces, but relations with Tokyo were strained by Wang's efforts to establish his own independent authority. Military deadlock and political fragmentation underscored the fact that there was no stable, China-wide outcome in sight.

World War II in Global Perspective, 1931–1953: A Short History, First Edition. Andrew N. Buchanan.
© 2019 John Wiley & Sons, Inc. Published 2019 by John Wiley & Sons, Inc.

The regional wars in Europe and Asia remained separate, but during 1940 stronger connections began to emerge. Britain, France, and the Netherlands all ruled Asian colonies threatened by Japanese expansionism, but the war in Europe meant that they lacked adequate resources to defend them. From Washington, President Roosevelt had stiffened America's opposition to Japanese expansionism with his 1937 call to "quarantine the aggressors," and the 1938 Navy Act called for a 20% expansion in the US Navy. Nevertheless, despite concentrating the American battle fleet in Pearl Harbor, Hawai'i, Roosevelt showed little enthusiasm for action against Japan. Washington did, however, became increasingly supportive of Nationalist China. This was a significant realignment for both parties, and it was paralleled by a rupture in the long-standing relationship between Chongqing and Berlin. Germany supplied weapons and military instructors to Chiang's armies throughout the 1930s. These ties were cut in 1938 after the Anti-Comintern Pact brought Berlin and Tokyo into closer alignment.

Winter War in Finland

While Phony War brought quiet to the Western Front, new conflicts flared in Eastern Europe. Under the terms of the Molotov–Ribbentrop Pact, Moscow incorporated former Polish territory east of the Bug River into the Soviet republics of Ukraine and Belorussia, and in October 1939 it forced the former Tsarist provinces of Estonia, Latvia, and Lithuania to accept Soviet troops on their territory. The Soviets also insisted that Finland withdraw its frontier on the Karelian Isthmus near Leningrad and asserted the Soviet Navy's right to use the Finnish naval base at Hanko. When the Finland government refused to comply, the Red Army invaded in November 1939. Despite their numerical superiority, poorly led Soviet forces failed to break through the defenses of the Mannerheim Line on the Karelian Isthmus, and in the forests and lakes of the north slow-moving Red Army formations were outmaneuvered by Finnish ski troops.

Berlin honored its pact with Moscow by blocking Italian arms shipments to Finland, but as Finnish resistance stoked their anti-communism Anglo-French leaders discussed taking time out of the Phony War to send troops to help the Finns. The British Royal Air Force (RAF) even planned to bomb oil installations in the Soviet Caucasus. Before the Allies could act, however, the Red Army regrouped for a massive assault on the Mannerheim Line, finally forcing the Finns to surrender in March 1940. Helsinki ceded extensive territory under the Moscow Peace Treaty, but Finland retained its independence and the Soviets shelved plans to install a client regime under Communist leader Otto Kuusinen. Despite its brevity, the Winter War was bloody, costing 50000 Finnish and 110000 Soviet lives, and the poor performance of the Red Army convinced observers in Berlin that the USSR was a second-rate military power.

During 1940, Moscow assimilated eastern Poland into its centrally planned economic system in an effort to strengthen the military defense of its western frontier. In a "top-down" assault on Polish capitalism, banks and businesses were expropriated, large landed estates were divided among peasant farmers, and Polish political, religious, and cultural institutions dissolved. One and a half million Poles were deported to collective farms in the USSR, while gangs of Ukrainian and Belorussian paramilitaries killed thousands more. In the Katyń Forest near Smolensk, Soviet secret police (NKVD) executed over 20 000 Polish army officers on Stalin's orders, and tens of thousands of private soldiers were marched off into Soviet prison camps. For the region's Jews, their numbers swollen by refugees from German-occupied western Poland, Soviet annexation appeared to offer relief from persecution, and many joined the new Soviet administrations.

German *Lebensraum* in Poland

Harsh though they were, conditions in Soviet-occupied eastern Poland paled in comparison to the brutality unleashed by German forces in the west. Here the consequences of the Nazi colonial project and its racialized contempt for Slavs and Jews became fully evident. Hitler had outlined the social goals of the Polish campaign to senior commanders: "Poland," he informed them, "will be depopulated and settled by Germans."[1] The German occupation was structured to facilitate this goal. In the west, Polish territory was annexed directly to Germany, becoming the Reich districts of Danzig-West Prussia and the Wartheland, while in the east the "General Government" administered the new colonial territory. Polish businesses in all of German-occupied Poland were expropriated, and in the new Reich districts Poles began to be evicted to make way for German settlers. Displaced Poles were crammed into the General Government where, as German planners well knew, food supplies were inadequate to support the enlarged population.

The German project in Eastern Europe bore a familial likeness to colonial ventures elsewhere in the world, and in the Nazi imagination it replicated the conquest and annexation of the American West. As in the United States, the aim was to connect vast, resource-rich, and contiguous colonial space directly to the country's industrial heartland. On this new frontier, Jews and Slavs replaced Native Americans as indigenous inhabitants worthy of extirpation. What was unique to Nazi-style colonialism was its compressed timeframe and the sustained intensity of its racialized brutality. A vision of *Lebensraum* in the East had inspired the Nazi movement since its inception, but its realization was an unfolding process in which new steps built pragmatically and opportunistically on previous accomplishments. In line with the overall operation of the Nazi state this was a surprisingly decentralized process, with rival leaders and their state, military, and party institutions taking their own initiatives as they competed for the resources that came with Hitler's approval.

Special Task Forces, or *Einsatzgruppen*, accompanied German military forces during the invasion of Poland. They were tasked with liquidating Polish political elites and others – especially Jews – deemed hostile to the new order. While nominally under military control, their independent command structure allowed army officers to disclaim responsibility for the *Einsatzgruppen* while tolerating or even encouraging their murderous activities. "Self-Protection" militias organized by German Poles and units of other German security organizations worked alongside the *Einsatzgruppen* in a generalized wave of violence that claimed over 65 000 civilian lives in 1939 alone. As the killing spread, regular German soldiers joined in, particularly younger men who had grown up under Nazi rule.

This orgy of violence was intertwined with a further radicalization of Nazi anti-Semitism. During the first six years of Nazi rule, thousands of German Jews left the country in the face of legalized persecution, economic dispossession, and physical assault. Nazi authorities encouraged this emigration, and over 55 000 German Jews moved to Palestine while a further 90 000 headed for the United States. Many more were denied American immigration visas. The 1935 Nuremberg Laws redefined German citizenship in explicitly racial terms: Jews were excluded from citizenship, while *Mischlinge* (people of mixed race) could hold citizenship but faced extensive legal discrimination. The new laws opened "full Jews," *Mischlinge*, and Romani (Gypsies) alike to further official and unofficial persecution.

By 1940, the Jewish population in Germany had fallen from over 500 000 to around 200 000, and the country seemed to be becoming *judenrein*, or "cleansed of Jews." In Poland, however, German soldiers encountered large Jewish communities that made up around 10% of the total population. Although they had long faced government anti-Semitism, Poland was home to long-standing Jewish communities that made up over half the population of some major cities. Among the occupying Germans, feelings of imperial and racial superiority combined with Nazi anti-Semitism to make these communities special targets. From the beginning of the occupation, random assaults and local pogroms proliferated, and in some places ethnic Poles joined German attacks on their Jewish neighbors.

As German rule in Poland was consolidated, anti-Semitic policies were clarified and codified. The drive to depopulate Danzig-West Prussia and the Wartheland in order to clear the way for German settlement fell particularly heavily on Jews. German planners discussed schemes to herd Jews into special reservations in the East or even to deport them to the French colony of Madagascar in the Indian Ocean, but they settled for concentrating them in urban ghettos scattered throughout the General Government. In Łódź and Warsaw, Jewish councils recognized by the German authorities administered walled-off ghettos, and this pattern was copied in many smaller towns. Jewish ghettos quickly became overcrowded, food and fuel were scarce, and typhus and other diseases were rampant. The death toll began to rise.

The German Domination of Scandinavia

The Phony War with Britain and France allowed Berlin to turn its attention to Denmark and Norway. Nazi leaders considered both countries to be populated by "Nordic" peoples who, like the Germans, were part of the "Aryan" master-race, and their occupation offered significant strategic advantages. Denmark's productive agricultural sector could be integrated into the Reich, while Norway's long west coast would shield German access to Swedish iron ore while providing naval and air bases from which to challenge British control of the North Sea.

German forces rolled into Denmark on April 9, 1940, and the government in Copenhagen capitulated just two hours later. The speed of the collapse reflected both the enthusiasm with which many Danish elites embraced integration into German autarky and the lack of any viable alternative course. Nazi leaders reciprocated by leaving Denmark's governmental structures intact, and throughout the war Danish farmers sold farm produce to the Third Reich at premium prices. The invaders faced a more difficult challenge in Norway, where the government organized brief but spirited resistance before escaping into exile in Britain along with King Haakon VII. German air, sea, and land attacks on strategic points across the country paralyzed defensive efforts, and the British and French troops who rushed to Norway's assistance were badly led, poorly equipped, and lacking air support. They were soon forced to evacuate. Only at sea did the defenders enjoy success. Norwegian coastal batteries capsized one German heavy cruiser, and at Narvik the Royal Navy sank eight destroyers. These losses severely weakened the *Kriegsmarine's* small surface fleet, making it impossible for it to support a projected invasion of Britain later in the year. Berlin had already canceled the March 1939 Z Plan, a program of surface warship construction directed towards global power projection, and German surface warships played little further part in the war.

Berlin installed a government in Oslo led by local fascist Vidkun Quisling. Quisling's name became synonymous with collaboration, but his National Unity movement enjoyed little popular support. Berlin worked with Quisling until October 1942 before jettisoning him in favor of governing directly through Reich Commissioner Josef Terboven. In both Denmark and Norway, the German takeover was eased by an absence of working-class opposition.

The invasions took place during the period of Nazi–Soviet cooperation, and the small but influential Scandinavian Communist parties were under strict orders from Moscow not to oppose the Germans. For Berlin, the drive into Scandinavia had the added benefit of strengthening its relationship with neutral Sweden. As in Denmark, Swedish elites enjoyed profitable collaboration with Germany, supplying iron ore and high-quality manufactured goods while violating their country's neutrality by allowing German troops to cross their territory.

Anglo–French Plans and Imperial Mobilizations

The military debacle in Norway precipitated a political crisis that forced the resignation of British Prime Minister Neville Chamberlain, who was replaced by the pugnacious Winston Churchill on May 10, 1940. Churchill represented the wing of the British elite that was most determined to resist German expansionism, and his appointment transformed Chamberlain's Conservative Party government into a genuine wartime alliance that included the opposition Labour Party. Labour's inclusion signaled Churchill's willingness to rally the country for war, and the party's support in the trade unions and among working-class voters was critical to this effort. In return, Churchill committed the new government to a far-reaching program of postwar social reform that was eventually codified in the 1942 Beveridge Report. The report – named after economist William Beveridge – proposed setting up a welfare state based on socialized healthcare, housing, and education. These measures embodied the promise of a better postwar society, and they helped to secure working-class support for the war effort.

Britain and France entered the war without a real strategic plan, and neither wanted to launch a major campaign in Europe. Along much of the Franco-German border, French troops hunkered down in the fortified Maginot Line. But the line stopped at the Luxembourg border, and Allies planned to secure their northern flank by advancing into neutral Belgium. While fighting on the defensive in Europe, the Allies intended to use their naval forces to blockade Germany and to launch "peripheral" operations against Norway and elsewhere. They hoped that this approach, combined with bombing attacks on Germany, would enable them to wage a protracted war against an enemy whose economy they judged to be fully stretched and susceptible to breakdown. In September 1939, Washington had expressed its support for this general approach by revising the Neutrality Acts to permit trade with belligerent powers. The new "cash and carry" agreement required that warring countries pay cash for American goods and carry them in their own ships – provisions that clearly favored the Allies and signaled Washington's desire to sustain the Anglo-French war effort.

Britain and France also took urgent steps to mobilize the human and material resources of their colonial empires. France's Colonial Army was organized primarily to defend its overseas colonies, but in 1940 West and North African troops were rushed to reinforce the Western Front. In the "White Dominions" of the British Empire, governments in Australia, Canada, and New Zealand quickly followed Britain into the war. In the Union of South Africa, Prime Minister Barry Hertzog advocated neutrality, but he was pushed aside by a revolt in the United Party that installed the pro-war cabinet of Jan Smuts and began mobilizing men and resources for the imperial war effort. During the war South Africa's industrial output doubled, coal exports quadrupled, and food shipments to Britain increased dramatically as the country's skilled workforce and its critical raw materials were harnessed to the war effort. Economic growth in South Africa drew in workers from other British colonies, and while the number of white workers grew by 21%, the black workforce leapt by 74%. The demand for African workers led to a relaxation of segregationist pass laws and prompted a construction boom as unregulated squatter towns grew up outside the major cities.

Britain also mobilized soldiers from its African colonies, starting with the long-service professionals of the Kings African Rifles recruited in East Africa and their counterparts in the Royal West African Field Force. Both forces participated in the British-led campaign against Italian East Africa starting in late 1940. As the war went on, the British authorities expanded recruitment in colonial Africa and began sending African troops overseas for the first time. Two West African divisions and one from East Africa were dispatched to fight the Japanese in Burma. West African recruits were trained by what Churchill described as a "white infusion" of nearly 300 Polish officers, some of whom then fought in Burma.[2] From southern Africa, men from the High Commission Territories of Basutoland, Swaziland, and Bechuanaland (now all part of South Africa) were recruited into the African Pioneer Corps and sent to work in support of British-Imperial forces in the Middle East. Imperial recruiters appealed to tribal loyalties, and recruits often had little understanding of the cause they were being asked to fight for. Nevertheless, military service overseas necessarily exposed soldiers to new experiences and ideas, and colonial officials fretted that soldiers would be "detribalized" by their service, with potentially dangerous consequences for colonial rule.

Éire (Ireland) was a British Dominion under the 1921 Treaty that recognized the country's independence from Britain. Despite this formal association with the British Empire, Éire had been established after a long and bitter struggle against British rule, and Taoiseach (Prime Minister) Éamon de Valera was determined to remain neutral in the world war. London's demands to use Éire's ports for naval operations were backed by economic sanctions, but despite the real hardship these measures produced Éire remained neutral throughout the war.

Despite formal neutrality, however, Dublin leaned informally towards Britain. Over 40 000 Irish citizens joined the British military, Allied aircraft were allowed to overfly a strip of Irish territory, and Dublin provided London with weather reports on conditions in the Atlantic. The ambiguities of Éire's position were illustrated by the Curragh prisoner of war camp, which housed 40 British and 200 German airmen and submariners who had crashed in Éire and were detained for the remainder of the war. In 1943 the Allied prisoners began to be quietly repatriated, while their Axis co-detainees were allowed to rent apartments in Dublin and to attend college, but not to leave the country.

The situation in British-ruled India was similarly complex. Most leaders of Gandhi's Indian National Congress (INC) favored supporting Britain against Germany, but they resented the fact that the British viceroy Lord Linlithgow took India into the war without consulting them. Linlithgow's snub was deliberate. Many British leaders – including Churchill – hoped that the war would allow them to push back against the growing influence of the INC. Benefiting from political reforms in the 1935 Government of India Act, Congress had won control of 8 of the 11 Indian provinces, and Linlithgow wanted to make it clear that despite these advances it would have no voice in foreign affairs. In November 1939, Congress provincial governments resigned in protest, and the British responded by stepping up their efforts to build up the Muslim League as a counterweight to the predominantly Hindu INC. Meanwhile, thousands of long-service Indian Army regular soldiers were dispatched to defend imperial outposts in Egypt, Singapore, Kenya, and Iraq, freeing British troops for the war in Europe.

Summer 1940: The Fall of France

The German invasion of France began on May 10, 1940. Barely six weeks later, the French government surrendered. In that time, the *Wehrmacht* routed the French army – the largest and best equipped in Europe – and drove the British Expeditionary Force (BEF) out of Europe. Ten million refugees took to the roads to escape the advancing Germans, and the French Third Republic was toppled and replaced by a right-wing collaborationist government. The astonishing speed of the French collapse led many contemporary commentators to argue that the Third Republic had been destroyed from within by the "dry rot" of communism, fascism, and pacifism.[3] More recently, historians have focused more on military factors and on contingent events. Both explanations have validity.

The German offensive began with airborne and ground forces moving into neutral Holland and Belgium. On May 14, German bombers attacked Rotterdam, killing nearly 1000 civilians, and the following morning the Dutch royal family fled to Britain as the government capitulated. Belgium held out until May 28 before the government surrendered and left for London, while King Leopold III remained in Belgium and cooperated with the German occupiers. As they had planned, the Allied forces responded to the German offensive by advancing deep into Belgium. This was exactly what German commanders wanted. On May 13, a second German force – Army Group A – broke out of the Ardennes Forest and began crossing the River Meuse *behind* the Anglo-French armies in Belgium. Allied planners had considered the Ardennes impassable, and were stunned by the sudden emergence of German tanks. Army Group A contained most of the *Wehrmacht's* new tank and mechanized infantry units, and it was supported by concentrated air strikes. Under General Heinz Guderian, German tanks broke through thin French defenses and raced towards the English Channel, cutting off the Allied armies in Belgium. This giant "sickle cut" was not without risk, and senior German commanders feared that Allied counterattacks would cut off Guderian's armored spearheads. Confident that speed was the key to victory, Guderian ignored orders to slow down, and on May 20 his tanks reached the English Channel.

The success of the German blitzkrieg relied on the skillful combination of fast-moving tanks, motorized infantry, and concentrated air support. Their rapid advances gave German troops an aura of invincibility, and their attacks shattered Allied command networks, broke morale, and unraveled organized resistance with shocking speed. As their armies collapsed, Anglo-French relations deteriorated in a welter of mutual recrimination, and on May 21 London decided to evacuate the BEF from the port of Dunkirk. Royal Navy warships operated under constant air attack, but between May 26 and June 4 they plucked 338 000 soldiers from Dunkirk, including over 100 000 Frenchmen. A flotilla of "little ships," including pleasure boats crewed by civilians, transferred soldiers from the beaches to larger ships waiting offshore. The BEF was forced to abandon its heavy equipment in France, but its irreplaceable soldiers survived to fight on.

After Dunkirk, German armies turned south, entering Paris on June 16. The French government had already fled to Bordeaux, where Prime Minister Paul Reynaud resigned in favor of Marshal Philippe Pétain, a national hero from World War I. The 82-year-old Marshal believed that surrender was unavoidable, and he rejected Reynaud's suggestion that the government carry on the fight from French North Africa. Pétain surrendered on June 22. Hitler's terms were relatively lenient: Germany occupied northern France and the Atlantic coast, while southern France – the so-called "French State" – remained unoccupied under Pétain's government, now based in the resort town of Vichy. The powerful French fleet was demobilized but remained under French control, and France agreed to pay the costs of the war and the German occupation. Berlin staked no claim on the French Empire, which remained under Vichy rule.

In line with these terms, rightist politician Pierre Laval disbanded the Third Republic, concentrated substantial dictatorial powers in Pétain's hands, and collaborated closely with Berlin and with German occupation forces. Vichy launched its own conservative and anti-Semitic "National Revolution," purging Jews from universities and the civil service and rounding up foreign Jews who had sought refuge in France. The shock of the military disaster and the willingness of much of the elite to collaborate with the Germans ensured that these measures provoked little opposition. Among government figures, only the recently appointed junior minister General Charles de Gaulle opposed the surrender, and he escaped to London to begin organizing opposition to the German occupation. Not surprisingly, Anglo-Vichy relations quickly broke down in a welter of mutual recrimination, and on July 3 London responded to the danger of the French fleet falling into German hands by bombarding warships anchored in Mers-el-Kébir, Algeria. Over 1300 French sailors died in the British attack.

Anglo-French armies were comprehensively outfought in summer 1940. General Erich von Manstein's planned advance through the Ardennes was a masterstroke, and its determined execution derailed the prospect of any coordinated Anglo-French response. These military factors unfolded within a broader political framework. Among French elites, nationalism had cohabited uneasily with admiration for Nazi Germany during the 1930s; many had little enthusiasm for the war, and they quickly accepted their new position as junior partners in a German-dominated Europe. On the left – and in contrast to the British Labour Party's enthusiastic support for Churchill – Moscow instructed the French Communist Party (PCF) to oppose the French war effort. As in Norway, the maintenance of Moscow's pact with Berlin took precedence over organizing opposition to a Nazi invasion. In response, the French government outlawed the PCF, persecuted its leaders, and interned communist refugees living in France. French elites were haunted by the ghost of the Paris Commune – the popular insurrection that erupted after France's defeat in the 1870–1871 Franco-Prussian War – and many feared domestic revolution more than German invasion.

The Battle of Britain

German leaders assumed that Britain would give in after the fall of France. The most pro-appeasement wing of the British elite shared this assessment, and led by Foreign Secretary Lord Halifax they responded to the crisis in France by pushing for a negotiated peace using Mussolini as an intermediary. It is possible that Berlin might have agreed to British peace proposals, particularly if they were sweetened by chunks of colonial territory. In the event, however, the successful evacuation of the British army from Dunkirk reinforced Churchill's refusal to seek immediate negotiations, and the War Cabinet backed his position. The attack on the French fleet at Mers-el-Kébir further underscored London's resolve, and Berlin had to adjust to this unwelcome new reality. In mid-July

Hitler ordered planners to prepare for an invasion of Britain later in the summer. German leaders recognized that a successful Channel crossing demanded control of both sea and air, but after its losses in Norway the *Kriegsmarine* was in no position to challenge the Royal Navy. Everything therefore rested on achieving air supremacy over the Channel, which Hermann Göring's *Luftwaffe* promised to deliver.

On August 13, 1940 – "Eagle Day" – the *Luftwaffe* launched a sustained attack on the RAF as German bombers pounded British airfields. Directed by a newly installed radar network, RAF fighters scrambled to oppose them. Over the following weeks, the RAF shot down 1887 German aircraft for the loss of 1023, and despite inflicting heavy losses German attacks did not, as is sometimes suggested, come close to destroying RAF Fighter Command. British aircraft production outpaced combat losses and this, combined with the determination of its pilots, the advantages of defending domestic territory, and the overall efficiency of its air defense network, enabled the RAF to win the Battle of Britain. The RAF itself was a multinational force: 10% of its combat pilots came from the British Dominions and another 10% from Poland and other parts of occupied Europe, while one of its key leaders – Air Marshal Keith Park – was a New Zealander.

In September, the *Luftwaffe* switched its attention to London. At first German bombers flew by day to attack specific targets, but as losses mounted they began indiscriminate nighttime bombing. These raids, and the attacks on many other British cities that followed during the "Blitz" of September 1940–May 1941, killed over 40000 civilians and did extensive physical damage. Nevertheless, *Luftwaffe* airplanes were designed to provide tactical support for German ground forces and they could not carry the heavy bomb loads necessary to inflict truly massive destruction. Britain's war-making capacity was not seriously threatened. Meanwhile, German commanders realized that they could not achieve air supremacy, and the planned invasion was canceled in early September.

New Strategic Choices

The German conquest of France redrew the political map of both Europe and the world in dramatic and unanticipated ways, forcing all the major states to redefine their strategic plans and priorities. Even in Berlin, the speed of the victory took Nazi leaders by surprise, and they, along with their Italian and Japanese partners in the emerging Axis alliance, saw new prospects for strategic advance. Their actual or potential opponents – Britain, the Soviet Union, and the United States – faced a more substantial challenge. They had all assumed that France would fight a long war against Germany, and the Nazi victory provoked a frantic scramble to revise their own plans and preparations. At this critical moment, the broad outlines of the coming global war began to take shape, and it is for this reason that historian David Reynolds refers to 1940 as the key "fulcrum" (or turning point) of the war.[4]

The Soviet Union faced the most direct threat from Germany, and it had the least strategic flexibility. Moscow never believed that the Molotov–Ribbentrop Pact would permanently defuse the Nazi threat, but it had anticipated that a protracted Franco-German war would exhaust the combatants and buy time to strengthen the Red Army. While the Pact had moved the Soviet frontier westwards, it also brought the *Wehrmacht* and the Red Army face-to-face along a border that crossed potentially hostile populations of Poles, Ukrainians, and Byelorussians. Clearly, the Pact also precluded a strategic rapprochement with London. On the other hand, the Soviet victory over Japan on the Khalkhyn Gol and negotiations for a neutrality pact with Tokyo allowed Moscow to concentrate its forces in the west. Here, the Soviets annexed Latvia, Estonia, and Lithuania and strengthened their defenses in occupied Poland. Nevertheless, in January 1941 Soviet leaders estimated that the Red Army needed two more years to prepare for war, and until then Moscow aimed to avoid provoking Berlin by maintaining the shipments of grain, oil, and cotton agreed under the Pact.

Britain's decision to fight on did not mean that British leaders had any plan for victory beyond a vague combination of strategic bombing, naval blockade, and a propaganda campaign aimed at stirring anti-Nazi rebellions. Moreover, despite his pugnacious public pronouncements, Churchill did not exclude the possibility of a negotiated peace once Britain had demonstrated its capacity to survive. France had been the "one firm rock" on which British strategy was based, and once it was swept away London was left without a major ally.[5] Given its vast empire, Britain was never truly alone, but even with its colonial resources it lacked the economic and military means to defeat Germany. As a result, the British government turned towards the United States. Wartime and postwar rhetoric has made the Anglo-American axis seem entirely natural, but during the interwar years the two countries had viewed each other with distrust that verged on outright hostility. As British leaders recognized, the rising power of the United States threatened London's global standing. Yet as the new political situation unfolded in summer 1940 Churchill argued forcefully that Britain now had to rely on "the New World, with all its power and might" to rescue "the Old."[6] Churchill championed this new Anglo-American (or Atlanticist) orientation throughout the war, even as it became clear – as some British elites feared all along – that it would ease America's rise to global hegemony.

Like their British and Soviets counterparts, American leaders had anticipated protracted French resistance, and they now faced the unpalatable prospect of a German-dominated Europe – precisely the threat that had pulled America into war in 1917. Initially, American military chiefs fell back on a strategy of "continental defense," premised on securing the Western Hemisphere from invasion, but they soon came around to the idea of a strategic alliance with Britain favored by President Roosevelt. Roosevelt's problem was that many Americans were hostile to involvement in another European war. Formed in September 1940, the isolationist America First Committee (AFC) soon claimed over 800 000 members, and many more Americans opposed overseas military entanglements for a variety of reasons. In response to this anti-war sentiment, Roosevelt waged a "cautious campaign" that moved slowly and incrementally towards greater involvement in the war.[7]

By summer 1940, a consensus was forming among American elites in favor of supporting Britain, although many still hoped to avoid armed intervention. Roosevelt signaled this convergence by appointing two top Republicans, Henry Stimson and Frank Knox, to his cabinet. Wendell Willkie, the Republican candidate in the 1940 presidential election, was also an avowed "internationalist," and Roosevelt's reelection for a third term confirmed this growing elite consensus. Meanwhile, Congress introduced a peacetime military draft, and the July 1940 Two-Ocean Navy Act doubled the size of the US fleet.

These measures reflected a growing conviction in elite circles, nurtured by collaboration between the Council on Foreign Relations – an influential non-governmental think-tank – and the State Department, that American global hegemony could not be achieved by economic means alone. Instead, economic predominance had to be backed by a willingness to use military force on a world scale. This understanding gave new force to Wilsonian liberal internationalism, and it was popularized by a February 1941 *Life* magazine editorial on the "American Century" written by publisher Henry Luce. Luce envisioned the United States as the world's leading superpower whose "Good Samaritan" behavior, economic benevolence, and cultural influence were backed by economic muscle and military might.[8]

American military thinking evolved alongside this growing internationalism. In November 1940, Chief of Naval Operations Admiral Harold Stark presented a new strategic plan to the president; Plan Dog envisaged supporting Britain in a war to overthrow Nazi Germany while assuming a defensive posture in response to Japanese threats in the Pacific. This "Germany First" approach would – at least nominally – govern Washington's entire wartime strategy, and in spring 1941 it framed secret ABC-1 talks with British and Canadian military planners. Step by step, the United States was getting closer to the war in Europe. These steps were accompanied by practical measures to support Britain. In September 1940, Roosevelt responded to British requests for convoy escort ships by transferring 50 aging destroyers to the Royal Navy. In exchange, the United States gained long rent-free leases on British bases in Canada and the Caribbean. The "destroyers for bases" deal set the stage for more US military aid, culminating in the March 1941 Lend-Lease Act. Based on the convenient fiction that the United States was simply lending military equipment to Britain and would get it back at the end of the war, Lend-Lease ultimately resulted in the shipment of over $50 billion worth of supplies to Britain, the USSR, and other Allied countries. The program took time to ramp up, and in 1941 it supplied barely 1% of British munitions, but its existence demonstrated Washington's increased commitment to the British war effort.

As Anglo-American cooperation deepened, US naval vessels began escorting supply convoys bound for Britain across the North Atlantic. These forces operated within the Pan-American Security Zone established by the American-inspired Declaration of Panama in 1939 and then extended into the mid-Atlantic by President Roosevelt in 1941. In May 1940, British forces violated Icelandic neutrality and occupied the country in order to deny Germany access to its strategic harbors. The following summer, US Marines took over the occupation and began building air and naval bases for forces combating German submarines in the Atlantic. In April 1941, the United States also occupied the Danish colony of Greenland, effectively turning it into an American protectorate. American military base construction was soon underway there, too, and in 1942 American forces ejected several small German weather stations. At the same time, American forces strengthened the Pan-American Security Zone in Latin America by occupying the Dutch colony of Surinam in November 1941; acting with the consent of the Dutch government-in-exile in London, US forces secured important bauxite (aluminum ore) mines against the threat of invasion from Vichy-ruled French Guiana.

The Tripartite Pact

The fall of France also prompted Italy, Japan, and Germany to rethink their strategic plans and to accelerate their expansionist drives. Italy joined the war on June 10, 1940, invading France when German troops were already well on the way to victory. After a brief but bloody Alpine campaign, Italian troops established a small occupied zone in southern France. Rome now eyed military operations in the Balkans and North Africa, making Britain's position in the Mediterranean look suddenly vulnerable. In Asia, the collaborationist Vichy government opened new opportunities for an extension of Japanese power into French Indochina, while in Berlin discussion began on ambitious new plans for an invasion of the Soviet Union. These projected moves argued for closer cooperation among the emerging Axis powers, and in September 1940 the German, Italian, and Japanese governments signed the Tripartite Pact. The Pact hailed German and Italian efforts to establish a "new order in Europe" and welcomed those of Japan to do likewise throughout "Greater East Asia," and the signatories pledged mutual assistance in the event of an attack by any country not yet engaged in either war.[9] The country they all had in mind was the United States.

In practical terms the Tripartite Pact accomplished little. The wars in Europe and Asia were geographically distant, making coordinated action between Japan and its Western allies virtually impossible. Even where German and Italian interests overlapped, their governments showed little interest in serious strategic coordination. Special Tripartite military and economic commissions met in Germany to promote cooperation, but they did little beyond dividing the world into defined spheres of interest. In essence, the Pact envisioned the three Axis powers pursuing separate but mutually supportive imperial projects. Together, these efforts would overturn the existing political order in Europe and Asia, and the signatories had a common interest in opposing American intervention in either sphere; as such, and despite its practical limitations, the Tripartite Pact marked another step towards a globalized conflict. It was certainly seen that way by the British and American governments, which both responded to the Pact by stepping up their support for Nationalist China.

Berlin Turns East

Britain's decision to fight on posed Berlin with the strategic challenge of maintaining the momentum of victory. Even before the Battle of Britain, a cross-Channel invasion was a dubious proposition, and some German leaders looked instead to an "indirect" approach that aimed to weaken Britain by attacking its power in the Mediterranean. Inspired by the German victory in France, Spanish dictator Francisco Franco seemed ready to join the war, and German planners proposed advancing through Spain to seize the British base at Gibraltar. Before this plan could be enacted, however, the RAF victory in the Battle of Britain made Franco think again, and despite a personal meeting with Hitler in October 1940 he refused to sanction the attack. Franco continued to cheer the Germans on, and he encouraged thousands of Spanish soldiers to join the ostensibly all-volunteer Blue Division sent to fight alongside the *Wehrmacht* in Russia, but Madrid remained formally non-belligerent.

The conquest of France allowed the *Kriegsmarine* to base submarines on the Atlantic coast, strengthening its ability to attack British shipping by cutting out the long and dangerous transit from Germany to the Atlantic around Scotland. The first U-boats arrived at their new bases in July 1940, but the campaign took several months to move into high gear. German naval construction in the 1930s had focused on surface warships, only shifting in favor of submarines in 1939. In fall 1940, Admiral Karl Dönitz only had 65 U-boats ready for action out of the 300 planners deemed necessary to cripple British shipping. German strategists hoped that attacks on British shipping and the bombing of its industrial cities would bring Britain to its knees, making an invasion unnecessary. The stakes were very high. If the submarine campaign failed, then even with much of Europe under its control Germany would lack the resources to win a protracted attritional struggle against a defiant Britain backed by its empire and by the United States. Secure access to the coal, oil, iron, and grain required to win such a struggle could only be found in the USSR, and their acquisition now became the critical strategic priority. It was a strategic judgment that meshed with long-standing Nazi plans for colonial *Lebensraum* in the East.

Initial plans for Operation *Barbarossa*, an invasion of the Soviet Union slated to begin in May 1941, were approved in December 1940. They called for Germany to attack the USSR *before* defeating Britain, thereby deliberately initiating the two-front war that had long been Berlin's worst strategic nightmare. This audacious move was justified on two premises: first, while Britain was not defeated, it could not intervene in continental Europe; and second, that a rapid victory over the USSR was likely. Speed was critical because the German economy was not geared for a long attritional warfare, and a short campaign would minimize the economic demands of a two-front war. The gamble seemed justified militarily. The Red Army's weaknesses had been showcased in Finland, and German officers judged that the blitzkrieg operational methods perfected in France would guarantee a speedy victory in the Soviet Union.

Berlin aimed to secure *Barbarossa*'s southern flank by strengthening its diplomatic position in the Balkans. In November 1940, Admiral Miklós Horthy's conservative government in Hungary signed the Tripartite Pact, followed three days later by Marshal Ion Antonescu's rightist dictatorship in Romania. This diplomatic coup for Berlin required the settlement of complex territorial rivalries between the two countries, and it secured German access to Romania's Ploesti oilfield. Berlin developed a close relationship with Antonescu that gained it the commitment of two Romanian armies to the invasion of the USSR on the promise of territorial gains at Moscow's expense. Pragmatism triumphed over ideology when Berlin backed Antonescu against a January 1941 coup attempt launched by the Iron Guard, Romania's homegrown fascists and the dictator's former coalition partners. Unlike their Italian counterparts, Romanian officers were included in the planning of *Barbarossa*, while German advisers trained Romanian troops and a *Luftwaffe* mission strengthened the air defenses of the Ploesti oilfields.

Tokyo Turns South

Berlin's decision to march east was paralleled in Tokyo by a deepening conviction that a drive into Southeast Asia offered the way out of the strategic impasse in China. The military stalemate there had deepened during 1940. In August, the Communist-led Eighth Route Army launched the Hundred Regiments Campaign, a major offensive against Japanese lines of communication in northern China.

Initial Communist successes provoked a ferocious Japanese counter-offensive under the banner of the "Three Alls" – kill all, burn all, and destroy all. In the light of the widespread devastation inflicted on their base areas, Communist leaders suspended conventional military operations and concentrated instead on guerrilla actions. Despite its defeat, however, the Hundred Regiments Campaign showed how far Tokyo was from pacifying even those areas of China nominally under its control. This realization strengthened the emerging consensus among senior Japanese officers in favor of taking radical action to break the deadlock.

This process was intertwined with a further militarization of Japanese politics, signaled by the formation of a new government by Prince Konoe Fumimaro in July 1940 and by the dissolution of all political parties except for a coalition of rightist groups known as the Imperial Rule Assistance Association. Since 1938, Konoe had championed the creation of a Greater East Asian Co-Prosperity Sphere that would unify East and Southeast Asia under Japanese leadership. This sphere, including the European and American colonies in Burma, Malaya, Indonesia, Indochina, and the Philippines, would provide the food and raw materials needed to wage a protracted war in China. Above all, Japan would break its dependence on oil imports from the United States by seizing the oilfields of the Dutch East Indies. As with Germany's drive for *Lebensraum*, Japan's push to create an imperial-autarkic bloc in Asia had a strong ideological element. Propagandists pictured Tokyo rallying the peoples of Asia against their colonial masters, disguising its power grab behind an aura of anti-imperialist solidarity.

Japanese agents worked to give this vision some substance by forging links with anti-colonial fighters, including nationalist politicians Ba Maw and Aung San in Burma, and nationalist groups in Malaya, the Dutch East Indies, and French Indochina. Tokyo was also keenly interested in the activity of Indian nationalist Subhas Chandra Bose, leader of the left-wing Forward Bloc within the INC. Bose had been elected president of the INC in 1938 but was forced out by Gandhi and Jawaharlal Nehru the following year for advocating the violent overthrow of British rule. Unlike most INC leaders, Bose was hostile to the British war effort, and while remaining skeptical of Japan's own imperialist war aims he viewed the Axis powers as potential allies in India's struggle against colonialism. After leading a series of anti–British protests at the start of the war, Bose escaped from house arrest in Calcutta in January 1941 before surfacing first in Berlin and then in Tokyo. In both Axis capitals he sought backing for the construction of an anti-colonial Indian army.

Japanese leaders understood that their offensive in Southeast Asia would provoke war both with Britain and Holland – the major colonial powers in the region – and with the United States. Britain was preoccupied in Europe and was unlikely to send substantial reinforcements to Asia. Its weakness was signaled by London's decision to bend to Japanese pressure by closing the critical Burma Road into Nationalist China from July to October 1940. The United States was a different matter. Washington was reshaping its strategy along the lines of "Germany First," but its navy remained concentrated at Pearl Harbor with the explicit aim of deterring Japanese expansionism. Japanese commanders knew that warships ordered under the 1938 Navy Act would soon reinforce the US Pacific Fleet, tipping the naval balance against them and closing their window of military opportunity. When Japanese troops moved into the north of Vichy-ruled Indochina in September 1940, Washington responded by imposing a partial ban on the export of scrap metal and oil to Japan. Since the country was dependent on imported American oil, this move threatened Japan's vital interests, and Japanese planners concluded that if they were going to move into Southeast Asia, they needed to move quickly, protecting their advance by landing a stunning blow on American forces in the Pacific.

Rome's "Parallel War"

In June 1940, Mussolini used a brief moment of popular enthusiasm for war to launch a series of campaigns to secure Italian dominance of the Mediterranean and create a new Roman Empire. Mussolini hoped to fight a "parallel war" that would complement German expansionism without being subordinate to it. Italian plans for an attack on neutral Switzerland were soon shelved, and Berlin's desire for peace in the Balkans in the run-up to *Barbarossa* forced Rome to put an invasion of Yugoslavia on hold. Even so, the Italian military was ordered to make simultaneous attacks on British Somaliland, British-dominated Egypt, and Greece. The demands of these divergent and strategically unfocused offensives overwhelmed Italy's limited logistical capacity, and these difficulties were compounded by Mussolini's popular but militarily unwise decision to send half the army home to help bring in the harvest.

The first and most successful Italian offensive was the August 1940 drive into British Somaliland from Italian-ruled Ethiopia. Italian troops overwhelmed a scratch British-Imperial force that including the Somali Camel Corps and units from the Punjab, Rhodesia, and Nigeria in the critical Tug Argun Gap. From there, Italian troops quickly secured the port of Berbera, forcing the evacuation of the surviving British-led troops. The two-week conquest of British Somaliland was Italy's most successful land campaign of the entire war. This land offensive was accompanied by a long-range bombing campaign. On July 29, Italian aircraft took off from the Aegean island of Rhodes to bomb the oil refinery at Haifa in British-ruled Palestine, starting a blaze that halted production for over a month. Italian aircraft also struck Tel Aviv, killing 137 civilians. In an ambitious operation on October 18, heavily laden bombers flew from Rhodes on a 15-hour and 3000-mile mission to attack an oil refinery in British-ruled Bahrain and (by mistake) an American-operated facility in Dhahran, Saudi Arabia. After causing minor damage, the bombers landed in Italian Eritrea. Despite their limited success, these daring Italian raids obliged overstretched British forces to strengthen their air defenses throughout the Middle East.

In September 1940, Italian forces under a reluctant General Rodolfo Graziani launched an invasion of Egypt. Graziani's four divisions, which included tanks and motorized infantry, advanced 50 miles along the coast road from Italian Libya into Egypt before halting at Sidi Barrani, where they set up defensive positions. It was not a good place to halt. British forces had fallen back in the face of the Italian advance, but as Graziani dug in they regrouped for a counter-attack. British theater commander General Archibald Wavell's initial goal was to eject the Italians from Egypt, but as Graziani's forces disintegrated British-Imperial troops began an all-out offensive. By the time Operation *Compass* ended in February 1941, Wavell's forces had destroyed the Italian Tenth Army, capturing over 130 000 prisoners and occupying Cyrenaica, the eastern half of Italian-ruled Libya.

The Italian invasion of Greece was equally disastrous. After Berlin vetoed his planned invasion of Yugoslavia, Mussolini launched an attack on Greece in late October without informing the Germans. Italian troops advanced into Greece from Italian-ruled Albania, but they lacked numerical superiority, their tanks were unsuited to the mountainous terrain, and poor weather negated their air power. The Greeks rushed reinforcements to the front, and by early December they were pushing the Italians back into Albania. In response, Mussolini declared a full military mobilization, sending newly raised units to Albania and throwing them straight into battle. Italian troops finally stopped the Greek advance in January 1941, but their attempts to resume the offensive failed dismally.

As the Italian offensives stalled, Britain attacked Italian forces in Ethiopia and Somalia. This area came under Wavell's sprawling Middle East Command, and he assembled a polyglot imperial army that included units from the British, Indian, and South African armies together with white settlers from Rhodesia (Zimbabwe) and British-led colonial troops from East and West Africa. They were joined by detachments from the Belgian Congo and the Free French. In late 1940 and early 1941 these forces moved into Ethiopia in a giant pincer movement, advancing from Kenya in the south and from Sudan in the north. Well supplied with trucks and backed by effective air support, their speed and mobility unhinged the Italian defenses. Ethiopian "patriot" insurgents joined the attack, along with Gideon Force, a band of Sudanese irregulars commanded by British major and guerrilla warfare visionary Orde Wingate. After what one participant described as the "fastest and longest advance in the history of the British Army," British-Imperial and Ethiopian troops entered Addis Ababa in May 1941 and restored Emperor Haile Selassie to the throne (Figure 3.1).[10]

The East Africa Campaign was an unmitigated disaster for Rome, which lost 300 000 men (most of them captured) and all of Italian East Africa. Coming on

Figure 3.1   Indian troops enter Asmara, Eritrea, on April 1, 1941, during the successful British-Imperial offensive in East Africa. (*Source*: Andrew Stewart, private collection.)

top of reverses in Greece and North Africa, it signaled the unraveling of Rome's parallel war. The British-Imperial victory protected southern Egypt and secured control of the Red Sea. In April 1941, this enabled President Roosevelt to declare that the sea was no longer a war zone, opening it to American merchant shipping and allowing Lend-Lease supplies to be shipped directly to Egypt. In addition to these strategic advances, London saw the victory as an opportunity to extend imperial control in Ethiopia, where it had little regard for the independent-minded Haile Selassie. Under the January 1942 Anglo-Ethiopian Agreement, London retained rights and privileges in Ethiopia that limited the country's sovereignty, particularly in financial matters. Keen to weaken British imperial predominance, Washington pushed back by extending Lend-Lease to Ethiopia in 1942 and then pressuring London into dropping many of its claims in a renegotiated treaty signed in 1944. Prompted by Washington, London now recognized Ethiopia as an allied power, giving it a place at international conferences on the postwar order. Meanwhile, in July 1945 American influence led to the adoption of a new currency – the Ethiopian dollar – that was pegged to its US namesake. Even in victory, the war began to unravel Britain's imperial power.

Notes

1.   Quoted in Evans (2008), 11.
2.   Churchill, W.S. (1950). *The Second World War*, Vol. III, 686. Boston: Houghton Mifflin.
3.   *New York Times*, July 26, 1940.

4. Reynolds (April 1990), 325–350.
5. Lord Halifax, quoted in Reynolds (April 1990), 329.
6. Winston Churchill, quoted in Stoler (2005), 13.
7. Casey (2001).
8. Luce (Spring 1999), 170.
9. The text of the Tripartite Pact is available at: http://avalon.law.yale.edu/wwii/triparti.asp.
10. Quoted in Stewart (2016), 232.

References

Casey, S. (2001). *Cautious Crusade: Franklin D. Roosevelt, American Public Opinion, and the War against Nazi Germany*. New York: Oxford University Press.

Evans, R.J. (2008). *The Third Reich at War*. New York: Penguin.

Luce, H.R. (Spring 1999). The American Century. *Diplomatic History* 23 (2)): 159–171.

Reynolds, D. (April 1990). 1940: fulcrum of the twentieth century. *International Affairs* 66 (2): 325–350.

Stewart, A. (2016). *The First Victory: The Second World War and the East African Campaign*. New Haven: Yale University Press.

Stoler, M.A. (2005). *Allies in War: Britain and America Against the Axis Power*. London: Hodder Arnold.

Further Reading

Bungay, S. (2000). *The Most Dangerous Enemy: A History of the Battle of Britain*. London: Aurum Press.

Horne, A. (2007). *To Lose a Battle: France 1940*. New York: Penguin.

Knox, M. (2000). *Hitler's Italian Allies: Royal Armed Forces, Fascist Regime, and the War of 1940–1943*. New York: Cambridge University Press.

Nord, P. (2015). *France 1940: Defending the Republic*. New Haven: Yale University Press.

Paine, S.C.M. (2012). *The Wars for Asia, 1911–1949*. New York: Cambridge University Press.

Reynolds, D. (1985). Churchill and the British 'decision' to fight on in 1940: right policy, wrong reasons. In: *Diplomacy and Intelligence During the Second World War* (ed. R.D. Langthorne), 147–167. New York: Cambridge University Press.

Reynolds, D. (2001). *From Munich to Pearl Harbor: Roosevelt's America and the Origins of the Second World War*. Chicago: Ivan R. Dee.

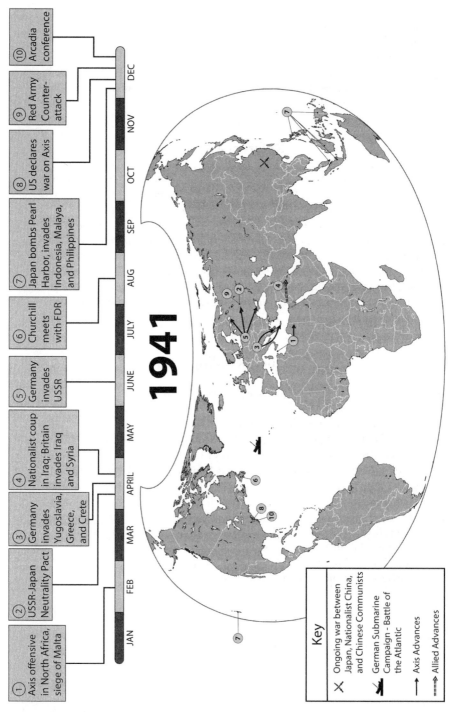

Map: 1941.

4

1941–1942: Axis Flood Tide

During 1941, Germany and Japan deliberately launched multi-front wars, and Italy had been involved in one since fall 1940. Yet all three Axis countries were "short-war powers" whose relative lack of resources militated *against* involvement in protracted multi-front struggles. Leaders in all three countries hoped to resolve this contradiction by winning rapid victories that would avoid getting drawn into long attritional struggles. In Berlin, this expectation seemed reasonable: the *Wehrmacht* had achieved dramatic recent successes, and its Soviet opponents had performed poorly in Finland. Tokyo's optimism also seemed plausible. Despite the extended war in China, the Imperial Japanese Navy was at peak efficiency, and its potential opponents in Southeast Asia were either distracted in Europe or – so the Japanese hoped – too decadent to fight. In Italy's case, however, the army was neither well equipped nor well led, and it faced a determined opponent in Britain. As we have seen, defeats in Egypt, Ethiopia, and Greece had already scuppered Italy's short-war gamble by early 1941, with drastic consequences for Germany.

Italy Pulls Germany into the Mediterranean

By the beginning of 1941, the Italian campaigns in Greece, North Africa, and Italian East Africa were all in serious trouble, as was the Italian navy's – the *Regia Marina* – campaign for naval supremacy in the Mediterranean. On November 11, 1940, carrier-based British torpedo bombers attacked the Italian fleet at anchor in Taranto, sinking one battleship, damaging two more, and forcing the *Regia*

World War II in Global Perspective, 1931–1953: A Short History, First Edition. Andrew N. Buchanan.
© 2019 John Wiley & Sons, Inc. Published 2019 by John Wiley & Sons, Inc.

Marina to withdraw its major warships to the safety of Naples. Successful code-breaking allowed the Royal Navy to strike again in March 1941, damaging one battleship and sinking three heavy cruisers in a running battle off Cape Matapan in southern Greece. London expected these victories to establish its dominance of the Mediterranean, but Italian forces proved resilient, mounting air and sea attacks on convoys bringing supplies to the British-ruled island of Malta while defending their own supply routes to North Africa.

Despite the tenacity of the *Regia Marina*, the crises facing Italian forces in Greece and North Africa forced Rome to abandon its parallel war and ask Berlin for help. Hitler observed with brutal accuracy that defeat had "compressed Italian claims to within the natural boundaries of their capabilities," and he agreed to send German forces to the Mediterranean to bail them out.[1] German airplanes arrived in Sicily in January to join Italian attacks on Malta, and their bombs soon reduced the port of Valetta to rubble. Many civilians fled to the countryside or sought refuge in caves. With Malta under siege, Axis air attacks closed the central Mediterranean to British shipping, forcing London to ship supplies to its armies in North Africa via the long haul around southern Africa.

Berlin also sent ground troops to support the Italians in North Africa and the Balkans. General Erwin Rommel's Afrika Korps arrived in Libya in February, and the *Wehrmacht* launched invasions of Yugoslavia and Greece in April. Rommel quickly took the offensive against British-Imperial forces overextended by their pursuit of the Italians, and his task was eased by London's decision to send 60000 men (including British, Australian, New Zealand, and Palestinian Jewish units) from North Africa to help defend Greece. British-Imperial troops offered little effective resistance to German forces experienced in blitzkrieg warfare, and they were quickly evicted from much of Libya. Rommel was poised for an advance into Egypt, but Axis troops were unable to overcome the joint Australian/Indian (later Polish/Czechoslovak) garrison in the key port of Tobruk. This failure worsened an already precarious logistical situation, with supplies for frontline Axis forces traveling over 1000 miles from Benghazi along a coastal road that was under constant attack by the British Desert Air Force.

With Axis forces advancing in North Africa, German armies rolled into Yugoslavia and Greece. When German commanders began planning Operation *Barbarossa* in late 1940, Hitler urged a secondary operation to secure the southern flank in the Balkans and to eliminate Greece, Britain's last ally in the region. This project was given new urgency by the collapse of the Italian invasion of Greece. The German campaign followed a diplomatic effort that convinced the Yugoslav government to join the Tripartite Pact in March 1941. The pro-German government was quickly overthrown by a military coup prompted by British agents and carried out by Serbian nationalists loyal to the young King Peter II. Nine days later, the Germans invaded. Heralded by an aerial bombardment of

Belgrade, German columns advanced into Yugoslavia from staging areas in Ostmark (Austria), Hungary, and Romania. German troops also attacked from Bulgaria, which had joined the Axis in March in exchange for promises of Greek and Yugoslav territory. In a now familiar pattern, Yugoslavia's surrender on April 18 ended a short offensive war against a divided country, some of whose leaders were openly sympathetic to the Axis.

After the Axis victory the Kingdom of Yugoslavia that had been cobbled together after World War I was broken into its constituent parts. In the north, Germany annexed Slovenia, while Italy occupied the Dalmatian coast and expanded its Albanian outpost, and Hungary and Bulgaria both grabbed chunks of Yugoslav territory. Two large regions – German-occupied Serbia and the Independent State of Croatia – remained nominally self-governing under pro-Axis governments. In Croatia, Rome sponsored a new government with the absentee Italian Duke of Aosta assuming the throne as King Tomislav II. Real power lay with the fascist Ustaše party of dictator Ante Pavelić, and under his rule rightist gangs launched a genocidal campaign against Serbs, Jews, Muslims, and Romani whose brutality astonished even hardened Nazis.

The German invasion of Greece followed quickly. In the north, German troops advanced from Bulgaria to outflank the Metaxas Line, a Maginot Line-like series of fortifications named for Ioannis Metaxas, the rightist dictator who ruled Greece from 1936 to January 1941. Metaxas had attempted to maintain Greek neutrality, but this effort collapsed following the Italian invasion in fall 1940. Fast-moving German mechanized units now outmaneuvered Greek and British-Imperial forces, entering Athens on April 27. Greece was subjected to a tripartite occupation: Italy seized much of the mainland and the islands in the Ionian and Aegean seas; Germany secured vital zones around Athens; and Bulgaria annexed Thrace. Axis demands for food soon produced rural famine, while throughout the Balkans German troops responded to the smallest acts of resistance with brutal reprisals, particularly against Jews.

As Greece fell, the Royal Navy evacuated British-Imperial troops from continental Europe for a second time, transporting 42 000 men to the island of Crete. The Germans were hard on their heels, and on May 20 airborne troops began landing on Crete. Again, British-Imperial defenses collapsed quickly, and the Royal Navy was soon braving punishing air attacks to conduct another evacuation. Nearly 20 000 men were transported to Egypt, including King George II of Greece and the Greek government-in-exile. The 17 000 British-Imperial soldiers captured by the Germans were generally treated properly, but Cretans who had fought alongside them faced ferocious reprisals. Over 500 were executed by the Germans. Despite capturing Crete, the heavy losses suffered by the German paratroops dissuaded Berlin from launching an airborne assault on Malta. This respite allowed British air and naval forces based in Malta to mount effective attacks on Axis shipping in the central Mediterranean, particularly after German airplanes were withdrawn from Sicily for the invasion of the Soviet Union.

War and Nationalism in the Middle East

Axis advances in North Africa and the Balkans generated political shock waves that reached deep into the Middle East. During the 1930s Germany and Italy had conducted propaganda campaigns presenting the Axis powers as champions of the Arab world against British and French imperialism. In particular, they cultivated a relationship with Mohammed Amin al-Husseini, the Grand Mufti responsible for Muslim holy places in Jerusalem. Husseini was an advocate of pan-Arab unity, a leader of the 1936–1939 Arab Revolt in British-ruled Palestine, and a fierce opponent of Jewish settlement. While their shared anti-Semitism facilitated cooperation between Husseini and Axis leaders, theirs was an alliance of convenience based on opposition to British imperial power in the Middle East, and for many Arabs anti-imperial sentiment was weightier than anti-Semitism. Arab students and workers saw Axis military advances weakening British rule, and the Afrika Korps' advance on Egypt sparked popular demonstrations in Cairo. British authorities in Palestine deepened religious tensions by encouraging Jewish militants in the *Haganah* (Defense) organization to attack Husseini's supporters, and officials in Egypt used British-Imperial troops to suppress nationalist demonstrations there.

Al-Husseini had fled to Baghdad after the suppression of the Arab uprising in Palestine, where he forged ties with nationalist-minded politicians and army officers. Under the 1930 Anglo-Iraqi Treaty, London recognized the country as an independent state ruled by the pro-British Hashemite monarchy, but it continued to enjoy privileged commercial standing and to maintain a military presence that included RAF bases at Habbaniya (near Baghdad) and Basra. Inspired by Axis advances, nationalist politician Rashid Ali al-Gaylani and four Iraqi colonels seized power in Baghdad, setting up the National Defense Government on April 1, 1941. Concerned that the nationalist government would cut the oil pipeline between Iraq and Haifa and inspire nationalist revolts throughout the region, the British responded quickly. Churchill pushed General Wavell to act despite the competing crises in Greece and North Africa, and in late April Indian troops landed in Basra while a scratch force led by the British Arab Legion raced across the desert from Palestine.

Faced with this British counterattack, al-Gaylani attacked the Habbaniya airbase and appealed to the Axis for support. Vichy prime minister Admiral François Darlan, then collaborating closely with Berlin, offered Germany the use of bases in Syria to move troops and airplanes to Iraq. But – like the British – Axis forces were heavily committed elsewhere, and their assistance to al-Gaylani was limited to a contingent of 30 aircraft and some weapons shipped by train from Syria. These forces were insufficient to change the outcome of the fighting, which quickly tipped in Britain's favor. British aircraft repulsed Iraqi attacks on Habbaniya, and after a fierce battle at Fallujah British-led forces entered Baghdad in late May. Al-Gaylani and the Grand Mufti fled to Iran and then to Berlin, while London restored the monarchy, reestablished political control, and secured supplies of Iraqi oil.

London used the momentum of its victory in Iraq to invade French-ruled Syria. Again, Churchill was the driving force behind this audacious move, and his goal went beyond simply ending Vichy rule in Syria. German advances in the Balkans had persuaded neutral Turkey to adopt the pro-Axis slant signaled by the signing of a non-aggression pact with Germany in June 1941. London hoped that by taking control of neighboring Syria it could force Turkey to reverse its slide towards the Axis. Promising independence for Syria and Lebanon, British-Imperial troops and units of de Gaulle's Free French advanced from Palestine and Iraq. Despite the lack of Axis support some Vichy forces fought fiercely, and while Anglo-Free French forces quickly captured Damascus, they took several more weeks to secure Beirut. The Free French assumed control, appointing General Georges Catroux as High Commissioner of the Levant. The Free French recognized Syrian independence but – as with the British in Iraq – they maintained control over all major aspects of Syrian life. They also fell out with their British allies, accusing them – not implausibly – of conspiring with Syrian nationalists against French rule.

During 1941, London responded forcefully to rising nationalist sentiment in the Arab world, launching successful military interventions that were conducted with limited forces amidst numerous other crises. These actions shored up British predominance in the Middle East, safeguarded oil supplies, and secured vital air routes to India, but they won London no friends in the Arab world. Instead, Britain's actions stoked the opposition to imperialist domination that would erupt throughout the region after the war.

Operation *Barbarossa*

The German invasion of the Soviet Union began early on June 22, 1941. Fearing a ruse to provoke war, Stalin dismissed British intelligence reports that an attack was imminent, allowing the *Wehrmacht* to achieve complete operational surprise. The initial fighting reprised earlier blitzkrieg operations on a vast scale, with nearly four million men advancing on a front that stretched from the Baltic to the Black Sea. Supported by concentrated air attacks, German tanks tore through holes punched in Red Army lines, plunging deep into Soviet territory to encircle the disoriented defenders in huge "pockets" that were then crushed by slower-moving infantry divisions. At Minsk in July and Smolensk in August, the Red Army suffered staggering losses, and between June and December nearly three million Soviet soldiers were killed or captured. Soviet air forces also suffered heavily, losing nearly 4000 aircraft in the first days alone, most of them destroyed on the ground.

Despite these crushing victories, German officers soon noted with concern that amidst all the chaos and confusion Soviet soldiers continued to fight fiercely. Some fought to the death where they stood, some launched determined local counterattacks, and others formed guerrilla bands behind German lines, while German tank commanders found that combat with technically superior Soviet KV-1 and T-34 tanks could prove deadly. It soon became clear that *Barbarossa* was not going to be a large-scale re-run of France, but German strategic planning hinged on it being just that. In the euphoria following the fall of France, and with their judgment warped by ethnic and political prejudices, German leaders had convinced themselves that they could defeat the Soviet Union in less than two months. They assumed that if they could destroy the Red Army in a blitzkrieg-style campaign fought close to the border, Soviet rule would come crashing down.

More sober-minded planners recognized that it would be difficult to win a decisive victory in the borderlands, while a protracted war deep in Soviet territory would put German supply operations under enormous stress. The German army had grown from 165 divisions in May 1940 to 209 in June 1941, but less than one-third of the units committed to the invasion were fully motorized, and over 600 000 horses were employed moving supplies and pulling artillery pieces (Figure 4.1). As the army advanced, its tanks, trucks, and wagons were forced to operate over vast distances on unpaved roads, and its critical armored formations were soon weakened by mechanical breakdowns and fuel shortages. The *Luftwaffe*, whose ground-attack aircraft were indispensable to blitzkrieg warfare, also faced significant problems. Frontline air units had been weakened by campaigns against France and Britain, and like the tanks they were now operating at the end of long supply lines where shortages of fuel, munitions, and spare parts could quickly erode efficiency.

To make matters worse, German forces became *less* concentrated as they advanced into the USSR. The *Wehrmacht* attacked on three divergent axes: Army Group North crashed through the Baltic States towards Leningrad; Army Group Center drove towards Smolensk and Moscow; and space Army Group South – reinforced by Romanian troops – pushed into Ukraine. Given this lack of strategic focus, the great German victories at the start of *Barbarossa* reflected the abysmal failures of Soviet political and military leadership as much as the competence and skill of the invaders. Moreover, as the inherent flaws in *Barbarossa*'s design began to be felt, the underlying strengths of the Soviet system started to emerge. Soviet leaders were badly shaken by the German attack – Stalin seems to have suffered a breakdown – but they soon rallied and reorganized. In contrast to France, no

Figure 4.1   German horse-drawn supply column rests for lunch deep in the Soviet Union, September 1942. Over 600 000 horses accompanied invading German armies, and horse-drawn wagons moved the bulk of supplies between railheads and the frontlines. (*Source*: Bundesarchiv, Bild 183-B22147.)

section of the Soviet hierarchy sought a compromise peace and nor, given the systemic gulf between the warring states, was one on offer.

Senior Soviet officials formed the State Defense Committee, a powerful new executive body that unified military, economic, and political decision making, and set up the *Stavka*, a centralized top-level military command. On its orders, over 1500 industrial enterprises were dismantled and moved out of the path of the advancing Germans, with entire factories being uprooted and shipped east of the Ural Mountains. Twelve million workers – many of whom took local initiatives to speed the evacuation – accompanied their machines, and production soon restarted; amazingly, Soviet war production *increased* during 1942. The USSR also mobilized its vast pool of reservists, expanding the Red Army from five million to eight million by the end of 1941.

These measures were made possible by a combination of top-down decision making and a broad upwelling of popular support for the defense of the Soviet Union. Government decrees were enforced by harsh police action, but popular support for measures to strengthen Soviet resistance was deep and widespread. Despite the horrors of Stalinist political repression, many Soviet citizens retained a deep loyalty to the legacy of the Russian Revolution. They were still proud of

71

their revolution and of the leap from economic backwardness into modernity that had unfolded during their lifetimes, and they valued the access to education and culture that it brought with it. Moscow bolstered resistance with nationalist propaganda framing the newly named Great Patriotic War in terms of Russia's victory over Napoleon in 1812. Moscow lifted restrictions on the Orthodox Church, whose leaders responded by endorsing the Soviet war effort. The success of drastic economic measures reflected the strength of the centrally planned economy in which individuals and enterprises were used to acting – and to taking initiative – within the framework of nationally determined priorities. It is hard to imagine a capitalist state, in which governments lead through incentivized negotiation with private businesses, responding so quickly and effectively to the existential crisis that faced the USSR in 1941.

With the war with Germany raging, Moscow took steps to secure control of the oilfields of northern Iran by launching a surprise attack on the country in collaboration with British forces. Citing the allegedly pro-Axis views of monarch Reza Shah Pahlavi and the presence of around 1000 German nationals, British and Soviet diplomatic protests were followed in late August by a full-scale invasion. By mid-September Iranian military resistance was crushed by British and Soviet forces that enjoyed complete air superiority and bombed several Iranian cities. After Tehran capitulated, Reza Shah was forced to abdicate, and he was replaced by his more pliable son, Mohammad Reza Pahlavi. British and Soviet forces occupied and partitioned the country, securing control of key oilfields and the Trans-Iranian Railway, the backbone of the future "Persian Corridor" linking Persian Gulf ports to Soviet Azerbaijan.

The *Shoah*

German leaders understood the battle to the death unfolding on their *Ostfront* as a struggle between different socio-economic systems, conceptualized both as a racial war against Slavs and Jews and as a political war against communism. This racialized vision of German superiority was shared by Nazi officials and *Wehrmacht* officers alike, and it was expressed in Hitler's call for a "war of extermination" against the USSR.[2] In this sense, the assault on the Soviet Union was qualitatively different from the war against France. In a series of pre-invasion orders, soldiers were urged to take ruthless action against Red Army officers, communist officials, and ordinary Soviet citizens who offered the slightest opposition. It was clear from the beginning that the normal rules of war would not apply. Units of *Einsatzgruppen* and other paramilitary police followed the combat units to impose German control over newly occupied territory through a reign of terror. These forces specifically targeted Jews, but prisoners of war and local Ukrainian and Belorussian peasants also received harsh treatment. As random killings escalated, the entire operational area became one vast killing field.

At the start of the invasion, some Ukrainians welcomed the advancing Germans as liberators. Many were deeply hostile to the Soviet Union as a result of the catastrophic famine produced by forced collectivization and by Moscow's repression of Ukrainian national independence. It has been argued that Germany failed to use this anti-Soviet sentiment to help topple the USSR. The problem with this argument is that Berlin had no interest in promoting Ukrainian independence; on the contrary, Nazi leaders aimed to depopulate the region in order to open space for German settlement, and their autarkic-colonial project precluded any ongoing alliance with Ukraine. The German military did recruit Ukrainian volunteers, often dubbing them "Cossacks" to mitigate the ideological contradiction posed by enlisting Slavs, but after the *Reichskommissariat Ukraine* was established to administer the occupied territory in September 1941, the true character of Nazi intentions quickly became clear.

The "war of extermination" in the Soviet Union was intertwined with a further radicalization of Nazi anti-Semitism as officials worked out how to deal with the large numbers of Jews coming under German control. The precise chronology is unclear, and it is unlikely that there was a single decision to launch a genocidal "final solution," but during the summer of 1941 German leaders concluded that systematic mass killing was the answer to their "Jewish problem." Continuous mass executions by gunshot tended to demoralize even hardened Nazis, and by October plans for purpose-built extermination centers using poison gas had been approved for sites at Belzec and Chelmno in occupied Poland. As the march towards Judeocide gathered momentum, senior officials led by Reinhard Heydrich's Reich Main Security Office met at Wannsee near Berlin in January 1942 to coordinate the work of the various government agencies involved. Their decisions ensured that across the bloodlands of Eastern Europe, the Holocaust – or *Shoah* (catastrophe) in Hebrew – developed into a systematic and highly organized slaughter on a vast scale. This acceleration of Nazi Judeocide intersected with an assault on the entire civilian population as officials requisitioned food for German use and left local peasants to starve. The aptly named Hunger Plan, drafted by SS officer Herbert Backe prior to *Barbarossa*, aimed to eliminate "useless eaters" with ruthless efficiency, and an estimated 4.2 million Soviet citizens died of starvation during the German occupation.

At the time when the final solution was initiated, Berlin still anticipated a quick victory over the Soviet Union, but the *Shoah* actually unfolded in the context of deepening military difficulties on Germany's *Ostfront*. In August 1941, Army Group South's drive into Ukraine ran into determined Soviet resistance around Kiev. Against the advice of senior officers eager to advance on Moscow, Hitler decided – not unreasonably – that Kiev had to be taken before advancing further east. Armored units were detached from Army Group Center to complete the encirclement of Kiev, where another 700 000 Red Army soldiers were killed or captured. The battle of Kiev was another major German victory, but it also delayed the advance on Moscow by a month. Stubborn Soviet resistance stoked German anger and frustration, which were vented on Jews in particular, as SS task forces and Ukrainian auxiliaries rounded up over 33 000 Jews and massacred them in the Babi Yar Ravine outside of Kiev. In the south, Romanian forces had already begun bloody anti-Semitic pogroms in the former Soviet territory annexed to form the Governorate of Transnistria.

The intensification of the *Shoah* intersected with the growing recognition that *Barbarossa* would not produce a quick victory in the USSR. This realization was underscored by developments on two key fronts. In early September, German armies encircled Leningrad, where Soviet defensive efforts were complicated by a renewed struggle with Finland known as the Continuation War. Despite repeated assaults, however, German forces could not take the city. The Siege of Leningrad dragged on for two years and cost the lives of at least 1.6 million soldiers and civilian Leningraders – many dying of starvation – but their resistance denied Germany one of its key goals. Army Group Center's assault on Moscow also failed. The *Wehrmacht* killed or captured a further 500 000 Soviet soldiers once their march on Moscow resumed in October, but autumn mud, early winter snows, and Red Army counterattacks slowed progress. The German advance ground to a halt in late November; German officers could see the spires of Moscow, but they could not advance towards them.

As temperatures plunged, the lack of any preparation for winter and the crisis of the overstretched supply system weakened German frontline units. A lack of spare parts rendered tanks unserviceable, fuel was in short supply, and men suffered frostbite or froze to death for lack of winter clothing. Then the Red Army struck back. In October, Marshal Zhukov, the victor of Khalkhyn Gol and the organizer of the defense of Leningrad, was appointed to lead the defense of Moscow. Zhukov assembled a strategic reserve east of the capital by drawing on Siberian units released by the non-aggression pact with Japan. After the German advance stalled, Zhukov unleashed the Soviet counterattack on December 5, 1941. The battle raged into early 1942, and the *Wehrmacht* finally stabilized the front in late February. But it was a desperate struggle, and Soviet forces came close to overwhelming Army Group Center. The myth of German invincibility was shattered.

Barbarossa and the Emerging World War

The German–Soviet war had major global implications. The nature of the Axis alliance precluded effective joint strategic planning, but Berlin hoped that it's invasion of the USSR would encourage Tokyo to accelerate its own expansionist efforts, tying America down in the Pacific and preventing it from interfering in Europe. Japanese leaders were inspired by *Barbarossa*, and temporarily revived their interest in attacking the Soviet Union. As German difficulties mounted, however, advocates of war with the USSR were marginalized by those favoring a "southern strategy." Prince Konoe's warnings that war with the United States would be disastrous were dismissed, and he resigned in October 1941. Konoe's successor, Army Minister Tōjō Hideki, was committed to the drive south and to war with America. In a sign of the growing interconnection between the regional wars in Europe and Asia, when the news of this decision reached Moscow courtesy of its spy network in Tokyo, it convinced Soviet leaders that the danger of a Japanese attack had passed and that it was safe to redeploy Red Army units from Asia for Zhukov's counterattack around Moscow.

The embattled British government quickly saw that the new war between Germany and the USSR ended its own isolation within Europe, and a formal military alliance – the Anglo-Soviet Agreement – was signed on July 12. Churchill proclaimed enthusiastically that "any man or state who fights on against Nazidom will have our aid."[3] In fact, the British had little aid to give, but with London's encouragement Władysław Sikorski's Polish government-in-exile signed an agreement with Moscow that freed thousands of Poles from Soviet prison camps and encouraged them to join a new Polish army being formed in the USSR. Tensions with the Soviets soon resurfaced, and in early 1942 the "Anders Army" – named after its leader, General Władysław Anders – was relocated to British-ruled Palestine after an arduous journey through Iran and across the Middle East. These troops, minus the 3000 Polish Jews who elected to remain in Palestine, went on to fight alongside British-Imperial forces in Italy.

At the start of *Barbarossa*, senior officers in Washington shared Berlin's belief that the invasion of the Soviet Union would be over within weeks, and some American politicians and newspaper editorialists openly hoped that the USSR and Nazi Germany would destroy each other. President Roosevelt took a different approach. He argued that the Soviets could play a decisive role in the war against Germany and, encouraged by Churchill, he sent key adviser Harry Hopkins on an arduous factfinding mission to Moscow. Hopkins's enthusiastic reports on the Soviet response to *Barbarossa* reinforced the president's decision to permit the shipment of military supplies to the USSR. At first, the Soviets were simply allowed to purchase equipment on a cash-and-carry basis, but in October they began to receive Lend-Lease aid. By this time, US military chiefs had come to see support for the Soviet war effort as a central component of American strategy, recognizing that the Soviets "had by far the best opportunity [to] launch a land offensive against Germany."[4] Put bluntly, Roosevelt and his military chiefs hoped that a well-supplied Red Army would bear the brunt of the fighting against Germany.

These developments were intertwined with Roosevelt's cautious campaign towards greater American involvement in the war. In his January 1941 State of the Union speech, the president had proclaimed "Four Freedoms" – freedom of speech, freedom from want, freedom of worship, and freedom from fear – that should be enjoyed by all the world's people. Given deep class and racial divisions within the United States, this list of vague generalities was freighted with hypocrisy, but it served to frame Washington's march towards war in terms of liberal internationalism. It was also unclear whether Roosevelt envisaged direct military involvement in the war. British leaders welcomed aid, but they wanted America to join the fighting, and Churchill hoped to secure a firm military commitment when he met Roosevelt in Newfoundland in August 1941 for their first wartime summit conference.

Instead of an American declaration of war, the summit produced nothing more than a statement of Anglo-American war aims that was quickly dubbed the Atlantic Charter. The Charter offered a vision of a postwar world based on free trade, equal access to world markets, national self-determination, and international disarmament. Despite the genial bonhomie that blossomed between Churchill and Roosevelt, London had fundamental disagreements with a vision that – to say the least – implied American global leadership. It did not plan to give up its empire, abandon Imperial Preference in favor of free trade, or allow self-determination in its colonies. Nevertheless, if it got the United States into the war, the Atlantic Charter seemed a small price to pay.

Alongside this ideological preparation for war, American rearmament began to move into high gear; naval construction expanded dramatically after the fall of France, and with the development of the Lend-Lease program in spring 1941 military spending jumped to 11% of gross national product (GNP). In July, the War and Navy departments drafted a "Victory Plan" that projected expanding the army from 10 active-service divisions into a 215-division force backed by massive air power. This huge army was designed to win a land war in Europe; whatever the strategic weaknesses of this vision, it articulated a willingness to fight. Even as the Victory Plan was being drafted, the US Navy was getting drawn into a shooting war in the North Atlantic. In September, a US destroyer operating from Iceland was attacked by a German submarine, and in response Washington ordered warships to shoot at U-boats on sight. Further attacks led to the sinking of the destroyer *Reuben James*, and by December 1941 American warships were fighting an undeclared naval war in the Atlantic.

America's march towards war was framed by the Germany First strategy adopted after the fall of France. This required postponing a clash with Japan, and during 1941 Washington tried to deter Japanese expansionism by concentrating the fleet in Pearl Harbor and by imposing economic sanctions. Japanese forces continued to advance, moving into southern Indochina and occupying the key Cam Ranh airfield in July. These moves were viewed as preparation for further advances into Southeast Asia, and Washington replied by imposing a total trade embargo, cutting off oil shipments, and dispatching new B-17 Flying Fortress bombers to reinforce the defenses of the Philippines. London sent the battleships *Repulse* and *Prince of Wales* to Singapore in the hope of deterring a Japanese attack. American military commanders hoped to buy time by making short-term diplomatic concessions, but Roosevelt was concerned that they might free up Japanese forces to attack the USSR, and in late November the State Department reiterated American demands that Japan withdraw from China and Indochina, recognize the Nationalist government, and quit the Axis alliance. These demands were clearly unacceptable to Tokyo, and they pointed unambiguously towards war. Clearly, Washington now felt able to fight a two-front war and was willing to risk provoking a clash with Japan while continuing to prioritize the struggle against Germany.

Pearl Harbor and World War

War soon followed, heralded by Japan's surprise attack on the American naval base at Pearl Harbor on December 7, 1941. The attack was designed to eliminate the US Pacific Fleet, making it impossible for Washington to block the main Japanese advance into Southeast Asia. This drive, and the resulting establishment of the Co-Prosperity Sphere, was the principal goal of Japanese strategy; the preemptive attack on Pearl Harbor was essentially a secondary operation, critical to the success of the main assault but subordinate to it. Tokyo hoped that by the time America's "new navy" – the product of the shipbuilding programs initiated by the 1938 and 1940 Navy Acts – was ready, the resources of the Co-Prosperity Sphere would have been integrated into a Japanese economy and protected by a chain of island outposts across the Central Pacific. Japanese leaders anticipated that Washington would lack the resolve for a protracted war and instead would seek an accommodation with Tokyo that recognized Japan's predominance in China and Southeast Asia. This, of course, was a tremendous gamble, but Japanese leaders concluded that with American sanctions choking off oil imports, there was nothing to gain by waiting. What is surprising is not how far-fetched this plan was, but how close it came to at least partial success.

The Japanese attack on Pearl Harbor and America's declaration of war on Japan the following day finally fused several regional wars into a genuinely global conflict. For the first time, there was a combatant nation that not only had vital interests in both Europe and Asia, but also possessed the capacity to fight simultaneously in both spheres. On December 11, 1941, Germany declared war on the United States. This move is often viewed as a great strategic blunder, and it undoubtedly came as a relief to the British government, which feared that a wave of popular enthusiasm for war with Japan would force Washington to abandon the Germany First strategy in favor of an all-out war with Tokyo. But the German declaration was not irrational. German leaders had long viewed the United States as their ultimate global opponent, they knew that American aid was keeping Britain fighting, and they were well aware that the US Navy was already fighting an undeclared war against their submarines in the North Atlantic. In this context, a formal declaration of war allowed Berlin to begin systematic attacks on American merchant shipping with the aim of cutting Britain's trans-Atlantic lifeline. In December a long-range U-boat left France for an extended patrol off the eastern seaboard of the United States. More soon followed, and in the first half of 1942 German submarines sank three million tons of unescorted merchant shipping in American waters. German submariners referred to this as their "happy time," and the losses they inflicted were among the highest of the entire three-year Battle of the Atlantic.

America's entry into the war had dire consequences for Japanese Americans. In February 1942, President Roosevelt's Executive Order 9066 permitted the exclusion of specific civilians from newly designated "military areas" and facilitated the expulsion of 120 000 Japanese Americans from the West Coast in response to unproven assertions that many were loyal to Tokyo. For the rest of the war, Japanese Americans removed from the coast on the sole basis of their ethnicity were housed in makeshift prisons euphemistically known as "relocation" camps. Over two-thirds of the detainees were second-generation *nisei* who were American citizens, and many lost homes, prosperous farms, and small businesses. In December 1944, the Supreme Court ruled on a case brought by Japanese American activist Fred Korematsu, upholding the constitutionality of the exclusion order on the grounds that national security outweighed democratic rights. In his dissenting opinion, Justice Frank Murphy argued that the court ruling legitimized institutionalized racism. Many detainees remained in the camps until 1945.

In a parallel move, the Canadian government ordered the removal of 27 000 Japanese Canadians from a 100-mile-wide "protected zone" on the coast of British Columbia. Many were detained throughout the war in internment camps, while others were forced to work on farms and construction projects in the interior. The government confiscated the property of Japanese Canadians – including houses, farms, and fishing boats – and sold them to cover the costs of internment. In 1944, Japanese Canadians were given the choice of moving permanently east of the Rocky Mountains or being repatriated to Japan – a country many of them had never visited. At the end of the war, nearly 4000 were shipped to Japan, many against their will. The policy was finally rescinded in 1947, by which time many Japanese Canadians had permanently relocated to Toronto while others had returned to the West Coast as the exclusionary policy gradually crumbled.

America's formal entry into the war was accompanied by an upwelling of popular nationalism that swept aside isolationist and anti-war sentiment. Major news organizations adopted a wartime policy of self-censorship, but Washington also moved to silence domestic opponents of the war. In June 1941, the government prosecuted the Trotskyist Socialist Workers Party (SWP) under the 1940 Smith Act, which made it illegal to advocate the overthrow of the American government. The day after Pearl Harbor, 18 SWP leaders were sentenced to jail for their anti-war stance, and throughout the war the party's *Militant* newspaper faced repeated government attempts to silence it. Black-owned newspapers that challenged segregation and institutionalized racism in the armed forces also faced intense government pressure. During 1942, several African American papers joined the *Pittsburgh Courier*'s popular "Double V" campaign that linked fighting for victory over fascism abroad to victory over racism at home. Campaign articles featured protests against segregation and racial violence within the military. Concerned that this campaign presented the war effort – and American society more broadly – in a bad light, Attorney General Francis Biddle threatened black-owned newspapers with closure, and by the end of the year criticism of segregation within the military had virtually disappeared from their pages.

Japan's Centrifugal Offensive

The Pearl Harbor attack was planned by Admiral Yamamoto Isoroku, the commander of the Combined Fleet, and executed by the six aircraft carriers of Admiral Nagumo Chūichi's Mobile Strike Force, or *Kidō Butai*. American code-breakers gave Washington extensive knowledge of Japan's war preparations, but they failed to detect the movements of the *Kidō Butai*. Operational surprise allowed Nagumo's pilots to sink two American battleships, damage six more, and destroy nearly 200 aircraft on the ground. But the attack was only a partial success: the American aircraft carriers were not in Pearl Harbor at the time of the attack and escaped destruction. As Yamamoto planned, American losses prevented the US Navy from blocking the Japanese advance into Malaya and the Philippines, but the chance survival of the American carriers allowed it to oppose subsequent Japanese advances in New Guinea and the central Pacific. And, as the Japanese attack itself demonstrated, aircraft carriers – not battle-ships – would play a decisive role in the Pacific War.

With the Pearl Harbor operation underway, Japan struck at British, American, and Dutch colonies in the Philippines and Southeast Asia in a spiraling series of attacks sometimes described as the Centrifugal Offensive. In the first phase, Japan attacked British-ruled Hong Kong and the Gilbert Islands, the American-ruled islands of Guam and Wake, and Australian-ruled islands of New Britain in the Bismarck Archipelago and Bougainville in the Solomon Islands. Japanese forces also invaded the Philippines and British Malaya. Defending forces fought fiercely in Hong Kong and on Wake but were quickly overwhelmed. In the Philippines, most of the B-17 bombers sent to bolster the defense were destroyed on the ground, but the invaders still faced stiff resistance from numerically superior Filipino and American forces. Pushed back into defensive positions in Bataan and Corregidor, Filipino and American troops braved starvation before finally surrendering on May 6, 1942. Their commanding officer, General Douglas MacArthur, had already been ordered to evacuate to Australia, and President Manuel Quezon, head of the American-sponsored Filipino administration, escaped to form a government-in-exile in Washington. In his place, Tokyo set up the Second Philippine Republic under Supreme Court justice José Laurel in 1943.

Japanese troops invaded British Malaya by sea from their new bases in southern Indochina and by land via Thailand, which abandoned its neutrality and cooperated with Japan. For much of the war the Thai government maintained its formal independence and remained outside the Tripartite Pact, but it functioned as Tokyo's junior partner in the Co-Prosperity Sphere and expanded its borders at the expense of neighboring states. In Malaya, Japanese forces under General Yamashita Tomoyuki faced poorly organized British-Imperial contingents, including Australian troops ordered to Singapore by London over Canberra's opposition. Although heavily outnumbered on the ground, the Japanese enjoyed air superiority, decisive leadership, and high morale. Yamashita's troops moved south on jungle tracks and in commandeered coastal boats, infiltrating and outflanking the road-bound defenders and spreading panic and confusion. British-Imperial forces were soon in full retreat towards Singapore.

On December 8, the British battleships *Repulse* and *Prince of Wales* sortied from Singapore to intercept a Japanese invasion fleet heading for Malaya. The battleships sailed without air cover, and two days later they were attacked by Japanese aircraft flying from Cam Ranh Bay in Indochina. Japanese airplanes were operating at the very limit of their range, but they succeeded in sinking both battleships. Their loss weakened the defense of Malaya and dealt a terrible blow to British morale and prestige, and it also demonstrated that even well-armed warships maneuvering at high speed were vulnerable to air attack. Yamashita's advance continued unimpeded. By the end of January 1942, the Japanese had ejected Imperial troops from Malaya, and after a short siege the island city of Singapore, fortified by London at great expense during the 1930s, surrendered on February 15. Over 80 000 Imperial soldiers became prisoners of war, including large numbers of Australian and Indian soldiers. Forty-five thousand Indian prisoners were recruited into the anti-British Free India Army, which came under Subhas Chandra Bose's leadership in 1943.

After the surrender of Holland in May 1940, colonial officials in the Netherlands East Indies (NEI) remained loyal to the Dutch government-in-exile in London, and as tensions with Japan intensified they joined the American oil embargo. After Pearl Harbor, the modest Dutch forces in the region were integrated into the new ABDACOM (America, Britain, Dutch, Australia Command) established by British and American leaders at the *Arcadia* conference (see below). By the time British General Wavell arrived in Singapore in early January to assume command, the military situation was already unraveling. ABDACOM was charged with defending the Malay Barrier, a defensive line running through Malaya, Borneo, and the NEI. As Malaya crumbled, Japanese forces began landing in Borneo and then in NEI, where small Dutch garrisons were quickly overwhelmed. In late February, Allied naval forces were defeated in the Java Sea, and on March 9, the Dutch authorities surrendered. As Japanese forces breached the nominal Malay Barrier, Wavell resigned after barely a month in office and ABDACOM ceased to exist.

The Japanese offensive continued. Japanese troops invaded Burma from Thailand in January 1942, capturing Rangoon (Yangon) in early March and advancing north towards the Indian border. In Rangoon, the Japanese freed nationalist leader Ba Maw from prison, and units of Aung San's Burma Independence Army fought alongside Japanese forces throughout the campaign. The Japanese faced a scratch force of British, Burmese, and Indian Army units, many of them poorly trained, badly equipped, and without adequate air support. The defenders were reinforced by a Chinese expeditionary force commanded by American General Joseph Stilwell that was dispatched by a reluctant Chiang Kai-shek to defend the critical Burma Road supply route. Stilwell was Roosevelt's personal representative in Chongqing and Chiang's chief of staff, but his relationship with the Chinese leader was already strained, and defeat in Burma did not help matters.

As in Malaya, Japanese forces outmaneuvered British-Imperial defenders, who were soon in full retreat towards India. Retreating troops were joined by thousands of Indian plantation workers. Even in rout, British officials maintained the racial hierarchies of empire, holding back Indian refugees to allow the escape of British soldiers and administrators. Many Indian laborers were rounded up by the Japanese and forced to work on the notorious Thai–Burma railroad and other projects. In May, the defeated British, along with Stilwell and part of the Chinese army, crossed the border into India. Other Chinese units retreated towards Yunnan, but many were cut off by Japanese and Thai troops advancing into Burma to occupy the northern Shan States. As British-Imperial forces in Burma collapsed, the aircraft carriers of the *Kidō Butai* raided into the Indian Ocean, attacking naval bases at Colombo and Trincomalee in British-ruled Ceylon (Sri Lanka), sinking several warships, and bombing Indian ports. The raid forced the Royal Navy to make a demoralizing withdrawal from the Bay of

Bengal, a sea that it had dominated since the 1760s; the psychological shock of this defeat on the British elite was enormous.

Japan's Centrifugal Offensive overthrew European colonialism across a great arc of Southeast Asia. It is hard to overstate the significance of this tectonic shift in a region that had long been ruled from Europe and the United States, particularly as the Western imperialists had been routed by an Asian power, shattering the aura of European superiority. Throughout the region, local populations were indifferent to the fate of their colonial masters, and many welcomed the Japanese as liberators. Some, like those who flocked to Aung San's new Burmese Independence Army, even took up arms against their old colonial rulers. In Aceh, on the northern tip of Dutch Sumatra, Japanese agents encouraged a Muslim revolt against Dutch rule, and throughout the archipelago they collaborated with Sukarno and other Indonesian nationalists. Tokyo hoped to work with local nationalists to exploit the region's oil reserves, and Sukarno seized on collaboration with the invaders to popularize Indonesian nationalism, even though it meant helping to recruit forced laborers – *rōmusha* – for Japanese construction projects.

War also loosened the ties of empire between Britain and Australia. The Statute of Westminster, adopted by the British parliament in 1931, recognized Australia as a self-governing commonwealth, but the British monarch remained the head of state and London expected Canberra to follow its lead on major questions of foreign policy. After Pearl Harbor, however, John Curtin's Labor Party government recognized that Britain could not protect Australia from Japanese invasion, and it turned instead to the United States. Increasingly, Australia functioned as America's junior partner in the region, and even as its wartime "client state."[5] Canberra was furious when Britain delayed the return of Australian troops fighting in North Africa, particularly after Japanese air raids on the northern port of Darwin in February 1942 heightened invasion fears. After leaving the Philippines, General MacArthur arrived in Australia to take command of the newly formed South West Pacific Area (SWPA). As SWPA forces battled for survival and then began a counteroffensive in New Guinea in 1942–1943, the war in the South Pacific became an American–Australian joint effort, and Australia also functioned as a staging area for US forces moving into the region.

The outbreak of war with Japan had a major effect on Indian politics. Since 1939, the British had been mobilizing Indian men and material for war without any collaboration with the Indian National Congress. As British rule in Malaya and Burma collapsed, however, London worried that a Japanese attack on India might spark an anti-colonial rebellion, so it launched a political initiative to draw the INC into the war effort. Senior Labour politician Stafford Cripps traveled to India in March 1942 with a promise that India would be granted self-governing "dominion" status after the war if Congress agreed to mobilize support for the war effort. Cripps did not, however, offer the INC an opportunity to participate in foreign policy or military decision making during the war. Denied any real say in the conduct of the war, Congress rejected Cripps's offer.

The *Arcadia* Conference

Days after America formally joined the war, Churchill and the British chiefs of staff crossed the Atlantic to meet with Roosevelt and top American military leaders. This summit conference, codenamed *Arcadia*, established the basic strategy and organizational structures of the Anglo-American alliance. As the conference assembled, the Allies were scrambling to respond to the Japanese offensive, but the British were pleased to find that Pearl Harbor had not over-turned Washington's commitment to the "Germany First" strategy. *Arcadia* reaffirmed this approach and adopted a vaguely defined plan to begin operations against German-dominated Europe by launching an attack on French North Africa later in 1942. Conference participants also discussed how to keep trans-Atlantic shipping lanes open to maintain the flow of supplies to the embattled Soviet Union, where Zhukov's counterattack around Moscow was underway.

In addition, the *Arcadia* conference established a centralized military leadership for the Anglo-American alliance in the form of the Combined Chiefs of Staff (CCS). Based in Washington and composed of senior military leaders from both countries, the CCS oversaw numerous subcommittees working on strategic planning, war production, and shipping. In addition to its day-to-day work in Washington, CCS members met with Roosevelt and Churchill at the series of conferences that shaped Allied strategy. The Combined Chiefs were also empow-ered to set up regional or "theater" commands in which a single Allied supreme commander – who could be from either country – would have authority over all Allied land, sea, and air forces in the region. The first such command was the short-lived ABDACOM discussed above. After the conference, US leaders formed the Joint Chiefs of Staff in February 1942 in order to coordinate American mili-tary efforts and to participate effectively in the Combined Chiefs organization.

These measures established a historically unprecedented degree of military integration between wartime allies. Moreover, Anglo-American military coop-eration was at the center of a broader set of alliances. London and Washington were committed to supporting the Soviet war effort, and that involved establish-ing close diplomatic relations with Moscow and ensuring the involvement of Soviet leaders in a number of wartime conferences. Despite this collaboration, however, Moscow was never integrated into the "combined" military command structure of the Anglo-American alliance. British and American leaders recog-nized the decisive role of the USSR in the military struggle with Nazi Germany, but they never lost sight of the deep systemic divide between the capitalist West and their Communist ally in the East.

As the *Arcadia* conference was taking place, representatives of 26 countries met in Washington on January 1, 1942 to sign the Declaration by United Nations. The signatories, including the USSR, China, and several governments-in-exile, as well as nine countries in the Americas and five British dominions including India, pledged their support for the liberal internationalist principles articulated in the Atlantic Charter. At one level, the Declaration simply created attractive ideological packaging for the Anglo-American bloc at the heart of the United Nations alliance, and several signatories made no active contribution to the struggle against the Axis during the entire war. At the same time, however, the statement sketched the outline of a postwar order based on liberal internationalist principles and led by the United States, and as other states signed on it popularized the idea of a "United Nations" organization.

Notes

1. Hitler, quoted in Knox, M.G. (2000). *Hitler's Italian Allies: Royal Armed Forces, Fascist Regime, and the War of 1940–1943*, 18. New York: Cambridge University Press.
2. Hitler, quoted in Stahel (2009), 96.
3. Churchill, W.S. (1950). *The Second World War*, Vol. III, 332. Boston: Houghton Mifflin.
4. US Joint Board, quoted in Stoler, M.A. (2007). *Allies in War: Britain and America Against the Axis Powers, 1940–1945*, 31. New York: Hodder Arnold.
5. Murray, W. and Millett, A.R. (2000). *A War to be Won: Fighting the Second World War*, 188. Cambridge, MA: Harvard University Press.

Reference

Stahel, D. (2009). *Operation Barbarossa and Germany's Defeat in the East*. New York: Cambridge University Press.

Further Reading

Bayly, C. and Harper, T. (2004). *Forgotten Armies: The Fall of British Asia 1941–1945*. Cambridge, MA: Harvard University Press.

Browning, C.R. (2004). *The Origins of the Final Solution: The Evolution of Nazi Jewish Policy 1939–1942*. Jerusalem: Yad Vashem.

Browning, C.R. (2017). *Ordinary Men: Reserve Police Battalion 101 and the Origin of the Final Solution in Poland*. New York: HarperCollins.

DiNardo, R.L. (2005). *Germany and the Axis Powers: From Coalition to Collapse*. Lawrence, KS: University Press of Kansas.

Evans, R.J. (2009). *The Third Reich at War*. London: Penguin Books.

Hilberg, R. (1985). *The Destruction of the European Jews*. New York: Holmes & Meier.

Ienaga, S. (1978). *The Pacific War, 1931–1945*. New York: Pantheon Books.

Overy, R. (1997). *Russia's War: A History of the Soviet War Effort, 1941–1945*. London: Penguin Books.

Porch, D. (October 2004). The other Gulf war: British intervention in Iraq, 1941. *Joint Forces Quarterly* 35: 134–140.

Spector, R.H. (1985). *Eagle Against the Sun: The American War with Japan*. New York: Vintage Books.

Wood, J.B. (2007). *Japanese Military Strategy in the Pacific War: Was Defeat Inevitable?* Lanham, MD: Rowman & Littlefield.

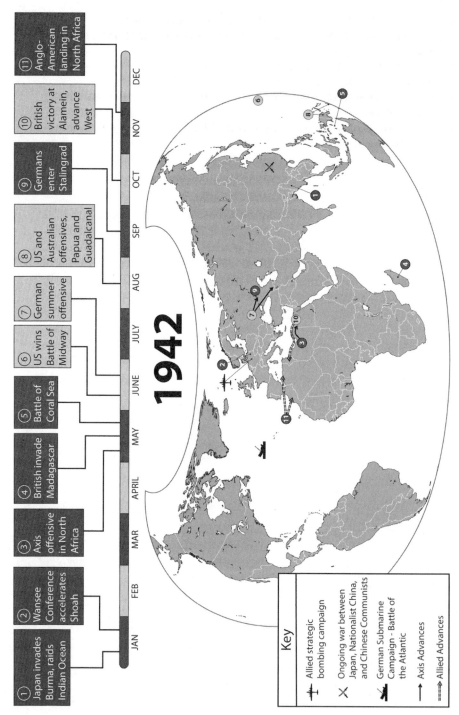

1942

| JAN | FEB | MAR | APRIL | MAY | JUNE | JULY | AUG | SEP | OCT | NOV | DEC |

1. Japan invades Burma, raids Indian Ocean
2. Wansee Conference accelerates Shoah
3. Axis offensive in North Africa
4. British invade Madagascar
5. Battle of Coral Sea
6. US wins Battle of Midway
7. German summer offensive
8. US and Australian offensives, Papua and Guadalcanal
9. Germans enter Stalingrad
10. British victory at Alamein, advance West
11. Anglo-American landing in North Africa

Key

✈ Allied strategic bombing campaign

✕ Ongoing war between Japan, Nationalist China, and Chinese Communists

✈ German Submarine Campaign - Battle of the Atlantic

→ Axis Advances

═➤ Allied Advances

Map: 1942.

5

1942–1943: Turning Points

A World War

The formal entry of the United States into the ongoing wars against Germany, Italy, and Japan brought these disparate struggles together and imparted global cohesion for the first time. A genuine *world* war was emerging. This new world war was a uniquely American construction, and while it placed existing regional conflicts in an overarching framework, it did not negate their specificity: China and the Soviet Union continued to resist Japanese and German invasions, while the Axis powers struggled to establish colonial-autarkic empires in Eastern Europe, East and Southeast Asia, and the Mediterranean. Nazi leaders certainly *thought* in terms of a *Weltkrieg* or world war to establish a new world order, but they recognized that a fight for global hegemony was a long-term project that first required the construction of a secure autarkic bloc in Europe. This understanding was reflected in Berlin's 1939 decision to cancel major warship construction, effectively abandoning transoceanic power projection for many years. Likewise, Japanese leaders never thought of conquering America; instead, their goal was simply to keep it out of their new Co-Prosperity Sphere.

Britain was capable of fighting in both Europe and Asia, but its goal was to defend its existing empire, not to carve out a new world order, and it lacked the resources to fight major wars in both regions simultaneously. In contrast, the United States had both the resources and – after Pearl Harbor – the political will to fight a *world* war and, as publisher Henry Luce had pointed out in his influential "American Century" editorial in February 1941, fighting a world war and establishing a world peace go hand-in-hand. Even as it mobilized for war,

World War II in Global Perspective, 1931–1953: A Short History, First Edition. Andrew N. Buchanan.
© 2019 John Wiley & Sons, Inc. Published 2019 by John Wiley & Sons, Inc.

Washington began to organize for the peace. In April 1942, the State Department set up the Advisory Committee on Postwar Foreign Policy, an influential body that involved senior diplomatic and military figures along with top businessmen, journalists, and academics. Many of the committee's extensive and detailed proposals for a new American-led world order were later modified or shelved entirely, but others, like those dealing with the formation of the United Nations, helped to inform postwar policy. Moreover, the formation of the Advisory Committee underscored the Roosevelt administration's conviction that the war would give rise to a new global order under American leadership, a conclusion that seemed to make it legitimate for the United States to determine the postwar fate of numerous individual countries.

Sea Lanes, Air Ways, and Networks of Connectivity

Anglo-American leaders structured the emerging global war through the "combined" command structures set up at the *Arcadia* conference in December 1941. Headquartered in Washington, the Combined Chiefs of Staff managed the worldwide deployment of Allied military forces, while subcommittees of industrial and transportation specialists organized production priorities and planned the movement of personnel and equipment. These bodies oversaw the establishment of robust networks of global connectivity that could move people and supplies around the world in large quantities and at unprecedented speed. From their inception, the contrast between these global pathways and the fragile connections between Japan and its Axis partners in Europe could hardly have been greater.

The most important strands of this global network were the trans-Atlantic convoys that carried food, oil, and war matériel from the United States to Britain. Cutting these supply lines was the German *Kriegsmarine*'s primary strategic mission, and its efforts to do so resulted in the 1939–1943 Battle of the Atlantic. At first, the *Kriegsmarine* was poorly prepared for this task. Under the 1939 Z Plan, Berlin had embarked on the construction of a powerful surface navy, but this project was abandoned when the war in Europe forced Germany to concentrate resources on its land and air forces. German plans to use its existing surface warships against Allied shipping were an almost complete failure. In December 1939, the small battleship *Graf Spee* was scuttled by its crew in the Uruguayan port of Montevideo after being trapped by a British squadron. The following year the *Kriegsmarine* suffered heavy losses in Norway, and in May 1941 the powerful new battleship *Bismarck* was sunk in the North Atlantic. After these losses, Berlin conserved its remaining surface warships, and by spring 1941 its campaign against Allied shipping was entirely dependent on submarines. Berlin's earlier emphasis on surface warships, however, meant that the prewar

U-boat fleet was too small for a long attritional struggle, and it took time to ramp up production.

Operating from bases in occupied France, German U-boats enjoyed considerable initial success in their campaign against the Atlantic convoys, particularly after extending their operations into American coastal waters in December 1941. This "happy time" for U-boat crews came to an end after the US Navy began organizing coastal convoys in April 1942. Nevertheless, Allied forces still faced a protracted struggle against German submarines in the mid-Atlantic. In February 1942, the *Kriegsmarine* improved their Enigma cipher machine, denying Allied codebreakers information on the location of U-boat "wolfpacks." This loss of intelligence, combined with an "air gap" that was beyond the range of land-based escort aircraft, created a mid-Atlantic danger zone. U-boats inflicted heavy losses on Allied merchant shipping during 1942, sinking 134 ships in November alone, and by the end of the year Allied shipping losses (around eight million tons) were outstripping new construction (about seven million tons).

During 1942, Allied convoy defenses were strengthened by new anti-submarine weapons, better detection equipment (radar and sonar), and new long-range aircraft, while convoy escorts were being built in American shipyards in large numbers. In December, analysts at Britain's Bletchley Park codebreaking center cracked the improved Enigma code, and the resulting intelligence allowed convoys to be routed around U-Boat wolfpacks. The crisis in the Battle of the Atlantic was at hand. In January 1943, Admiral Dönitz had 400 U-boats at his disposal, and merchant ship sinkings spiked upwards again. But submarine losses were also rising, with 41 boats sunk in May. Suddenly and dramatically, the scales tipped against the *Kriegsmarine*, which began losing submarines faster than it could build them. Dönitz recognized the new reality and withdrew his U-boats from the North Atlantic in May 1943. Germany had lost the Battle of the Atlantic. In retrospect, and with the exception of the crisis months of late 1942, the *Kriegsmarine* never came close to overwhelming Allied merchant shipping, particularly as American shipyards moved into top gear. Nevertheless, the battle cost the Allies the lives of 36 000 merchant seamen and 3500 ships; over 30 000 German submariners died, around 75% of the all-volunteer force.

Following Roosevelt's August 1941 decision to send military supplies to the USSR, the Allies established new convoy routes through the Arctic Sea to the ports of Archangel and Murmansk. Convoys had to sail past German-occupied Norway, and frigid winter weather added to the threat posed by German aircraft, submarines, and surface warships. In June 1942, fear of an attack by the German battleship *Tirpitz* caused Convoy PQ-17 to scatter, allowing U-boats and aircraft to sink 24 of its 35 cargo ships. After this disaster, Arctic convoys were suspended until long winter nights shielded them from German attack. Arctic convoys carried nearly four million tons of supplies and accounted for around 25% of all Allied aid to the USSR. Lend-Lease supplies also flowed into the Soviet Union along two other pathways, one that crossed the Pacific to Vladivostok and carried around 50% of all shipments, and one that entered Soviet Azerbaijan overland via the road and rail lines of the "Persian Corridor" through Iran.

Trans-Pacific supply shipments began in late 1941 and – remarkably – the Soviet–Japanese Non-Aggression Pact allowed them to continue uninterrupted despite the outbreak of war between America and Japan. Shipments were liable to inspection by Japanese patrols, so they had to be made in Soviet ships and could not include war matériel. In fact, many of the "Soviet" vessels were American-built Liberty ships supplied to the USSR under Lend-Lease. Several ships were mistakenly sunk by American and Japanese submarines, but around eight million tons of food, railroad equipment, and other non-military supplies were delivered to Vladivostok. This effort was supported by the construction of giant warehouse complexes in California and Washington State operated by civilian workers and Italian prisoners of war.

The Persian Corridor route also required substantial infrastructural development, including building ports in the Persian Gulf and constructing the network of highways and railroads that connected them to the Soviet Union. The US Military Mission to Iran (later Persian Gulf Command) organized thousands of US military construction workers for these projects, and they also built a factory in Abadan where airplanes shipped across the Atlantic in crates were assembled before flying on into the USSR. American and British railroad workers arrived to operate the new long-distance trains (Figure 5.1). This giant logistical operation was made possible by the 1941 Anglo-Soviet invasion and partition of Iran. As the war progressed, however, America's large military presence and the fact that it was not already a colonial power in the region allowed Washington to establish considerable influence in Iran. In May 1942, Tehran was made eligible for Lend-Lease aid, and in August Colonel Norman Schwarzkopf, formerly superintendent of the New Jersey State Police, was sent to Iran to train the country's new national police force.

American shipping to Australia also increased dramatically as men and equipment poured in to support offensive operations launched by General MacArthur's new South West Pacific Area Command. These inflows reflected Canberra's decision to position itself as Washington's junior partner in the region, but relations between well-paid and sometimes domineering American personnel and Australian soldiers and civilians were often far from smooth, and in November 1942 they erupted into two days of deadly rioting in the so-called "Battle of Brisbane."

The Imperial Japanese Navy (IJN) decided not to launch a submarine campaign against merchant shipping in the Pacific, and as a result the American military buildup in Australia was virtually unopposed. In contrast, the US Navy used long-range submarines to attack Japanese merchant shipping. Tokyo had established the Co-Prosperity Sphere to secure raw materials including oil, iron

Figure 5.1 American and British railroad workers and US-supplied locomotive at work moving Lend-Lease supplies to the USSR via the Persian Corridor route through Iran in 1943. (*Source*: Library of Congress, Office of War Information, Digital image number fsa 8d29398.)

ore, rubber, and bauxite, but it still faced the challenge of shipping them back to Japan. Due in part to poor quality torpedoes, the American submarine campaign got off to a slow start, sinking only 180 merchant ships in 1942. Once these problems were fixed, US submarines inflicted heavy losses on Japanese shipping that could not be replaced by Japan's shipyards. American attacks were aided by the fact that the IJN was reluctant to organize convoys, and by 1945 the Japanese merchant marine had been reduced to a mere 25% of its prewar size. Although overshadowed in public perception by events on and above the Pacific, America's undersea campaign succeeded in imposing the kind of devastating economic blockade on Japan that the *Kriegsmarine* failed to inflict on Britain.

Aerial Highways

Allied sea lanes were complemented by an extensive network of air routes. President Roosevelt worked through a private corporation to circumvent the Neutrality Acts, prompting Pan American Airlines (Pan Am) boss Juan Trippe to begin work on a trans-Atlantic air route to Africa after the fall of France in 1940. Pan Am built new airfields at Natal and Belém in northern Brazil and took over the trans-Africa Takoradi Air Route from the overstretched British RAF. The trans-Atlantic leg of the route was improved in 1942 by an airfield on British-ruled Ascension Island. From there, pilots made landfall at Takoradi in the British Gold Coast or at Bathurst in Liberia before crossing Africa to Khartoum in Sudan via a string of airfields in Free French- and British-ruled colonies. From there, some aircraft flew on to India via Aden and Karachi, while others turned north to Egypt. Twelve hundred employees of two special Pan Am subsidiaries operated the bases in Africa, and they brought with them the infrastructure of American modernity from refrigerators and chilled soda to movie theaters. Americans interacted with Africans in contradictory ways, often absorbing the racialized practices of British colonial officials while insisting that their project marked a "complete departure" from British imperial rule.[1]

A parallel air route crossed the North Atlantic. Here, too, work began before America formally joined the war, with US military engineers constructing airfields in Greenland and Iceland in 1941 while London built an airbase on the Danish-ruled Faroe Islands. Despite this string of bases, bad weather often made flying across the North Atlantic a dangerous proposition, and hundreds of aircraft were lost in transit. New air routes also traversed the Pacific. In the north, aircraft supplied under Lend-Lease were turned over to Soviet pilots in Alaska before being flown across the Bering Strait into the USSR. To the south, aircraft flew from America to Australia via a series of long hops from Hawai'i to the Christmas and Cook Islands and on to Tonga. In Asia, the loss of the Burma Road meant that American aid for the Guomindang government in Chongqing could only get into China by air. The India–China Ferry began operation in April 1942, with transport aircraft flying from Assam in eastern India over the "Hump" of the Himalayas to Kunming in Yunnan province. This demanding route pushed aircrews and airplanes to their limits, and despite a massive effort the tonnage arriving in Chongqing fell well short of the government's needs.

To manage these sprawling airways, the US Army Air Force created the Air Transport Command (ATC) in July 1942. American Airlines President C.R. Smith was appointed to lead the new organization. From 37 000 personnel, the ATC grew to 210 000 in 1945. In late 1942, the new organization took control of Pan Am's military supply routes, and many Pan Am employees were simply commissioned into the Air Force. Other civilian airline executives and pilots joined Smith in the new command, applying their experience to the task of organizing an integrated global supply network. The presence of these commercial airline executives stoked British fears that in addition to meeting the Allies' worldwide logistical needs, the Americans were building the infrastructure and gaining the operational experience necessary to dominate postwar commercial aviation. These concerns were not misplaced: as American businessmen stepped in to relieve the overstretched British, *postwar* aviation was never far from their minds.

The creation of these global transportation networks required the commitment of enormous resources, beginning with the production of ships and airplanes and extending to the construction of harbors, airfields, warehouses, roads, railroads, repair bases, and barracks. Construction projects were undertaken in dense jungles, on coral atolls, in ice-bound fjords, and in arid deserts. Military construction workers in the Army Corps of Engineers and US Naval Construction Battalions – or Seabees – did much of the work. American engineers learned about the management of "native" labor from British colonial administrators, and they used this knowledge to mobilize large gangs of local workers to do everything from moving dirt and breaking rocks to unloading ships and fueling airplanes. On many sites, modern heavy equipment was put to work alongside gangs of forced laborers working under conditions of semi-slavery. As they created this war-winning global infrastructure, American engineers established the worldwide archipelago of military bases that underpinned America's postwar global hegemony.

The contrast between these networks of global connectivity and the chronic communications difficulties faced by the Axis powers could hardly have been greater. Japan did carry out some large-scale transportation projects, driving the Thai–Burma railroad through dense jungle in just 15 months using the forced labor of 60 000 Allied prisoners of war and 200 000 *rōmusha* workers from across Southeast Asia. Nevertheless, since there was no joint strategic planning between the Axis powers there was little incentive to develop robust connections between them. Before June 1941, Axis officials could travel between Germany and Japan on the Trans-Siberian Railroad, but Operation *Barbarossa* severed this route across the USSR. With Anglo-American naval forces dominating the oceans, further contact between Germany and Japan relied on radio messages and on long-range submarines, and only six such undersea missions were completed successfully. The inability of the Axis powers to maintain anything but the most minimal of contact underscores the fact that their alliance was based on building parallel colonial empires in their own distinct spheres, not on a coordinated bid for world domination.

Military Turning Points: The Pacific

As these international pathways were being established, the military balance was turning against the Axis in three major warzones in the Pacific, the Soviet Union, and the Mediterranean. Only in China did strategic deadlock continue. These shifts occurred at different tempos, but in all three warzones it was a protracted process rather than the result of a single battle. Moreover, these shifts did not mean that the strategic initiative – the ability to take actions that set the military agenda – passed directly from one side to the other. Instead, what opened up was a period in which both sides struggled to seize the initiative.

Japan's dramatic victories in late 1941 and early 1942 filled Tokyo with enormous confidence, but this sense of invincibility – sometimes described as a "victory disease" – distorted its strategic decision making. The *Kidō Butai*'s rampage through the Indian Ocean had already taken the IJN beyond the parameters of the Co-Prosperity Sphere, and in spring 1942 Tokyo wanted to push further into the Pacific to create a front line that stretched from the Aleutian Islands in the north, through Midway – or even Hawai'i – in the central Pacific, to the Solomon Islands in the south. Some naval officers also wanted to invade Australia, but when the army and Prime Minister Tōjō vetoed this scheme it was agreed to isolate the continent by a push into Fiji, Samoa, and New Caledonia. These far-reaching expansionist schemes were intertwined with Admiral Yamamoto's desire to provoke a major naval battle that would allow the IJN to complete the destruction of the US Pacific Fleet.

In April 1942, the US Navy exposed the weakness of Japan's Pacific frontier by launching a bombing attack on Tokyo from the aircraft carrier *Hornet*. Colonel James Doolittle's raid inflicted little damage, but it boosted American morale and underscored the urgency of Tokyo's efforts to strengthen its defensive perimeter. In the early summer the Japanese launched two offensive operations, the first aimed to deepen the isolation of Australia by seizing Port Moresby in New Guinea and the second to capture the American island outpost of Midway in the central Pacific. Codebreakers gave American commander Admiral Chester Nimitz the information he needed to deploy his limited forces, and two major battles followed. In early May, the US Navy fought the IJN to a tactical draw northeast of Australia at the Battle of the Coral Sea. Strategically, the Coral Sea was an American victory. The shock of hitting effective American resistance convinced Japanese commanders to abandon their attack on Port Moresby, breaking the momentum of the Japanese advance for the first time.

The second battle was fought around Midway on June 4–5. Yamamoto hoped that his advance on Midway would lure US forces into a trap, but American codebreakers allowed Nimitz to organize an effective counterattack. Thanks to shipyard workers at Pearl Harbor – and to the mechanized equipment that boosted their productivity – the aircraft carrier *Yorktown*, damaged at the Coral

Sea, was repaired in time to join the battle. As in other major battles, chance events helped to tip the balance. US pilots were lucky to locate the Japanese carriers when their flight decks were crammed with weapons and fuel lines as they prepared to launch another airstrike. All four of the *Kidō Butai*'s aircraft carriers were sunk, while the Japanese finally succeeded in sinking the *Yorktown*. It was a devastating blow to the Japanese navy. The losses in ships and aircraft (322 Japanese airplanes to 147 American) were bad enough, but the Japanese also lost many irreplaceable highly skilled pilots. The United States was already producing pilots on an industrial scale using mechanical Link flight simulators and rotating experienced combat pilots home to serve as instructors. The US Navy was able to train fliers in just 18 months; it took the IJN fifty, and after Midway pilot shortages were a constant problem.

Yamamoto had fought the great battle he had sought, but he had lost it. After Midway, Japan was increasingly forced onto the defensive in the Pacific. Nevertheless, it would take the United States time to assemble the naval forces needed to seize the strategic offensive. In the meantime, Washington launched limited counterattacks, including a hard-fought American–Australian offensive to open the Kokoda Track across the Owen Stanley Mountains in Australian-ruled Papua and a US Marine landing on Guadalcanal. Tokyo's attempt to defend this outpost in the Solomon Islands demonstrated the impossibility of securing a defensive perimeter so far from Japan. Japanese forces resisted the American landings with determination, besting the US Navy in a series of ferocious night battles around Guadalcanal. But Japanese bombers faced a five-hour flight from Rabaul just to get into the battlespace, while carrier- and land-based American fighters could be in combat within minutes. The fighting tipped slowly in America's favor, and in February 1943 the Japanese evacuated their remaining troops. Guadalcanal was a costly victory – the Americans lost two carriers, 20 smaller warships, and nearly 15 000 men killed and wounded – but, together with the battles of the Coral Sea and Midway it opened the way for a broader counteroffensive. Perhaps even more importantly, these battles ended the myth of Japanese invincibility, convincing the Americans that they could win.

While the Americans were blunting Japanese advances in the Pacific, a second Allied counteroffensive unfolded in the Indian Ocean. After the Japanese evicted the Royal Navy from the eastern Indian Ocean in early 1942, British leaders feared that Tokyo would establish a submarine base in Vichy-ruled Madagascar. With the Mediterranean already closed to Allied shipping, such a force could cut the vital supply routes running to Egypt via South Africa. London ended this threat by invading Madagascar in May 1942. British commandos quickly captured the port of Diego Suarez, but a British-Imperial army that included East African, South African, Rhodesian, and Indian units took until November to secure the entire island. To de Gaulle's understandable annoyance, Free French forces were excluded from the invasion, although civil governance was later turned over to a Free French commissioner. Japanese submarines, working with German U-boats assigned to the Monsoon Group and based in the Malay port of Penang, did wage a limited campaign against Allied shipping on the east coast of Africa, but by summer 1942 the threat of a major Japanese offensive in the Indian Ocean had passed.

Deadlock in China

As the war turned against Japan in the Pacific, Tokyo's seemingly unwinnable war in China became even more burdensome. Japanese forces conducted a ferocious campaign in central China to punish the Guomindang for sending troops to Burma, and as Japan's drive into the Co-Prosperity Sphere wrapped up, units were redeployed to strengthen the army in China. Despite these moves, Tokyo lacked the resources to transform the strategic situation in China. Japan's difficulties did not directly benefit the Guomindang. Instead, the deadlocked struggle accelerated the unraveling of effective governance across much of the country, creating new opportunities for the advance of Communist influence.

In Nationalist China, endemic government corruption combined with rising inflation as Chongqing tried to solve its economic difficulties by printing money. Government efforts to collect farm produce in lieu of taxes worsened the consequences of drought, and in the resulting famine as many as three million people starved to death in Henan alone. Conditions were also bad in Communist-ruled areas, with peasants suffering poor harvests, high taxes, and runaway inflation, but the corruption and outright destitution evident in Guomindang-ruled areas were much less pronounced. The poorest peasants paid no taxes, and the CCP funded initiatives that boosted grain production and promoted modest industrial development. The sense of progress and optimism generated by these policies was in sharp contrast to the pervasive desperation elsewhere in China. It also underpinned the consolidation of Mao Zedong's personal control over the CCP, made evident when the party's 1942 Rectification campaign promoted the study of Mao's own writings over the classic works of Marxism.

Even as the Guomindang's domestic crisis was deepening, Washington was working to elevate the international standing of Chiang's government. When Soviet Commissar for Foreign Affairs Vyacheslav Molotov visited Washington in May 1942, President Roosevelt floated the idea of a postwar world order based on four regional "policemen" – America, Britain, the USSR, and China. Since Roosevelt anticipated that both Britain and China would be beholden to the United States, this arrangement would also give Washington a preeminent position on the world stage. To advance this goal, Washington lionized China's Nationalist leaders and touted their supposed enthusiasm for liberal democracy. Neither London nor Moscow shared Washington's enthusiasm for the Guomindang, but their reliance on American aid made it impolitic to reject Roosevelt's plan outright. Chiang took advantage of America's backing to boost his international standing, visiting Gandhi in February 1942 to express support for Indian independence while urging Congress to back the British war effort. London wanted to ban Chiang's visit, but American support for the Guomindang and its enthusiasm for the decolonization of India made this impossible.

Washington's efforts to build up Chongqing's military capacity were weakened by a sharp disagreement between the two leading American officers in China. General Joseph Stilwell, Roosevelt's personal representative to Chongqing and Chiang's chief of staff, favored creating a strong Chinese army, while Colonel Claire Chennault, Chiang's air adviser and leader of the semi-official American Volunteer Group (AVG) of fighter pilots, envisaged building a large air force. In April 1942, Chennault was promoted to general, and in July the AVG was incorporated into what would become the American 14th Air Force. Chennault had Chiang's backing, while Stilwell – who always had a difficult relationship with the Guomindang leadership – was close to Roosevelt, and their rivalry triggered intense competition for the limited resources arriving from India over the Hump. This fight exposed Washington's bigger problem in China where, as Stilwell reported, unchecked corruption undercut American efforts to strengthen the Nationalist regime.

Military Turning Points: The German–Soviet War

The Red Army's counterattack around Moscow in winter 1941–1942 forced German leaders to recognize that there would be no quick victory in the Soviet Union and that they now faced a protracted multi-front war against increasingly powerful opponents. This realization had several consequences: firstly, steps were taken to gear the German economy for total war; secondly, the *Wehrmacht* planned a major offensive to regain the strategic initiative in the Soviet Union; and thirdly, the Nazi regime intensified its genocidal assault on European Jewry.

German planners had been so confident of their blitzkrieg in the USSR that they had *decreased* the amount of steel allocated to the army prior to *Barbarossa*, shifting resources towards building the large submarine fleet needed to win the Battle of the Atlantic. Now vehicle losses on the *Ostfront* through combat and breakdown began to demotorize the *Wehrmacht*, increasing its dependence on horse-drawn transport and long foot-marches. Clearly, Berlin could not fight a long land war without a massive increase in armaments production. The armaments crisis began to be resolved following the appointment of Albert Speer as Reich Minister of Armaments following Fritz Todt's death in an airplane crash in February 1942.

Albert Speer was an architect whose grandiose designs for the rebirth of Berlin as a "world capital" gave physical expression to Hitler's vaulting political ambition. He was also an ardent Nazi and a modernizing technocrat. Speer believed that centralized economic planning could bring about an "armaments miracle," and with Hitler's backing he began to streamline armaments production. His efforts faced bureaucratic resistance from rival centers of economic and political power within the Nazi state apparatus, and General Plenipotentiary for Labor Deployment Fritz Sauckel battled Speer for control over the allocation of industrial personpower. With expanded military recruitment draining the supply of German workers, this was a critical question. Sauckel's solution was the forced conscription of foreign workers, many of them prisoners of war from Poland, France, and the Soviet Union. Of the eight million foreign workers employed in Germany during the war – nearly 30% of the workforce – only 200 000 came voluntarily. Forced laborers often lived under harsh conditions, living on near-starvation diets in closely guarded camps. From spring 1942, hundreds of thousands of Jewish concentration camp inmates were also forced to work in German war plants, where many died of starvation and exhaustion.

German plans for its new colonial territory in the East were codified in the *Generalplan Ost*, drafted in early 1942 by Heinrich Himmler's office of the Reich Commissioner for the Consolidation of German Nationhood and by Reinhard Heydrich's Reich Main Security Office. The plan envisaged the forced depopulation of the conquered territory to make room for settler-farmers moving from Germany and from *Volksdeutsche* communities throughout Eastern Europe. This impulse towards widespread ethnic cleansing intersected with the mounting demand for forced laborers *and* with the intensification of the *Shoah*. Organized Judeocide – the "Final Solution" – began while Germany was basking in the euphoria of its early victories, but it accelerated in the context of the struggle against the Soviet Union going badly awry and of the United States' formal entry into the war. Nazi leaders saw the August 1941 Atlantic Charter as confirmation that a world Jewish conspiracy stretching from Wall Street financiers to Soviet Communists was waging a world war against Germany.

By the summer of 1942, six extermination camps – Auschwitz, Bełżec, Chełmno, Majdanek, Sobibór, and Treblinka – were operational. Purpose built for mass killing, they received regular shipments of Jews from the Polish ghettos of the General Government, from the occupied Soviet Union, and from Germany's European allies. Jews were joined by other victims of Nazi violence, and over the next three years as many as 500 000 Romani were killed in the death camps, or around 50% of the prewar population. The accelerating *Shoah* combined anti-Semitism and ethnic cleansing with the drive to create autarkic-colonial *Lebensraum* in the East, but it also conformed to an economic rationalism that aimed to conserve food for the German people by eliminating millions of "useless eaters." The development of the *Shoah* was thus closely tied to the overall course of the war, a fact appreciated by ghettoized Jews who understood that the longer it went on, the more remote their chances of survival became.

Major military operations in the Soviet Union resumed as the spring mud dried. By June, German forces completed the conquest of Crimea after storming the port of Sevastopol, and they blunted a Soviet counterattack against Kharkov in battles that resulted in the death or capture of another 250 000 Red Army soldiers. The *Wehrmacht* was now ready to launch its major offensive of the year. German forces lacked the resources to attack along the whole front as they had in 1941, but instead of making another push towards Moscow – as Soviet leaders anticipated – they chose to drive south. Codenamed Operation *Blau* (Blue), the German plan aimed to seize the oilfields of the Soviet Caucasus, giving Germany direct control of virtually inexhaustible reserves of fuel.

Germany committed over 1.2 million men to *Blau*, and their Axis partners added another 200 000. In spring 1941 Germany was trying to meet its manpower shortages by drafting young men 18 months ahead of schedule, and of the 41 new divisions assembled for *Blau*, 6 were Italian, 10 Hungarian, and 5 Romanian. Such was the animosity between the Romanian and Hungarian forces that German commanders considered it prudent to deploy other troops between them. Contrary to popular images of a monolithic force, the "German" army on the *Ostfront* was, as one general noted ironically, an "absolute League of Nations army."[2] The army's multinational character was underscored by the large-scale use of Soviet "Hiwis," or *Hilfswillige* ("willing helpers"). Of the tens of thousands of Hiwis in the *Wehrmacht* by summer 1942 – including 50 000 in Sixth Army alone – some were ideologically motivated volunteers, but most were former Red Army soldiers who enlisted to escape the brutal conditions in German prisoner of war camps. Initially, most Hiwis were assigned to logistical and support duties, but as manpower shortages bit many were reassigned to frontline units.

Albert Speer's drive to reorganize German industry had yet to produce tangible results, and the numbers of tanks, airplanes, and artillery were all lower than they had been in 1941. The offensive began in late June and German armored forces initially made rapid progress, particularly in the south where Army Group A advanced across rolling steppe grasslands into the Caucasus. Learning from their disasters the previous year, Soviet forces retreated, trading space for the time needed to prepare effective resistance. German troops advanced 300 miles in just two weeks, but their haul of prisoners was small. As in *Barbarossa*, the Germans advanced along divergent axes, with Army Group A racing towards the Caucasus while Army Group B advanced eastwards towards Stalingrad.

Stalingrad was a key transportation hub on the Volga, and its capture would shield German forces in the Caucasus from Soviet counterattacks. With both men and equipment in limited supply, however, the attempt to secure Stalingrad while simultaneously invading the Caucasus weakened both efforts. These negative consequences were not immediately apparent. In the south, the *Wehrmacht* closed in on Grozny and sent elite Alpine troops high into the Caucasus Mountains, but when special engineering units arrived to begin oil production they found a landscape dotted with oil wells wrecked by the Red Army. No Caucasian oil was ever shipped to Germany. Four hundred miles to the north, Sixth Army entered Stalingrad in early September. Rapid movement over the open steppes now gave way to fierce street fighting in which progress was measured in city blocks or even in individual houses.

The *Stavka* instructed General Vasily Chuikov's 62nd Army to defend Stalingrad at all costs. They did just that, beating back three German offensives supported by heavy air strikes. The 62nd Army's sacrifice bought Soviet commanders time to organize a major counterattack, and in mid-November Red Army tanks broke through poorly equipped Romanian forces on the northern and southern flanks of Sixth Army. The Romanian Third and Fourth Armies were shattered, and thousands of Romanians were left stranded behind Red Army lines; Russian peasants treated them well, largely because they were not Germans. Within days the Soviet pincers closed, trapping Sixth Army in the ruins of Stalingrad. The encirclement of Stalingrad now created the possibility of trapping Army Group A in the Caucasus. Hitler allowed German forces to retreat, but their withdrawal was dependent on the Soviets being tied down around Stalingrad. From this point of view, Hitler's insistence that Sixth Army fight on in Stalingrad was not irrational, and while the *Luftwaffe* never delivered the quantity of supplies promised by Göring, it did keep food and ammunition trickling in.

The Germans still fighting in Stalingrad finally surrendered on February 2, 1943. The Red Army captured 91 000 men, only 5000 of whom ever returned home. Among the prisoners were thousands of Hiwis, who accounted for nearly 50% of the frontline strength of some German infantry divisions, and many now faced death at the hands of their Soviet captors. Precise figures are hard to ascertain, but well over 500 000 German and Axis soldiers were killed or wounded at Stalingrad, and tens of thousands more died in the subsequent Red Army offensives. In January, the Italian Eighth Army and the Hungarian Second Army fought fiercely to defend the Don River before being forced to make a long and harrowing retreat: both armies lost over 80 000 men, and the survivors were withdrawn from combat and repatriated. In addition to these staggering human losses, the *Luftwaffe*'s air transport force was savaged. Stalingrad was not, as is often suggested, *the* turning point of the German–Soviet war. In fact, under General Manstein skillful *Wehrmacht* counterattacks stabilized the front in February 1943 and even recaptured some of the territory lost after Stalingrad. But Stalingrad gave the Soviet people – and their allies worldwide – both a powerful symbol of resistance to Nazi aggression and a bellwether of their coming victory.

With America's formal entry into the war, the Soviet government began pushing for a "Second Front" in Western Europe. The idea of an Anglo-American front in France appealed strongly to Moscow as it would plunge Berlin into an active two-front war and limit the resources available for its *Ostfront*. Moscow also hoped that its military alliance with the United States might underpin ongoing postwar collaboration. Concern for the shape of the postwar world also informed Stalin's insistence on retaining former Tsarist territory acquired under the 1939 Molotov–Ribbentrop Pact and his desire, expressed in the May 1942 Anglo-Soviet Treaty, to destroy Germany's war-making capacity. These proposals focused exclusively on the security of the USSR and – postwar rhetoric notwithstanding – they had nothing to do with the extension of communism.

Churchill accepted Stalin's territorial proposals, including the cession of Polish territory, but Roosevelt argued that they smacked of the kind of Great Power horse-trading that could discredit American claims to global leadership. When People's Commissar for Foreign Affairs Molotov visited Washington in spring 1942, Roosevelt sweetened his rejection of Moscow's territorial demands by pledging to launch a second front by the end of the year. Stopping over in London on his way home, however, Molotov was shocked to find that Churchill would not guarantee British support for such a project. In this way, the question of a second front – although it was unclear exactly what Roosevelt had in mind – was inserted into the intense strategic debate that was already unfolding between British and American leaders. This debate, which determined much of the future course of the war, centered on Allied strategy in Europe and the Mediterranean.

Military Turning Points: The Mediterranean

The military turning point in North Africa was particularly protracted, with the strategic initiative changing hands several times as fighting surged back and forth along the coastal highway between Egypt and Libya. The arrival of the German Afrika Korps in early 1941 had turned the tables on the British-Imperial army, driving it back to Egypt in disorder. Then in late 1941, the newly organized Eighth Army counterattacked, relieving the garrison of Tobruk and pushing Axis forces back across Libya. The German–Italian Panzer Army Africa launched a renewed drive towards Egypt in May 1942. Rommel's mechanized forces outmaneuvered the British-led Eighth Army in a series of freewheeling battles and stormed the port of Tobruk, and with Egyptian nationalists taking to the streets of Cairo to cheer Rommel on, British-dominated Egypt looked very vulnerable.

Panzer Army Africa's offensive was accompanied by an Axis resurgence elsewhere in the Mediterranean. In December 1941, elite Italian frogmen sank two British battleships at anchor in Alexandria, while Italian air attacks pounded

Malta and inflicted heavy losses on supply convoys heading for the beleaguered island. Aircraft transferred from Germany's *Ostfront* supported the Italian assault, and in early 1942 Axis forces regained the upper hand in the Mediterranean. Italian commanders argued that an invasion of Malta would consolidate Axis control of the Mediterranean, but German leaders, mesmerized by Rommel's advance and anxious to conserve their elite airborne forces, disagreed. Malta survived the onslaught, aided by the arrival of heavily escorted supply convoys and by fighter aircraft delivered by the American aircraft carrier *Wasp*. By late summer, Malta-based submarines, surface ships, and aircraft were attacking Axis convoys shuttling supplies for the Panzer Army across the Mediterranean.

The Eighth Army halted the Axis advance into Egypt at the First Battle of El Alamein, fought just 60 miles from Alexandria in July 1942. The two armies faced each other for the next three months, but the fighting capacity of the Axis forces stalled at the end of long and vulnerable supply lines was slowly eroding. In contrast, British-Imperial forces were growing in size and strength as reinforcements were rushed to Egypt and the Eighth Army was reorganized under General Bernard Montgomery. Meanwhile, British authorities took drastic measures to secure their political control in Egypt, staging what amounted to a military coup in February 1942 to force the pro-Axis King Farouk I to appoint a pro-British Wafd Party government.

British-Imperial forces in Egypt were strengthened by large quantities of American equipment. When Axis forces captured Tobruk in June, British and American leaders were in Washington for their second wartime conference, and President Roosevelt responded to the crisis by rushing 300 brand-new M4 Sherman tanks to Egypt along with United States Army Air Forces (USAAF) fighter and bomber squadrons. The Shermans gave the Eighth Army a tank equal to the German *panzers*, and American heavy bombers strengthened RAF attacks on Axis ports and shipping. These reinforcements helped to tip the military balance in the Eighth Army's favor when Montgomery attacked the Panzer Army at the Second Battle of El Alamein in late October. For more than a week, British-Imperial forces battered their way through Axis defensive positions before German commanders overrode Hitler's orders to stand fast and began to retreat westwards along the North African coast. For the first time in the war, Britain could celebrate a decisive offensive victory.

These events framed the major strategic debate that roiled Anglo-American relations during 1942. At the *Arcadia* conference, British and American leaders agreed to invade French North Africa in 1942, but within weeks American planners changed their minds, arguing instead for building up a large army in Britain and then launching a cross-Channel invasion of German-occupied France. For their part, British leaders insisted on so-called "peripheral" operations in the Mediterranean, aiming to secure French North Africa and defeat Italy *before* taking on the Germans in France. British opposition to a cross-Channel attack was reinforced by the disastrous experience of the large-scale raid on the French port of Dieppe in August 1942. Carried out mainly by Canadian troops, the attackers suffered heavy casualties for no appreciable gain.

This strategic debate posed Roosevelt with a dilemma. The president was sympathetic to a "Mediterranean strategy," not least because he saw the possibility of laying the groundwork for America's postwar predominance in the region. Since late 1940 he had been directly involved in organizing undercover operations in French North Africa designed to facilitate an American invasion. But Roosevelt could not side openly with the British against his own chiefs of staff, and the discussion followed a long and tortuous course before agreement to proceed with an American-led invasion of North Africa was finally reached – at Roosevelt's insistence – in August. The invasion, codenamed Operation *Torch*, was slated for November. While falling short of Stalin's hoped-for second front, *Torch* had the political merit of engaging American troops in the (broadly defined) European Theater. With US Navy chiefs pushing for the Pacific to have priority, *Torch* also reaffirmed Washington's commitment to a Germany First strategy.

American diplomatic efforts in North Africa were focused on the search for credible French leaders who might welcome an American landing. While the British had been on the brink of war with Vichy since their attack on the French fleet in July 1940, Washington maintained diplomatic relations with Pétain's collaborationist government. Under a special trade agreement with Vichy, America supplied the French colonies in North Africa with oil, and in exchange French officials turned a blind eye to the activities of the American spy network organized by the new Office of Strategic Services (OSS). Despite forming links with various Vichy officials and right-wing politicians in North Africa, however, American efforts produced no credible "invitation." As a result, when American and British troops came ashore in French-ruled Morocco and Algeria on November 8, 1942, they encountered fierce resistance from Vichy forces.

Facing a major political and military crisis, American officials turned in desperation to former Vichy prime minister Admiral François Darlan, who happened to be in Algiers visiting his son in hospital. Formerly a committed pro-Nazi collaborationist, Darlan was sensitive to the changing military balance, and he agreed to arrange a ceasefire in exchange for being recognized by the Allies as the head of French North Africa. As promised, Darlan quickly halted French opposition to the landings, allowing the Allies to begin to build up their forces in North Africa. The "Darlan Deal" presented the Allies with a major political problem as government leaders on both sides of the Atlantic faced a barrage of press criticism. How could it be, critics asked, that in the first territory "liberated" by the Allies, a fascist-minded politician had been put in power?

Fortunately for the Allies, Darlan was assassinated under mysterious circumstances a few weeks later. His death relieved domestic criticism of the deal, but it did not solve Washington's political problems in North Africa. American leaders wanted to avoid setting up an Allied military government in the region, not least because it might require handing political power over to the majority Arab population at the end of the war. Despite the Atlantic Charter's support for the principle of national self-determination, American leaders feared that its actual implementation in the colonial world would produce dangerous political instability. At the same time, Roosevelt also wanted to prevent the Free French from forming a provisional government in North Africa. De Gaulle's goal of reestablishing a strong France clashed with Roosevelt's vision of the country as a junior partner to the United States. In the short run, this complex problem was resolved by appointing the self-important but politically incompetent General Henri Giraud to lead the French colonial administration.

The Allied military campaign was almost as problematic as its troubled political counterpart. Planners had envisaged Anglo-American forces under the overall command of American General Dwight D. Eisenhower moving quickly eastwards into French-ruled Tunisia. There, it was hoped, they would crush Rommel's Panzer Army as it retreated westward after El Alamein. In practice, the Allied advance was delayed by supply difficulties and winter weather, while Berlin reinforced the Axis garrison in Tunisia by flying in airborne units and shipping tanks and ground troops by sea. As a result, Allied forces advancing into Tunisia suffered a series of sharp defeats, most notably that inflicted by Rommel's desert veterans on inexperienced American soldiers at the Kasserine Pass in February 1943. Typically, however, German planners had given little thought to logistics, and with Allied air and sea forces using accurate signals intelligence to destroy Axis convoys, the supply situation in Tunis deteriorated rapidly. German attempts to airlift supplies to Tunis were blocked by Allied fighter pilots, who shot down over 200 transport aircraft, completing the destruction of the *Luftwaffe*'s airlift capacity. In early May 1943, the 275 000 Axis soldiers trapped in "Tunisgrad" surrendered: the strategic initiative in the Mediterranean had passed firmly into Allied hands.

While fighting was still raging in Tunisia, British and American leaders met in the Moroccan port of Casablanca for their third wartime summit conference. Churchill and the British Chiefs of Staff arrived primed with arguments for pushing deeper into the Mediterranean by invading Italy. The US Joint Chiefs of Staff wanted to get out of the Mediterranean in order to prepare for their favored cross-Channel invasion of France, but they felt out-argued by the British and trapped into continued Mediterranean campaigning. It is striking that President Roosevelt made no attempt to resist this conclusion, suggesting that – for his own reasons – he also favored invading Italy. The conference took several other major decisions, including launching the Combined Bomber Offensive against Germany and stepping up Lend-Lease shipments to the Soviet Union. Finally, and in response to public criticism of the Darlan Deal, Roosevelt and Churchill declared that the Allies sought the "unconditional surrender" of the Axis powers. There would, they pledged, be no more compromise deals.

Notes

1. PAA-Africa manager Voit Gilmore, quoted in Van Vleck (2013), 164.
2. Gerd von Runstedt, quoted in Trigg, J. (2017). *Death on the Don: The Destruction of Germany's Allies on the Eastern Front, 1941–1944*, 119. Stroud: The History Press.

Reference

Van Vleck, J. (2013). *Empire of the Air: Aviation and the American Ascendancy*. Cambridge, MA: Harvard University Press.

Further Reading

Atkinson, R. (2002). *An Army at Dawn: The War in North Africa, 1942–1943*. New York: Henry Holt.

Ball, S. (2009). *Bitter Sea: The Brutal World War II Fight for the Mediterranean*. New York: Harper.

Beevor, A. (1998). *Stalingrad: The Fateful Siege, 1942–1943*. New York: Penguin.

Citino, R.M. (2007). *The Death of the Wehrmacht: The German Campaigns of 1942*. Lawrence, KS: University Press of Kansas.

Funk, A. (1973). Negotiating the 'deal with Darlan.' *Journal of Contemporary History* 8 (2): 81–117.

Glantz, D.M. and House, J. (1995). *When Titans Clashed: How the Red Army Stopped Hitler*. Lawrence, KS: University Press of Kansas.

Porch, D. (2004). *The Path to Victory: The Mediterranean Theater in World War II*. New York: Farrar, Straus & Giroux.

Stoler, M.A. (2000). *Allies and Adversaries: The Joint Chiefs of Staff, the Grand Alliance, and U.S. Strategy in World War II*. Chapel Hill: University of North Carolina Press.

Symonds, C.L. (2011). *The Battle of Midway*. New York: Oxford University Press.

Thorne, C.G. (1978). *Allies of a Kind: The United States, Britain, and the War Against Japan, 1941–1945*. New York: Oxford University Press.

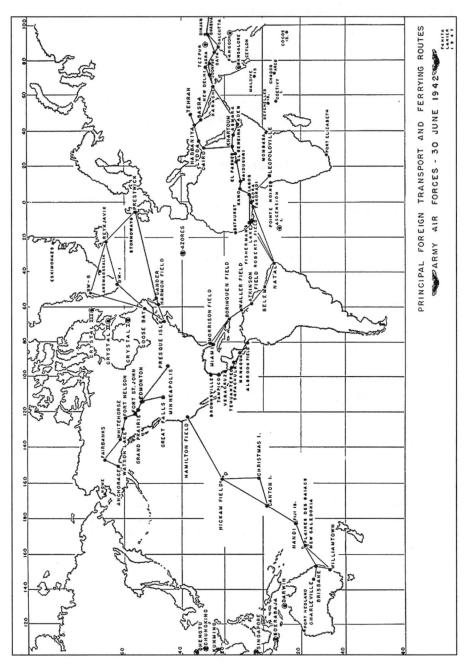

Map: US air transport command trunk routes, 1942.

6

War Economies

World War II armies consumed vast quantities of industrially produced matériel. Soldiers had to be fed, clothed, and equipped with everything from boots and backpacks to bullets. They and their equipment had to be moved around the world, using fleets of ships, tens of thousands of miles of railroad track, and enormous numbers of trucks. Military forces consumed huge quantities of oil, and some – like American, British, and late-war Soviet armies – were literally immobilized without it. The interlocking wars of 1931–1945 were not won *by* matériel – they were won by human actors – but they could not have been won *without* matériel. That simple fact made the control, transportation, and utilization of raw materials and human labor, the organization of large-scale factory production, and the production and distribution of food integral to the overall conduct of the war.

This intimate interrelationship between war and economics emerged during World War I when a long attritional struggle forced all the Great Powers to set up special government agencies – either civilian ministries or branches of the military – to organize war production. As international tensions built during the 1930s, governments again established specialized agencies to organize war production. Planners looked back to the experience of the Great War, but they were also inspired by the rapid industrialization of the Soviet Union under the Five-Year Plans and by the leap in industrial productivity in the United States achieved using assembly line techniques. This mélange of ideas, part Soviet central planning and part American "Fordism," convinced technocrats from New Deal America to Nazi Germany that nation-states should intervene in economic life to achieve specific social, political, and military goals.

World War II in Global Perspective, 1931–1953: A Short History, First Edition. Andrew N. Buchanan.
© 2019 John Wiley & Sons, Inc. Published 2019 by John Wiley & Sons, Inc.

All economic planning agencies struggled to satisfy competing demands for limited resources. Armies, navies, and air forces fought with each other to secure resources for their own projects and weapons systems, which they often presented as the key to victory. Resolving these inter-service rivalries was crucial to successful planning, but it was no easy matter. Determining the relative resources to be allocated to warship, tank, and airplane construction required top-level agreement on military priorities and strategic perspectives, and – given limited resources – on what should *not* be produced as well as what should be. To complicate matters, in every country other than the Soviet Union the bulk of war production was done by private corporations that existed to make a profit, and governments had to incentivize corporate involvement in the war effort by offering lucrative contracts, tax breaks, and direct state investment in plant and machinery.

The Soviet Union: Wartime Planning in a Socialized Economy

The absence of private capitalism differentiated economic planning in the USSR from every other major power. Private ownership of industrial capital was abolished following the 1917 Russian Revolution, and although Moscow engaged in some joint ventures with major Western corporations like the Ford Motor Company, overall control remained firmly in the hands of the state. When Stalin launched the headlong drive to industrialize the USSR in 1928, the State Planning Committee (*Gosplan*) was given responsibility for drawing up the Five-Year Plans. Harnessing the work of thousands of economists and statisticians, *Gosplan* monitored industrial performance using techniques that attempted to balance material inputs and outputs. In reality, Soviet planning was a blunt instrument. Administrators and factory managers struggled to expand industrial output, often using military-style "shock brigades" to achieve production goals and leveraging economies of large-scale production to offset low levels of technical skill and poor productivity. There was no critical oversight: independent trade unions were banned, and Soviet planning developed as a self-perpetuating bureaucratic machine riddled with corruption and inefficiency.

Despite these limitations and at tremendous human cost, centralized state planning did enable the rapid industrialization of the USSR. In doing so, it also created the structural framework of an economy that could survive the shock of the German invasion and the devastating loss of resources and industrial plant that accompanied it. Not surprisingly, *Gosplan's* carefully finessed plans collapsed under the hammer blows of war, but the habit of response to economic commands and the use of military-style industrial campaigns did not, and in the crisis of war local initiative and leadership flourished. Soviet planners had no private capitalists to negotiate with, compensate, or cajole. They could issue orders and expect to have them carried out. In summer and fall 1941, this allowed the rapid relocation of a large section of Soviet industry to safe areas east of the Ural Mountains. Naturally, there were numerous problems and difficulties with this large-scale industrial evacuation. The arrival of thousands of relocated workers often temporarily overwhelmed housing, health care, and education facilities in the host cities, but government insistence and local initiative combined to resolve most of these issues.

By spring 1942, all but 55 of 1500 relocated plants had resumed production. Many factories had dirt floors, workers were housed in makeshift camps, and working conditions were often dangerous, but war matériel was rolling off the production lines. The move of the Kirov tractor plant from Leningrad to the Siberian city of Chelyabinsk turned it into a giant tank-producing complex popularly known as "Tankograd." Here, and in other specialized centers, Soviet planners organized gigantic vertically integrated production complexes that turned raw materials into battle-ready products. This approach limited reliance on subcontractors and minimized the movement of semi-finished components on an already overstretched railroad network. The results were dramatic: in 1942, the Soviet Union outproduced Germany in every major weapons category, turning out over 24 000 tanks to the Reich's 6200. This production sustained the great defensive battles around Moscow and Stalingrad, anchoring the Allied military effort against Germany and buying time for the American war economy to move into top gear. As the military crisis passed, *Gosplan* – now based east of the Urals at Kuibyshev – began to reestablish comprehensive economic planning. By 1944, the favorable military situation and arrival of American Lend-Lease supplies allowed Soviet planners to throttle back arms production and to shift resources towards the repair of critical infrastructure and even to a limited increase in the production of consumer goods and workers' housing.

War and Business in America and Britain

In the capitalist countries, war planning required collaboration between government, the military, and major corporations, and this delicate balance was often undermined as different branches of the military tried to meet their own needs by dealing directly with industry. In America, the tsunami of orders issued by the War and Navy Departments in 1942 overwhelmed the efforts of the new War Production Board (WPB) to plan output, triggering a year-long struggle between military and civilian officials nicknamed the Battle of the Potomac. The "battle" was finally resolved in November 1942 with the establishment of the Controlled Materials Plan. This outcome forced the WPB to abandon efforts to set direct production priorities, requiring it instead to try to steer industrial output by controlling the distribution of critical raw materials. In May 1943, the intense political pressures generated by this process prompted the formation of another high-level agency, the Office of War Mobilization, headed by former senator and Supreme Court justice James Byrnes. Under Byrnes, a powerful politician who Roosevelt referred to as the "assistant president," government officials finally secured a degree of control over wartime production.

American business responded quickly to the surge in military orders. The output of combat aircraft jumped from 1400 in 1941 to over 24000 in 1942, while tank production leapt from 900 to 27000. This production boosted overall gross domestic product, which increased by a stunning 60% between 1940 and 1944. These increases were made possible by two major factors. First, continued Depression conditions in the late 1930s meant that there were plenty of idle plants and unemployed workers ready for war work, and second, "cost-plus" contracts incentivized corporate production by guaranteeing extraordinary profits. The war years were good years for business, with net corporate profits rising from $6.4 billion in 1940 to $11 billion in 1944. Washington eased the enforcement of anti-trust laws, allowing an accelerated process of mergers that concentrated the bulk of wartime contracts in the hands of a few giant corporations. Similarly – and as during the New Deal – government policy favored large-scale agribusiness over small farmers, and as average farm sizes increased the number of family farmers declined. The government also financed new plant and equipment that private companies used on a "Government-Owned, Contractor-Operated" basis. The vast Detroit Arsenal Tank Plant, for example, was funded by Washington but operated by the Chrysler Corporation. At the end of the war, the government sold off $17 billion worth of plant and equipment to private business at bargain-basement prices.

In Britain, centralized planning was even weaker than in America. Instead, the equipment procurement agencies of the Army and the Royal Air Force became the ministries of Supply and Aircraft Production, which functioned alongside the Royal Navy's long-standing Board of Admiralty. Each ministry placed its own orders with major corporations like Vickers, Avro, and Rolls-Royce. At the highest level, the cabinet set overall production priorities and – in typically British fashion – key officials from the different ministries met over lunch in the Carlton Hotel to iron out disputes over limited resources. Senior figures in government, the military, and the major corporations came from the same narrow social elite, and despite the carefully cultivated image of the war as a national endeavor, its direction remained firmly in the hands of the old ruling class.

These class connections also shaped the global network of colonial officials who ran the British Empire. During the war, colonial administrators worked through numerous newly formed bodies and committees including governor's conferences, supply councils, and production boards like the East African Production and Supply Council to manage the extraction and transportation of food and raw materials from the colonies to Britain. Wartime policy promoted industrial and agricultural development in the colonies, and in some parts of the empire – like the wheat-producing Punjab – farmers were able to make a good income. Elsewhere, the export of locally grown food to Britain benefited large-scale white-owned farms but left Africans hungry as food prices skyrocketed. In 1942, wartime inflation combined with drought to produce famine in Nigeria and Tanganyika, and by the end of the war some African peasants were reduced to eating roots and berries. At the same time, the recall of experienced officials to London at the start of the war forced colonial governors to promote Africans to administrative positions, and an emerging class of educated local elites administered the colonies in unequal partnership with their colonial masters. These reforms in imperial governance reshaped colonial administrations along quasi-national lines, creating African elites that had experience of running the state and that were trained to think in terms of top-down economic planning. In this way, and quite unintentionally, the wartime mobilization of the British Empire helped to lay the basis for the great tide of decolonization that swept across Africa and Asia in the postwar years.

Axis War Planning

Despite some *political* similarity to the Stalinist dictatorship in Moscow, the Nazi regime did not exercise direct *economic* control in Germany. Germany remained a capitalist country, and Berlin – like London and Washington – had to work with industrialists who were in business to make a profit. As in Britain and America, the military's own procurement agency – the War Economy Headquarters – placed orders directly with major corporations, but in Germany the picture was further complicated by the fact that other state agencies such as Hermann Göring's Office of the Four-Year Plan and Heinrich Himmler's SS also intervened directly in the economy. Explicitly based on the Soviet model, the 1936 Four-Year Plan was designed to end German reliance on imported iron ore, rubber, and oil. Some private corporations, like the chemical giant IG Farben, helped to develop synthetic products that boosted this drive for autarky, but steel manufacturers resisted plans to exploit low-grade German ores. Their resistance was pushed aside by the establishment in 1937 of the *Reichswerke Hermann Göring*, a giant industrial conglomerate that combined state and private capital to create the largest corporation in Europe. In launching the *Reichswerke*, Nazi leaders sought to follow a hybrid "middle road" between a socialized Soviet-style economy and free market capitalism.

By 1940, the German economy was fully mobilized for war. Forty percent of national income was dedicated to military production, and Nazi programs had already eliminated the pockets of unutilized plant and labor that facilitated the

111

rapid expansion of wartime production in America. This high preexisting level of mobilization made it difficult to expand production further as the unfolding multi-front war placed new demands on the German economy after 1941. The only way to increase output was to produce more efficiently, but Fritz Todt's Armaments Ministry, an outgrowth of an organization set up to administer large-scale construction projects during the 1930s, was poorly equipped to meet this challenge. As we have seen, the crisis began to be resolved when Albert Speer took over the ministry in February 1942. With Hitler's backing, Speer established centralized planning through a series of top-level committees that integrated government officials, military officers, and leading industrialists. As the deepening military crisis helped to enforce business compliance the results were impressive, with the 1944 output of tanks and airplanes quadruple that of 1941. This self-proclaimed "armaments miracle" resulted from a drastic reduction in the number of product lines, in the concentration of production in large plants where Fordist practices could be utilized, and in the employment of more efficient techniques. The new super-rapid-firing MG 42 machine gun, for example, was made from cheap stamped components rather than the high-precision machined parts used in earlier weapons. Despite these measures, the real key to the armaments miracle was Speer's own ruthless political drive and his willingness to use coercive measures to achieve results.

Nazi leaders envisioned Germany as the hub of an autarkic bloc that included its new colonial empire in the East as well as its subordinate allies in the Balkans. In addition, the conquests of 1940 brought the developed economies of France, the Low Countries, Denmark, and Norway under German control. This bloc and its allied periphery – stretching from Sweden to the Italian Mediterranean and from Spain to Turkey – had the resources, population, agriculture, and industrial base necessary to sustain a genuine world power. The problem was time. The genocidal depopulation of the eastern colonies proceeded rapidly, but the Red Army's "scorched earth" policy and the slow pace of German agricultural settlement rendered the region economically worthless. *Sturmabteilung* (SA) stormtroopers waged a vocal campaign to promote the migration of "armed peasants" from Germany into the occupied territories, but they garned little support. Meanwhile, the efforts of 2000 German miners and tens of thousands of forced laborers to get coal production going in the Donbass were a dismal failure. In occupied Europe, economic integration required negotiation with foreign capitalists, many of whom were quite willing to collaborate with their new rulers, but Nazi ideological imperatives and the pursuit of short-term gains led to economic looting rather than long-term collaboration. In 1943–1944, 55% of France's GDP went directly to Germany, while food requisitioning in Greece quickly produced famine in much of the country.

Japan faced a different set of challenges. Tokyo's conquest of Manchuria preceded Berlin's drive to the East by a decade, giving Japan more time to integrate colonial resources into a functioning warfare state. As with the German conquest of *Lebensraum* in the East, Tokyo promoted Manchuria as "Japan's life-line" and encouraged Japanese farmers to settle this "new paradise."[1] A 20-year plan adopted by the Kwantung Army in 1936 projected planting a million farmer-settler households in Manchukuo. In practice, the demands of military conscription and the difficulties of homesteading in contested territory limited emigration, but nevertheless 219 000 Japanese settlers moved to Manchukuo by 1945. Industrial investment in Manchukuo was channeled through the Kwantung Army, which funded construction of the giant Shōwa steel mill together with numerous regional infrastructure projects. Like many Nazi leaders, Japanese technocrats in Manchukuo hoped to find a hybrid "third way" between market capitalism and Stalinist "communism," vesting ownership (and profit) in private hands but giving the state control over planning and resource management.

This formula worked in Manchukuo, where military leaders collaborated with new business conglomerates like Nissan, and in other parts of the Co-Prosperity Sphere, where the Mitsubishi and Sumitomo corporations mined for coal, copper, gold, and other key minerals. The "third way" was less successful in the heart of the Japanese economy, where the "Big Four" family-owned corporations (*zaibatsu*) – Mitsui, Mitsubishi, Sumitomo, and Yasuda – held sway. In 1938, the Japanese government tried to establish a centrally planned war economy by setting up a Planning Board and initiating a Four-Year Plan. Despite this initiative, the "control associations" designed to regulate access to raw materials quickly came under the control of private-sector managers, while military procurement officers circumvented the entire planning process by placing orders directly with the *zaibatsu*.

One of the results of this tension between government planners, big business, and the military was that between 1939 and 1941, military production only expanded from 22% of gross domestic product (GDP) to 27%. This was not a problem as long as Japan was fighting a low-tech war in China, but the outbreak of war with America demanded a much greater economic commitment. Prime Minister Tōjō established a powerful new Ministry of Munitions in late 1943, and rigorous centralized planning, streamlined resource allocation, and the import of raw materials from the Co-Prosperity Sphere combined to produce a dramatic surge in war production. By 1944, fully 76% of Japan's GDP was devoted to war production. In a war with the United States, however, this was too little and too late. Even if full mobilization had been achieved earlier, the modest size of the Japanese economy placed strict limits on its productive capacity. As in Germany, this structural weakness might have been addressed over time through the integration of Japan's new colonial empire, but American military operations denied Tokyo that luxury.

In contrast to Germany and Japan, Italy achieved a relatively low level of economic mobilization. In 1939, only 8% of Italy's GDP was devoted to war production, rising to just 23% at the height of wartime mobilization in 1941. Like its Axis partners, Italy was constrained by chronic raw materials shortages, but although its economy was the weakest of the major combatants and less than half the size of Germany's, it did contain outposts of Fordist dynamism like the giant FIAT auto plants. As in other capitalist states, the Fascist government struggled to balance its need for an arms production program with the interests of its big business backers. Despite setting up a General Commissariat for War Production in 1935, Fascist officials were wary of imposing their plans either on business or on the military, and military departments continued to negotiate procurement contracts directly with industry. Long production runs of semi-obsolete tanks and airplanes meant that Italy entered the conflict entirely unprepared for high-tempo modern warfare, and – unlike its Axis partners – Rome could not hope to offset economic weakness with superior fighting ability. Nor could it anticipate short-term economic reinforcement from colonial conquest. There was no Italian armaments miracle, despite the establishment of a centralized Ministry of War Production in February 1943. Instead, as military pressure on Italy mounted in spring 1943, workers' protests and Allied bombing combined to produce a dramatic collapse in production.

China: War Production and Capitalist Modernity

During the "Nanjing Decade" from the formation of the Guomindang government in 1927 to the Japanese invasion in 1937, Nationalist leaders struggled to modernize the Chinese economy. All shared a vision of an autarkic or *minzu* economy, but where Chiang Kai-shek envisioned a militarized state, Wang Jingwei, his main rival in the Guomindang leadership, pushed for broader economic reforms. Wang advocated boosting industrial output in the coastal cities while developing cooperative food and raw material production in the rural hinterlands. Wang's view was inspired by Italian corporatist notions of class collaboration in the national interest, and in 1931 the Guomindang set up the National Economic Council (NEC) to advance this program. In practice, however, Nationalist leaders faced a fundamental contradiction, as economic modernization in the countryside threatened the interests of the traditional rural elites who were the very people that the regime relied upon to maintain social and political stability.

The 1937 Japanese invasion resolved this dilemma by tipping the balance within the Guomindang in favor of Chiang's militarized state. The following year Wang split from the Guomindang, setting up the collaborationist Reorganized National Government under Japanese protection in 1940. In place of the broad reforms advocated by Wang and the NEC, Chiang's Natural Resource Commission sponsored the development of war-related heavy industry in the rural interior. In the light of the loss of China's coastal industrial belt to the Japanese, this policy successfully stimulated the large-scale relocation of Chinese industry. Between 1937 and 1945 some 20000 plants employing 30 or more workers each were set up in the rural southwest, and despite shortages of modern machinery and low productivity they proved capable of sustaining the Nationalist war effort. As a result, the Japanese confronted unexpected Chinese economic resilience. At the same time, Chiang's rejection of the rural reforms advocated by Wang increased the Guomindang's reliance on conservative local elites, deepening divisions between the state and the peasantry. These divisions, exacerbated by military conscription, heavy taxation, and forced food requisitions, opened the door to the peasant-based revolution advocated by Mao Zedong and the Chinese Communist Party.

A War of Production

The goal of wartime planning was production, and here humanity registered stupendous accomplishments on a global scale. Between 1942 and 1944, worldwide output topped 31 million rifles, 220000 tanks, 415000 combat aircraft, and nearly 9000 warships and submarines. Much of this material was built in plants that were themselves brand new, carved like Tankograd from the Siberian steppes or, like the $1.3 billion-worth of new factories in the suburbs of Chicago, from the cornfields of the American Midwest. The key to the success of this mighty global enterprise was the widespread application of the assembly line techniques perfected in the automobile industry in the early twentieth century. The basic principles of Fordism are simple enough: an unfinished assembly moves down a production line from workstation to workstation, and at each one new components are added until a finished vehicle rolls off the line. Fordism breaks down complex manufacturing processes into a series of simple tasks that can be performed by workers with just a few hours' training, taking production out of the hands of highly skilled craftsmen and allowing it to be greatly speeded up.

The application of the automobile assembly line to tank production was fairly straightforward, and tank plants in America and the Soviet Union were organized on this basis from the start of the war. In both countries, production centered on a single rugged design – the M4 Sherman and the T-34 – and ruthless cost-cutting allowed the Soviets to halve unit costs between 1941 and 1943. Yet the application of Fordism to tank production was not entirely self-evident. Under Albert Speer's Adolf Hitler Panzer Program, German tank production doubled between fall 1942 and May 1943, partly due to the construction of a major new assembly plant near Linz. Despite this accomplishment, German tank production was not organized on an assembly line basis. Even after Speer's rationalization campaign, Germany produced numerous different tanks, each with several sub-variants, and further minor modifications were made at the army's request during production. The work was carried out largely by highly skilled workers, and every tank was to some degree hand-crafted. The use of assembly line techniques and large numbers of dedicated machine tools meant that it only took 10 000 person-hours to produce a Sherman tank, and 35 000 for a T-34, but it required 300 000 person-hours to build a German Tiger tank. Japan and Italy also clung to production techniques based on large inputs of skilled labor, while industrial conservatism in Italy led to the continued production of obsolete tanks despite being offered the designs, patents, and machine tools necessary to build more advanced German models.

The application of Fordism to aircraft production was more challenging, and here the innovative dynamism of American engineering came to the fore. Combat aircraft contained tens of thousands of parts and sub-assemblies – the B-24 bomber had 25 000 – and for assembly line production to work they all had to arrive at the right workstation at the right time and in the correct quantities. The absence of a single component could stall the entire line. These complex problems were solved by teams of process engineers working without the help of a single computer. It all took time, and for months Ford's mile-long Willow Run aircraft assembly plant near Detroit was nicknamed "Will It Run?" but when it all finally came together the results were truly impressive, with a finished B-24 Liberator bomber rolling off the line every 63 minutes.

In the new shipyards that sprang up around the coast of America from Maine to Mississippi and from Washington to San Diego, engineers struggled to apply mass production techniques to shipbuilding. The wartime shipping needs of America and its allies were met by building nearly 3000 Liberty ships, slow but reliable 14 000-ton maritime workhorses. Instead of building these ships from the keel up on dedicated slipways, workers in the shipyard operated by construction tycoon Henry Kaiser in Richmond, California prefabricated sub-sections of hull in giant assembly sheds before welding them together to form a complete ship. Welded construction, much of it done by women, was itself a radical departure from highly skilled and labor-intensive riveting. Using traditional shipbuilding methods, the first Liberty ships took over 350 days to complete, but by 1943 workers using Kaiser's mass production techniques were routinely "splashing" ships in just 41 days.

The difficulties of applying prefabricated assembly techniques to shipbuilding were highlighted by the German experience. After withdrawing from the Battle of the Atlantic in 1943, German commanders sought a wonder weapon that would enable them to relaunch their submarine campaign. The result was the Type XXI U-boat, a revolutionary design capable of extended underwater operation. Based on newspaper reports describing the production of Liberty ships, Speer decided to build the Type XXI using prefabricated sub-assemblies. Hull sections were manufactured throughout Germany and transported by rail for final assembly in a shipyard. As well as speeding construction, dispersed manufacture was designed to minimize disruption by Allied bombing. In practice, however, the program was a costly failure. Of 80 boats delivered in 1944 not one was fully seaworthy, and only two Type XXI's ever undertook combat patrols. Some of the problems resulted from rushing an innovative design directly into production, but many stemmed from the fact that the sub-assemblies were not manufactured with sufficient precision, leading to mismatches that weakened the critical pressure hull.

The Type XXI fiasco highlights the fact that while mass production techniques opened the road to high output, they were no shortcut. Assembly lines had to be set up and organized, and this time-consuming "make-ready" period required the production of thousands of job-specific gigs, fixtures, and dedicated machine tools. Make-ready was critical to the success of mass production, and many American plants had first begun to tool up for war production in response to British and French orders placed before the United States formally entered the war. The cost and complexity of make-ready meant that once a model was in production, it made sense not to make any substantial modifications. As a result, weapons systems like the B-24 bomber and the M4 Sherman remained in full production after they had been outclassed by enemy models, and even though superior replacements had already been designed. In both cases, these decisions reflected Washington's confidence that German defenses could be overwhelmed by weight of numbers; tank and airplane crews left operating outdated equipment often drew rather different conclusions.

The development of large-scale weapons production affected the basic structures of industry. In the USSR, it led to the development of vast vertically integrated complexes, but in the United States plants like that at Willow Run were sites of *assembly* where components and sub-assemblies manufactured elsewhere were put together. In America, as in Japan, Germany, and Britain, capital was increasingly concentrated in giant corporations that dominated entire industrial sectors, and assembly plants became the central nodes in dense and multi-layered networks of suppliers and subcontractors. Many subcontractors were small family-owned firms, and their particular skills and expertise helped to define the character of entire regions from Greater Los Angeles to Osaka-Kobe and the English Midlands; in Germany, many would go on to form the dynamic *Mittelstand* sector of the country's postwar economy.

Subcontracting also required the dissemination of knowledge in the form of blueprints and special tools, and it demanded high standards of accuracy and quality control; as the Type XXI fiasco demonstrated, contractor-built sub-assemblies were worthless if they didn't fit together properly. In America, the drive for accuracy stimulated the development of machine tools where punch cards rather than human hands controlled complex metal-cutting processes, and these advances laid the basis for the postwar development of Computer

Numerical Control (CNC) machining. Timing was as important as accuracy. Components and sub-assemblies had to be delivered on time or the assembly plants ground to a halt, and strict delivery schedules were baked into contracts. Again, wartime developments prepared the "just-in-time" inventory management and globalized supply chains critical to the long postwar expansion of capitalism.

In the United States, wartime advances in industry were paralleled by a great leap in agricultural productivity. Alone among the warring powers, America was able to produce both tanks *and* tractors, and the use of farm machinery – including combine harvesters and corn- and cotton-pickers – doubled during the war. At the same time, inputs of fertilizers, herbicides, and pesticides also increased dramatically, with 10 new synthetic nitrogen plants allowing the United States to manufacture inorganic fertilizers alongside explosives. Allied control of the seas also allowed the manufacture in America of insecticides based on the import of pyrethrum extracted from daisies grown in British-ruled Kenya. These developments in capital-intensive cultivation were matched by advances in large-scale food processing, with the quantity of vegetables grown for canning, freezing, or dehydration nearly doubling during the war. This cornucopia – together with the output of the 64 new Coca-Cola bottling plants set up around the world – meant that US forces were by far the best fed in the world. American combat troops could expect to consume nearly 5000 calories a day, while their Japanese opponents lived on a rice-based diet that, on the rare occasions that they received a full allocation, produced less than half that amount.

British and American naval power secured trade routes to Britain's colonies and to the markets of South America, giving Allied manufacturers access to a range of raw materials whose distribution was managed from Washington by the Anglo-American Combined Raw Materials Board. These global supply chains ensured that despite temporary bottlenecks Allied war production did not suffer from the chronic raw materials shortages that plagued the Axis. At the same time, American business took advantage of the difficulties of its British, German, and Japanese rivals to extend its economic hegemony in Latin America, where US companies dominated the markets for Chilean copper, Bolivian tin, and numerous other commodities. The government-funded Rubber Reserve Company promoted rubber production in Brazil in an effort to make good the loss of imports from British Malaya, and American officials worked with the Firestone Corporation to develop rubber plantations in Liberia. Here, Lend-Lease funds were used to develop ports and other critical national infrastructure, enabling a sixfold expansion in exports. Some supply chains were particularly complex: over 60% of the aluminum used in British aircraft plants was smelted in Canada by Alcan, a subsidiary of American Alcoa corporation, using bauxite mined in the British colonies of Guyana and the Gold Coast (Ghana).

Drawing on American-dominated resources and on those produced in its own empire, Britain was heavily dependent on imported food and raw materials.

In contrast, while both Germany and Japan dominated extensive imperial-autarkic spaces, the potential economic advantages of these conquests were never fully realized. Allied naval power made the movement of raw materials between the Axis powers extremely difficult. The only significant exception was Germany's 1940 agreement to supply Italy with coal shipped across the Alps by rail, a pledge honored until 1943 despite domestic shortages. In January 1943, Berlin and Tokyo signed an Agreement on Economic Cooperation that gave Germany preferential access to trade with the Co-Prosperity Sphere. German negotiators hoped to exchange technological innovations, including radar and jet engines, for critical raw materials including tin, rubber, and tungsten. To avoid Allied naval forces Axis commanders used cargo-carrying submarines, but nine of the 12 boats that left Southeast Asia for Europe in 1944 were either sunk or forced to abandon their missions. In 1944–1945 only 2606 tons of vital raw materials arrived in France; by comparison, a single Liberty ship carried nearly 11 000 tons of cargo.

Mobilizing Labor

Efforts to increase wartime production took place at the same time as governments were struggling to expand their armed forces, generating clashes over the allocation of personpower. In every major country, military conscription and war-related production quickly ended Depression-era unemployment, and states could only find additional workers by mobilizing sections of the population that had not previously been working in industry. Several sources presented themselves. Firstly, in every warring country women took on industrial jobs traditionally held by men, with many of them working outside the home for the first time. In the United States, their numbers were swelled by African Americans previously excluded from well-paid factory work by formal or informal "color bars." Secondly, imperial powers like Britain and Japan mobilized workers in their colonial empires, displacing the burden of war production and allowing more people in the imperial metropoles to be drafted into the military. Thirdly, all states had access to workers who could be forced to work under conditions of semi-slavery, including political prisoners, prisoners of war, and – particularly in Germany and Japan – workers acquired as a result of military conquest.

Combatant governments all took steps to organize the mobilization and allocation of labor, but their methods varied considerably. Since the first Five-Year Plan, Soviet planners had viewed labor as an economic factor that could be allocated in essentially the same way as other raw material inputs. The 1932 Labor Discipline Law reinforced this approach, making it difficult to change jobs without official approval and establishing harsh penalties for absenteeism. Labor laws were further strengthened in 1940, and in the year before the German invasion a remarkable 3.2 million Soviet workers were disciplined by the state for work-related offenses, with 633 000 serving prison time. During the war absenteeism was equated with desertion, and a new national Committee for Distribution of Labor established firm control over the deployment of labor. At the same time, many workers continued to be motivated by pride in the accomplishments of their revolution, and they often responded enthusiastically to the demands of wartime production. Reflecting both their patriotism and their attachment to a vision of women's equality, at least 800 000 women volunteered to join the Red Army, serving in many roles including as fighter pilots, tank crew, snipers, combat engineers, and frontline medics. The number of Soviet women in industry jumped from 40% of the workforce in 1940 to 60% in 1944, around double the proportion in Germany, Britain, or the United States.

If the centralized planning of the Soviet Union stood at one end of a spectrum of labor mobilization, the capitalist United States was at the other. The 1940 Selective Service Act made 43 million men eligible for the draft, but Washington made no attempt to control civilian labor. This was left to market mechanisms, with competitive wage rates and the promise of unlimited overtime attracting workers – both men and women – to jobs in key war plants. For many working-class Americans, the war brought economic prosperity, with average earnings rising by 27% in real terms – although corporate profits doubled in the same period. Many companies reinforced their efforts to get women into war work by providing childcare facilities and cheap 24-hour canteens, and government propaganda campaigns presented images of strong and self-confident women workers, including the archetypal Rosie the Riveter. Two million American women worked in industry during the war, making up over 30% of the overall workforce.

Over 700 000 African Americans left the rural South for war work in the industrial cities of California and the North. When a coalition led by black trade union leader A. Philip Randolph threatened a mass civil rights march on Washington in June 1941, President Roosevelt issued Executive Order 8802 banning racial discrimination in companies doing war work. In exchange, Randolph called off the march. Despite this limited reform African Americans continued to encounter discrimination and racist violence in the industrial North. The American military remained racially segregated, and for most of the war black soldiers were restricted to construction and transportation duties; only in 1944 did manpower shortages force commanders to use black soldiers in combat in large numbers. Despite continuing race and sex discrimination, war work opened new opportunities for good wages and economic independence for both African Americans and women. Deep racial divisions continued after the war, and many women were forced out of well-paid industrial jobs when men returned in 1945. Nevertheless, the experience of war work underpinned many of the changes in the social status of both women and African Americans that unfolded as a result of the postwar movements for Civil Rights and women's equality.

Over 350 000 women served in auxiliary branches of the American armed forces, but despite a setting up a secret trial unit to test the possibility of employing women in anti-aircraft batteries, none served in combat. Britain and the United States both employed women pilots to ferry aircraft from factories to frontline units. Over 150 women joined the 1100 pilots in the British Air Transport Auxiliary (ATA), and 1074 Americans flew as Women Airforce Service Pilots (WASPs). Female ATA pilots were paid the same as their male colleagues, but American WASPs earned only 65% as much as male pilots. In both countries, female pilots faced entrenched male prejudice, and despite their technical competence WASPs were not allowed to make transoceanic flights. In 1944, Congress rejected a proposal to militarize the WASPs – which would have required commissioning female pilots as officers – and as the availability of male pilots increased the program was terminated in December 1944.

American trade union leaders promised to avoid labor disputes during the war, and their "no-strike" pledges convinced government and business to collaborate with the heads of the mass unions built during the labor battles of the 1930s. Labor leaders were integrated into the War Production Board and other planning bodies, and in return they used their authority to promote no-strike agreements designed to ensure that shopfloor conflicts were resolved without work stoppages. Only the United Mineworkers bucked the trend, and 500 000 miners waged a successful strike to secure a wage hike in 1943. When Roosevelt threatened to use the army to break the strike, miners defiantly pointed out that "you can't dig coal with bayonets."[2] In 1944 the miners' example was followed by numerous other workers, and in response Congress adopted a series of legal constraints on trade union activity that were later embodied in the 1947 Taft–Hartley Act. In this light, the war was a contradictory experience for organized labor in America: union membership doubled to 12 million and union and militant action – continued in a great wave of postwar strikes – won significant wage raises, but union leaders were drawn into high-level government service in ways that paved the way for new legal constraints on union activity.

In Britain, Germany, and Japan, governments controlled the allocation of labor by making all male workers liable for military service or for assignment to specific civilian jobs. In Britain, 48 000 draft-age "Bevin Boys" were assigned to work in coal mines instead of going into the army. To an even greater extent than in the United States, the powerful British trade unions were integrated directly into managing the war effort, with Transport and General Workers Union leader Ernest Bevin heading the new Ministry of Labour and National Service. The involvement of trade union leaders in the wartime mobilization of labor helped to secure acceptance for measures that might otherwise have aroused opposition, such as the "dilution" of skilled work by the introduction of "semi-skilled" women workers. As in the United States, labor unions grew significantly during the war (from 4.5 million to 7.5 million), and official prohibition of strikes did not prevent numerous work stoppages for better wages, improved working conditions, and sometimes also for equal pay for women. Over 2000 strikes took place in 1944, prompting the imposition of Defence Regulation 1AA making it illegal to call for strike action; working closely with the government, trade union leaders supported this move.

In the Axis countries, independent trade unions were either forcibly abolished (Italy in 1926 and Germany in 1933), or else "voluntarily" dissolved under government pressure (Japan, 1940). Independent unions were replaced by mass organizations connected to party and state apparatuses – state-controlled syndicates in Italy, the German Workers Front (DAF) in Germany, and *Sanpo* (the Industrial Association for Serving the Nation) in Japan. These organizations embodied notions of corporatist collaboration between government, bosses, and workers for the benefit of the nation. In practice, the DAF held down wages and militarized factory work, sweetening these coercive tasks by encouraging workers to take part in the Strength Through Joy organization's promotion of mass tourism and other leisure activities. Despite the dissolution of their trade unions, however, German workers pushed back against government-sponsored wage cuts, increased workweeks, and the forced deployment of labor with informal "go-slows," local work stoppages, and an uncooperative attitude manifested in absenteeism and a general refusal to do overtime. Government-backed labor organizations in Italy and Japan were weaker than the DAF and lacked its ideological authority and its repressive power, and in both countries working-class resistance to wartime conditions continued to find new outlets. In 1939, workers at the FIAT Mirafiori plant in Turin greeted Mussolini with silence and folded arms, and in spring 1943 a strike wave in northern Italy signaled the demise of the Fascist dictatorship. Similarly, *Sanpo* battled local strikes and high absenteeism in Japan.

Britain, Germany, and Japan all made extensive use of women workers in war production. The move of women into war work was more pronounced in Britain, where female participation in the workforce rose from 25% in 1939 to 32% in 1944, than in Germany, where women *already* accounted for one-third of the workforce. In Japan, single women had long provided much of the labor in the textile industry, and after 1937 the government moved many women textile workers into machining and other war-related work. By 1945, Japanese women made up nearly 42% of the civilian workforce, with 120000 of them working in underground coal mines. In Germany, six million women worked on the small peasant farms that formed the backbone of German agriculture, and as men were drafted they – along with forced foreign workers – supplied the great majority of farm labor. Likewise, by 1944 eight million women made up the bulk of the workforce on the small farms typical of Japanese agriculture. British agriculture was more highly mechanized, but nevertheless over 80 000 women were conscripted into the Women's Land Army to do labor-intensive work like lifting potatoes, often working alongside German and Italian prisoners.

The large number of women workers in Germany and Japan suggests that government insistence that a woman's role should be bounded by family, children, and home was not designed to keep women out of the workforce. Rather, it was an attempt to assert traditional gender roles in a situation where many women were *already* playing key roles outside the home. In Japan, acute labor shortages led in 1944 to an effort to expand war work by conscription into the Women's Volunteer Corps. By 1945, over 472 000 women had been drafted into these ostensibly voluntary units, which assigned many to dangerous work in munitions factories. Britain and Germany also conscripted women into anti-aircraft defense units. By 1943, 56 000 women were assigned to Anti-Aircraft Command in Britain, while over 450 000 served in the German military, many in anti-aircraft units. In both countries women were used to operate searchlights and calculate ranges, but conservative notions of women's roles prohibited them from actually firing the guns.

All warring states made extensive use of forced labor. Over 378 000 German prisoners of war were transported to America where they were interned at 700 prison camps, many located in rural areas of the South and the Midwest. As labor shortages intensified during the war, German prisoners of war were hired out to local farmers for very low wages. Under the 1942 Mexican Farm Labor Agreement, American farmers also benefited from annual drafts of Mexican contract workers, whose numbers reached a wartime peak of 62 000 in 1944. Promised good wages and decent living conditions, Mexican migrant workers who traveled to America under the so-called *bracero* (manual worker) program found a very different reality. Wage agreements were frequently violated, and *braceros* often lived in poor conditions in isolated work camps; some observed bitterly that while they faced prejudice and discrimination, white Americans treated German POWs "like [their] own boys."[3] Mexican *braceros* participated in numerous strikes protesting these harsh conditions, and in one notable instance migrant cannery workers in Dayton, Washington joined forces with Japanese American internees to defeat racially motivated restrictions on their freedom of movement.

Germany and Japan made even more extensive use of prisoners of war, who lived and worked under appalling conditions. Some, like the tens of thousands of French prisoners in Germany, worked in coal mines and industrial plants, but others – mainly Poles and Soviets – did heavy manual work on the land. Thirty-two thousand Italians unlucky enough to be in German hands when their country changed sides suffered a similar fate. The economic exploitation of prisoners of war reinforced a broader effort to mobilize forced laborers recruited in Germany's new colonial empire in the East. Fritz Sauckel's General Plenipotentiary for Labor Deployment transported more than eight million foreign workers to Germany, where they eventually made up one-third of the entire workforce. By 1945, German women and forced foreign laborers were doing the majority of work in both agriculture and industry. As labor shortages bit in Japan, Korean workers were brought into the country, with several hundred thousand working in coal mining, construction, and munitions production. Tens of thousands fled their assigned worksites, eking out a marginal existence in Japanese cities through contact with black market labor-brokers. A further four million were mobilized into Japanese war work in Korea itself, while 200 000 Korean women were forced into sexual slavery as "comfort women" for Japanese soldiers.

Hundreds of thousands of workers and peasants in China, India, and throughout the Pacific were mobilized by the Allies to work on large-scale military construction projects (Figure 6.1). Poorly paid and subject to harsh discipline and racist abuse, their conditions were similar to those of forced workers in Germany or Japan. British colonial administrators intensified the use of forced labor in their African colonies, where gangs of workers labored on infrastructure projects – including building bases for the trans-Africa Takoradi Air Route – and

Figure 6.1 Indian workers constructing a new runway at an RAF bomber base in Dhubalia, Bengal, carry dirt in head-baskets, January 1945. (*Source*: Australian War Memorial, Image SEA 0110.)

on privately owned tea, cotton, rubber, and sisal plantations. Over 100 000 forced laborers toiled in the tin mines of Nigeria's Jos Plateau. These wartime mobilizations had important social consequences. In Africa, port cities like Bathurst (Gambia), Massawa (Eritrea), and Freetown (Sierra Leone) expanded to meet wartime needs, drawing in thousands of peasants to work on the docks and in ship repair facilities. In French North Africa, the arrival of Allied forces in 1942 triggered a similar development as poor farmers streamed into Casablanca and other port cities to work on the docks, building military bases, or in the new American-run assembly plants. Urbanization advanced as vast shanty towns sprang up to house this new working class, laying the basis for far-reaching social and political changes.

The USSR also made extensive use of forced labor, much of it extracted from the three million German prisoners of war in Soviet hands. Like their Red Army counterparts in Germany, *Wehrmacht* prisoners faced extremely harsh conditions, particularly before the military situation turned in Moscow's favor. Between 400 000 and one million German prisoners died in captivity, and some remained in the Soviet Union until 1955. Soviet authorities also utilized the labor of real or alleged political opponents of the regime imprisoned in the sprawling camps of the *Gulag* system. These forced workers were highly mobile and were often used for heavy labor such as the construction of new industrial plants in Siberia. Ironically, many Trotskyist prisoners worked willingly despite the terrible conditions, sustained by their belief in the necessity of defending the Soviet Union against the German invasion.

A War of Technology

Wars often accelerate the pace of technological development as states seek to weaponize new scientific advances. World War II saw the deployment of entirely new weapons, including jet-powered aircraft, medium-range ballistic missiles, and nuclear bombs, while weapons systems already existing in crude forms were simplified, miniaturized, and made widely available. Radar, for example, was already a key part of Britain's air defense system, but the Chain Home network was based on large immobile installations. During the war, miniaturized radar sets were mounted in aircraft or even – in the form of proximity fuses – in artillery shells. Other pre-existing technologies, including battlefield rocketry and underwater detection systems, also underwent rapid development.

Many of the basic scientific principles behind these developments were known before the war. During the 1930s, eight soon-to-be combatants (Britain, France, Germany, Italy, Japan, Netherlands, United States, USSR) developed some form of radar, and design teams in Britain and Germany were working on jet engines. German physicists understood the basic principles of nuclear fission and wrote about them in widely read scientific journals, and by 1939 scientists on both sides of the looming war saw the possibility of producing a nuclear bomb. The critical question in the development of usable weapons systems, however, was not a brilliant moment of scientific discovery but the capacity to transform scientific insight into a manufacturable product.

Success in this process demanded the fulfillment of two conditions. The first was the accelerated emergence during the 1920s and 1930s of national systems of Research and Development (R&D). These systems integrated government officials, academic scientists, military officers, and representatives of big business in formal or semi-formal organizations that had access both to public funding and to the resources of private industry. The precise physiognomy of these R&D networks varied from country to country: in America, businessmen and academics developed close links without much direct government participation, whereas in Britain military and scientific communities made the running.

The second condition was the availability of sufficient manufacturing capacity to develop and produce technologically advanced weapons systems. In theory, all of the major combatants except China had this capacity, but in practice the diversion of manufacturing capacity to the speculative task of producing new weapons meant *not* using it to produce tried and trusted products. The difficulty of fulfilling *both* conditions when regular arms production had to have undisputed priority meant that while Britain, Germany, Japan, and the USSR all had advanced R&D networks, none was able to do much advanced weapons development. At the height of the Battle of Britain, London entrusted the development of new weapons systems to the United States, sending a delegation led by chemist Henry Tizard to Washington with plans for innovative new technologies developed by British scientists. These included a prototype of the cavity magnetron, a device critical to the miniaturization of radar and (later!) to the development of microwave ovens.

Alone among the major combatants, the United States possessed both the R&D networks and the manufacturing capacity necessary for sustained military-technological development. In June 1940, Washington strengthened ties between the military and academia by forming the National Defenses Research Committee (NDRC). Led by Vannevar Bush, an engineer and the vice president of Massachusetts Institute of Technology (MIT), the NDRC processed the plans brought to America by the Tizard Mission. In October 1940, the NDRC oversaw the establishment of the Radiation Laboratory on the MIT campus in Cambridge. The "Rad Lab" was charged with developing the cavity magnetron to produce miniaturized radar sets for target location and gun-aiming systems. Likewise, the new Applied Physics Lab at Johns Hopkins University developed initial British work on the proximity fuse. In June 1941, the NDRC was incorporated into the new Office of Scientific Research and Development (OSRD), a federal agency created by executive order and also led by Vannevar Bush.

In addition to overseeing the development of a broad range of new weapons, OSRD also funded research into military medicine, particularly the penicillin and antibiotic sulfa that saved thousands of wounded Allied soldiers.

This extensive government-sponsored R&D effort was backed by America's prodigious industrial capacity. It was this powerful combination that enabled the development and mass production of new weapons systems, so that by 1945 many Allied warships and airplanes carried radar sets as part of their standard equipment. The production of radar and other innovative devices required the large-scale involvement of the American electronics industry. Over 22 million proximity fuses were produced by a network of contractors and subcontractors led by industry giants like Crosley, RCA, and Eastman. New components, like the first printed circuit boards, had to be developed from scratch, tested, and moved into production at breakneck speed. As output increased unit costs tumbled, with the cost of a single proximity fuse falling from $732 in 1942 to just $18 in 1945.

In addition to technological innovation and productive capacity, the development of effective new weapons systems often involved the initiative of men and women in what historian Paul Kennedy refers to as the "middle." These mid-level managers, "innovators, organizers, officers, bureaucrats [and] eccentrics," provided a critical transmission belt between military planners and big businessmen at the "top" and large-scale factory production.[4] The development of the P-51 Mustang fighter provides a case in point. In April 1942, British test pilot Ronnie Harker was asked to evaluate a problematic new fighter produced by North American Aviation. Harker's report recognized the P-51's excellent handling characteristics but noted that it was severely underpowered, and he suggested replacing the aircraft's Allison engine with a powerful Rolls-Royce Merlin. Acting on their own initiative, Rolls-Royce managers and mechanics carried out the modification. The result was dramatic. The P-51 Mustang emerged as one of the best high-performance fighter aircraft of the war, capable of escorting American bombers deep into German airspace. Full production still required a long bureaucratic struggle to overcome American resistance to producing an aircraft with a British engine. As a result of these delays, the P-51 was not available in large numbers until late 1943, but without the initiative and input of Harker and his Rolls-Royce coworkers it would likely have been written off as just another failed design.

German leaders recognized that they lacked the manufacturing capacity necessary for the large-scale development of new weapons technologies, but they continued to hanker after the allegedly war-winning potential of "wonder weapons" like the V2 ballistic missile. Berlin attempted to overcome its economic constraints by using slave labor, and prisoners of war and concentration camp inmates constructed and operated the massive Mittelbau underground assembly plant near Nordhausen in central Germany. Albert Speer's Armaments Ministry ran the plant in collaboration with the SS, which supplied slave labor from the nearby Mittelbau-Dora concentration camp. This brutal effort resulted in the production of 5200 V2 rockets, enabling long-range missile attacks to be launched against London and other cities. Nevertheless, the combination of limited numbers, unreliable technology, and a lack of operational planning meant that the V2 had no appreciable effect on the course of the war; the futility of the entire effort can be judged by the fact that a V2 warhead delivered only one-quarter of the explosives dropped by a single Lancaster bomber.

The V2 rocket demonstrates that the relationship between technological progress and military effectiveness is not necessarily straightforward; likewise with the jet-powered fighter aircraft. Unlike the British, who scaled back efforts to produce a manufacturable jet engine once it became clear that airplanes with conventional piston engines would be adequate to achieve victory, Berlin pushed ahead with the development of jet aircraft. The jet-powered Messerschmitt Me 262 entered service in 1944, and in the final months of the war the new fighters launched effective attacks on Allied bomber formations. But the Me 262 was not quite the modern technological wonder it was made out to be. One of the advantages of jet engines was that they were cheap to produce, using inexpensive sheet metal parts and requiring little skilled machine work; assembly line production of the Jumo 004 jet engine required 700 person-hours, while a high-performance piston engine took over 3000. Moreover, unskilled – and unwilling – slave workers could do much of the work on a jet engine. There was a trade-off: jet engines were unreliable, had a very short operational life, and were prone to catastrophic failure. Their main advantage was *not* superior performance, but the fact that in the final desperate months of the war Germany could still manufacture them in large numbers.

The relationship between industrial capacity and technological advance is perhaps most clearly illustrated by the development of nuclear weapons. By the start of the war in Europe the potential military significance of nuclear fission was widely known, and research programs were underway in Britain, Germany, Japan, and the USSR. All faced serious problems – Japan, for example, scoured its new Co-Prosperity Sphere for deposits of uranium ore – and it soon became apparent that the industrial resources needed to bring plans to fruition were simply not available in these taut wartime economies. In 1942, German leaders decided against organizing a major nuclear weapons program, while the British recognized that even with Canadian assistance they lacked the industrial capacity to build a nuclear bomb. In 1943 London rolled the Anglo-Canadian nuclear project (codenamed Tube Alloys) into the emerging American nuclear program in the hope of trading scientific expertise for access to a usable atomic weapon.

The American nuclear weapons program was initiated by President Roosevelt and the OSRD in October 1941, taking shape as the Manhattan Project under Army Corps of Engineers General Leslie Groves the following summer. The Manhattan Project integrated academic science – reinforced by exiles from

German-dominated Europe, many of them Jews – with the industrial capacity of American business. The strength of this combination was underscored by the fact that the Manhattan Project pursued two parallel tracks towards a usable bomb. The "uranium option" required the production of enriched uranium 235, extracted at the sprawling new Clinton Engineer Works in rural East Tennessee. By 1945, the plant employed 82000 workers, who were housed in the brand new, purpose-built, and racially segregated town of Oak Ridge. The "plutonium option" also required major new production facilities, with the Du Pont Corporation building three nuclear reactors at Hanaford, Washington. This, too, was a massive construction project, with upwards of 50000 construction workers camped out in the tiny township of Richland. Much of the uranium ore used in both projects came from the Belgian Congo, where American officials nego-tiated with the *Union Minière du Haut-Katanga* and the Belgian government-in-exile to purchase the entire output of the Shinkolobwe mine. American military engineers helped to boost production and to develop airport facilities at Léopoldville (Kinshasa) and Élisabethville (Lubumbashi). By 1943, 400 tons of uranium oxide were being shipped to America every month via a global supply chain that tied the brand-new technology under development at Oak Ridge and Hanaford to the exploitation of forced colonial labor in the Congo.

The first test of the plutonium bomb took place at Los Alamos on July 16, 1945, and an untested uranium bomb was dropped on the Japanese city of Hiroshima on August 6. Three days later, a plutonium bomb was dropped on Nagasaki. The precise timing of the availability of a usable nuclear weapon and its intersection with the complex military and diplomatic choreography of the war in the Pacific was entirely contingent. If the development of the bomb had taken a couple of months longer, or if Japan's leaders had accepted the inevita-bility of defeat a week or two earlier, the picture would have looked entirely different. As it was, events unfolded in a way that created the plausible and per-sistent optical illusion that the nuclear bomb was a war-winning weapon. It was not. Instead, the bomb bludgeoned an already-defeated enemy into surrender. What the atomic bomb did do, however, was to underscore the particular combination of technological innovation, industrial capacity, and government initiative that was at the heart of America's prodigious wartime economic growth. In this context, nuclear weapons emerged not as instruments of con-quest, but as enforcers of a new world order.

Notes

1. See Wilson (May 1995), 249–286.
2. Preis, A. (1972). *Labor's Giant Steps: The First Twenty Years of the CIO, 1936–1955.* New York: Pathfinder Press.

3. Heisler, B.S. (Summer 2007). "The 'other braceros': temporary labor and German prisoners of war in the United States, 1943–1946." *Social Science History*, 31 (2), 241.
4. Kennedy, P. (January 2010). "History for the middle: the case of the Second World War." *Journal of Military History*, 74, 38.

Reference

Wilson, S. (May 1995). The 'new paradise': Japanese emigration to Manchuria in the 1930s and 1940s. *The International History Review* 17 (2): 249–286.

Further Reading

Carson, C. (2015). Knowledge economies: toward a new technological age. In: *The Cambridge History of the Second World War*, vol. III (ed. M. Geyer and A. Tooze). New York: Cambridge University Press.

Collingham, L. (2012). *A Taste of War: World War II and the Battle for Food*. New York: Penguin.

Edgerton, D. (2011). *Britain's War Machine: Weapons, Resources and Experts in the Second World War*. New York: Oxford University Press.

Engerman, D.C. (2015). The rise and fall of central planning. In: *The Cambridge History of the Second World War*, vol. III (ed. M. Geyer and A. Tooze). New York: Cambridge University Press.

Fear, J. (2015). War of the factories. In: *The Cambridge History of the Second World War*, vol. III (ed. M. Geyer and A. Tooze). New York: Cambridge University Press.

Giffard, H. (2016). *Making Jet Engines in World War II: Britain, Germany and the United States*. Chicago: University of Chicago Press.

Hachtman, R. (2015). The war of cities: industrial labouring forces. In: *The Cambridge History of the Second World War*, vol. III (ed. M. Geyer and A. Tooze). New York: Cambridge University Press.

Harrison, M. (1998). The economics of World War II: an overview. In: *The Economics of World War II: Six Great Powers in International Comparison* (ed. M. Harrison). New York: Cambridge University Press.

Herman, A. (2012). *Freedom's Forge: How American Business Produced Victory in World War II*. New York: Random House.

Jackson, A. (2006). *The British Empire and the Second World War*. London: Bloomsbury Academic.

Kennedy, P. (2013). *Engineers of Victory: The Problem Solvers Who Turned the Tide in the Second World War*. New York: Random House.

Killingray, D. and Rathbone, R. (eds.) (1986). *Africa and the Second World War*. London: Palgrave Macmillan.

Kowner, R. (2017). When economics, strategy and racial ideology meet: inter-Axis connections in the wartime Indian Ocean. *Journal of Global History* 12,: 228–250.

Miyake, Y. (1991). Doubling expectations: motherhood and women's factory work under state management in Japan in the 1930s and 1940s. In: *Recreating Japanese Women* (ed. G.L. Bernstein). Berkeley: University of California Press.

Pennington, R. (July 2010). Offensive women: women in combat in the Red Army in the Second World War. *Journal of Military History* 74: 775–820.

Smith, W.D. (Fall 2000). Beyond 'The Bridge on the River Kwai': labor mobilization in the Greater East Asia Co-Prosperity Sphere. *International Labor and Working-Class History* 58: 219–238.

Symonds, C. (July 2017). For want of a nail: the impact of shipping on grand strategy in World War II. *Journal of Military History* 81 (3): 657–666.

Tooze, A. (2007). *The Wages of Destruction: The Making and Breaking of the Nazi Economy*. New York: Penguin.

Zanasi, M. (2006). *Saving the Nation: Economic Modernity in Republican China*. Chicago: University of Chicago Press.

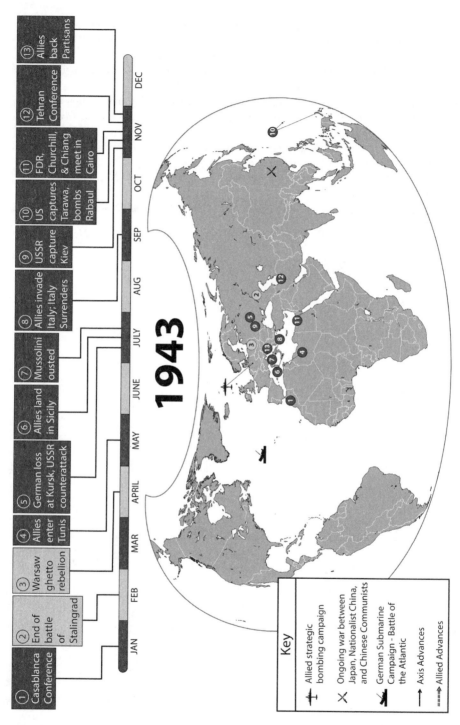

1943

① Casablanca Conference	② End of battle of Stalingrad	③ Warsaw ghetto rebellion	④ Allies enter Tunis	⑤ German loss at Kursk, USSR counterattack	⑥ Allies land in Sicily	⑦ Mussolini ousted	⑧ Allies invade Italy; Italy Surrenders	⑨ USSR capture Kiev	⑩ US captures Tarawa, bombs Rabaul	⑪ FDR, Churchill, & Chiang meet in Cairo	⑫ Tehran Conference	⑬ Allies back Partisans

JAN FEB MAR APRIL MAY JUNE JULY AUG SEP OCT NOV DEC

Key

✈ Allied strategic bombing campaign

✕ Ongoing war between Japan, Nationalist China, and Chinese Communists

⚓ German Submarine Campaign - Battle of the Atlantic

→ Axis Advances

===► Allied Advances

Map: 1943.

7

1943: Total War and the Emerging Contours of the Postwar World

During 1942 the Allies had seized the strategic initiative in the Pacific and in the Mediterranean, and in the Soviet Union the Red Army was gaining mastery over the *Wehrmacht*; only in China did deadlock persist. This broad shift did not lead directly to overwhelming Allied offensives – they would come in 1944 – but as an Allied victory started to come into view, so did a series of major geopolitical questions. As Germany crumbled, how much of Europe would the Red Army occupy? What kind of governments would emerge after the war in Western Europe? Would US military and economic power translate into political predominance, and how would that transform the relationship between Britain and America? And how, rulers in Washington, London, and Moscow all wondered, could the kind of revolutionary upsurges that had marked the end of the Great War be avoided?

The answers to these questions would help to define the postwar order in Europe. In early 1942 Allied leaders had discussed plans for an emergency invasion of France if the USSR was in danger of collapse, but by the following spring they were thinking about the opposite contingency and planning for a rapid cross-Channel attack in the event of a *German* collapse. The geopolitical premise behind these new plans was the need to rush Anglo-American forces into Germany and Central Europe in order to keep them out of Soviet hands. The aim, as Roosevelt put it, was "to get to Berlin as soon as did the Russians," and planners even wondered whether a defeated Germany might work *with* Anglo-American forces to contain the Soviet advance.[1] The Allied summit conference in Quebec in August 1943 approved several such contingency plans, known collectively as *Rankin*. As *Rankin* demonstrated, the political realities of the postwar order were starting to take shape.

World War II in Global Perspective, 1931–1953: A Short History, First Edition. Andrew N. Buchanan.
© 2019 John Wiley & Sons, Inc. Published 2019 by John Wiley & Sons, Inc.

The Combined Bomber Offensive

At the start of 1943, Allied leaders were still focused primarily on the military task of winning the war, not on establishing the postwar order. As discussed in Chapter 5, Anglo-American leaders meeting in Casablanca in January decided to push deeper into the Mediterranean, and they also agreed to use newly available squadrons of heavy bombers to step up the strategic bombing campaign against Germany. Waged from bases in Britain, the Combined Bomber Offensive involved RAF Bomber Command mounting nighttime attacks against German cities while the American Eighth Air Force launched daytime precision raids on key industrial plants. The result was the creation of a comprehensive aerial front that targeted German lives and economic activity, forced Berlin to devote substantial resources to air defense, and – eventually – significantly diminished the Reich's capacity to wage war.

After World War I, theorists of the new possibilities of airpower like Italian General Giulio Douhet argued that bombing attacks on enemy cities would undermine public morale and secure victory without the protracted slaughter of trench warfare. In Britain and America, Air Marshal Hugh Trenchard and General William "Billy" Mitchell embraced the idea that this strategic use of airpower was key to winning wars, not least because it would give their air forces a powerful independent role in future conflicts. There was less interest in strategic bombing in the Axis countries and the USSR, which built air forces designed primarily for tactical strikes in support of ground and naval operations. As a result, most Axis bombers could not carry the heavy bomb loads necessary for strategic bombardment. This limitation was highlighted by the relatively modest damage caused by German bombers during the 1940–1941 Blitz attacks on Britain.

At the start of the European war, British bombing attacks on Germany were constrained by a reluctance to endanger civilians or damage private property. After the fall of France, however, bombing offered one of the few ways of hitting back at Germany, and the Churchill government expanded Bomber Command with the aim of targeting German economic infrastructure. When daytime raids suffered heavy casualties, Bomber Command switched to nighttime operations, with predictably poor results: in August 1941 a government report concluded that only one-third of bombs landed within 5 miles of the target. In response, Churchill's science adviser and Oxford academic Frederick Lindemann proposed abandoning attacks on specific targets in favor of area bombing of German cities with the goal of "dehousing" German workers – a thinly veiled euphemism for killing them.

The decision to switch to area bombing coincided with the increased availability of four-engine heavy bombers and with the appointment of Air Marshal Arthur Harris to lead Bomber Command. Harris was a true believer in the war-winning potential of unrelenting "city-busting" attacks. In May 1942, Bomber Command launched its first 1000-bomber raid, destroying much of central Cologne and killing over 400 civilians. Over the following year, raids on cities in the industrial Ruhr region were followed by a devastating assault on Hamburg – Operation *Gomorrah* – in July 1943. Here, several nights of Allied bombing started a horrific firestorm that killed 38 000 civilians and forced 900 000 to flee the city. These shocking casualties shook popular morale. Low-level Nazi officials were abused on the streets, and some stopped wearing their uniforms in public. German leaders, too, were stunned by the destruction, but they recovered quickly. Nazi mass organizations mobilized aid for Hamburg and officials spearheaded a major rebuilding effort. Government propaganda blamed the "terror bombing" on Jews, rallying Germans to the idea that they were locked into a struggle with a brutal Jewish-led foe. As in Britain, civilian morale proved more complicated and more resilient than prewar theorists had anticipated (Figure 7.1).

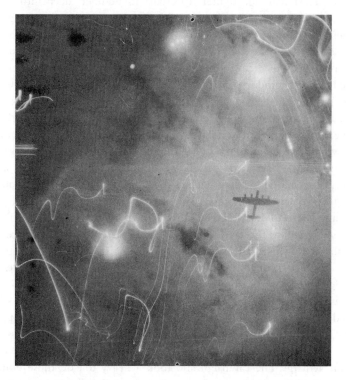

Figure 7.1 British Lancaster bomber silhouetted against flares, smoke, and explosions during attack on Hamburg, January 30–31, 1943. (*Source*: © Imperial War Museum, Image C 3371.)

The US Eighth Air Force began offensive operations in August 1942 armed with a detailed plan to unhinge the German economy by destroying key industrial sites. American bombers attacked specific factories – like the ball-bearing plant in Schweinfurt bombed in August and October 1943 – but the results were less decisive than predicted. Repair crews rebuilt damaged factories, and critical production was outsourced to neutral Switzerland and Sweden. German fighter aircraft inflicted heavy casualties on the unescorted bombers, downing 15% of the B-17 bombers attacking Schweinfurt. At night, massed anti-aircraft batteries and radar-directed night fighters savaged RAF bombers, defeating Bomber Command's attempt to obliterate Berlin in winter 1943–1944 by shooting down 1047 bombers with the loss of over 7000 crew members.

These unsustainable losses turned the strategic bombing campaign into a grinding attritional struggle in which the German defenders temporarily gained the upper hand. But the fighting also put the *Luftwaffe* under intolerable pressure. Aircraft were withdrawn from the *Ostfront* to reinforce Germany's defenses, but *Luftwaffe* casualties continued to climb. In early 1944, the Eighth Air Force began deploying P-51 Mustang fighters to escort its bombers deep into German airspace, and in February bombers based in Italy joined them for a "Big Week" of attacks on German aircraft plants. Attacking bombers continued to suffer heavy casualties, but the *Luftwaffe* lost nearly 18% of its fighter pilots in March 1944 alone, many of them to the long-range Mustangs. Allied losses could be replaced by newly produced aircraft and newly trained crews, but while German aircraft production held up, the supply of trained pilots did not. New jet-powered fighters caused Allied bombers further problems, but by early 1945 they were operating over Germany with increasing impunity. The final phases of the war in Europe unfolded under an umbrella of Allied air superiority, and "round-the-clock" attacks by British and American bombers finally unhinged the German economy while producing widespread apathy and demoralization among the civilian population.

It is impossible to determine exactly how many Germans died as a result of Allied bombing, but the best estimate is 353000, most of them civilians. It is impossible to fully grasp the physical and psychological scope of the destruction as raid after raid battered down the normal structures of everyday life. Some responded by trying to carry on as if nothing unusual was happening, cleaning house windows amidst seas of rubble and swarms of flies, clearing debris from a bombed-out cinema in preparation for a matinee that would never happen or, like my grandmother in Sheffield, dusting the mantelshelf in a roofless house. Others – their number increasing over time – were bombed into a state of profound lethargy. The campaign also took a heavy toll on those doing the bombing. RAF bomber crews – mostly Britons, Canadians, Australians, and New Zealanders – suffered a 44% death rate. Some broke down under the strain, displaying what the RAF called a "lack of moral fiber." Many more turned to magical thinking in the hope that personal rituals, like urinating on aircraft wheels or carrying a lucky charm, would get them through, and some drank heavily in off-duty hours.

For "Bomber" Harris, civilian deaths were not unfortunate collateral damage but the intended goal of the bombing. American commanders were more circumspect, insisting that their bombs were aimed at specific industrial targets. In practice, heavy cloud cover, smoke, and the confusion of battle reduced "precision" to a pious hope, often making the results of American bombing indistinguishable from British. Moral implications aside, Allied strategic bombing was undoubtedly effective, even though it took much longer and consumed many more resources than advocates had predicted. The cumulative effect of Allied bombing eventually dislocated the German economy, particularly after fuel and transportation infrastructures were targeted in early 1945 and as large numbers of refugees from previous raids required housing and feeding. Remarkably, 80% of German industrial equipment survived the bombing, but the workers who operated the machines and the houses they lived in were much less resilient. The campaign also had the unintended consequence of forcing Germany to concentrate fighter aircraft and anti-aircraft guns for domestic defense, relieving the pressure on Allied forces in the Soviet Union and the Mediterranean while locking the *Luftwaffe* into a losing battle for control of German airspace.

The Crisis on Germany's *Ostfront*

As the air war over Germany intensified, the situation on the *Ostfront* was worsening. General Manstein's counterattacks had contained the Red Army's post-Stalingrad offensive in early 1943, but as they contemplated plans for the summer German commanders recognized that they could no longer mount a major strategic offensive. Manstein proposed a defensive strategy aimed at tempting the Red Army to overextend itself before counterattacking, but Hitler rejected this approach as it meant abandoning the economically vital Donbass region of eastern Ukraine. German planners decided instead to launch a major attack on exposed Soviet positions around Kursk with the goal of disrupting preparations for a Red Army offensive and achieving a breakthrough that could lead to a broader advance. Berlin hoped that an offensive victory would capture thousands of prisoners who could be utilized as forced laborers and instill new resolve in its Hungarian, Italian, and Romanian allies. Evidence also suggests that Berlin hoped that a victory would advance the possibility of negotiating a peace deal with Moscow.

German commanders postponed the Kursk offensive – codenamed *Zitadelle* – to allow delivery of the powerful new Tiger and Panther tanks that they were relying on to achieve the breakthrough. Helped by accurate intelligence, the Red Army used the delay to prepare immensely strong defensive positions. The *Stavka's* plan was to grind the German offensive down in a deep defensive maze before launching a massive counterattack with forces already assembled behind the front lines. For the *Wehrmacht*, manpower shortages placed a premium on achieving a rapid breakthrough, and 17 well-equipped armored and motorized infantry divisions were committed to the attack. Of these, one-quarter were elite *Waffen-SS* units grouped together into the powerful II SS Panzer Corps. By 1943, this armed wing of the Nazi Party, composed largely of ideologically committed Nazis and well supplied with men and equipment, was effectively an elite parallel army that operated alongside the *Wehrmacht* and was used to spearhead critical assaults.

Zitadelle began on July 5 with German forces clawing their way forward through well-prepared Soviet defenses. In the north, they advanced around 8 miles; the II SS Panzer Corps made more progress in the south, breaking through two defensive lines before being contained by Red Army reserves in a swirling tank battle. As the attack ground to a halt, Allied landings in Sicily placed new demands on German reserves, and on July 12 *Zitadelle* was called off. Despite inflicting heavy casualties on the Soviet defenders, it was a costly failure. Germany's key armored formations were badly damaged, and Berlin was never again able to seize the strategic initiative against the USSR. The Red Army demonstrated a new level of operational competence, patiently exhausting German attacks before launching a cascading series of attacks that overwhelmed the *Wehrmacht* and produced a blitzkrieg-style breakthrough.

Soviet advances after Kursk were speeded by Lend-Lease supplies that were now arriving from America in substantial quantities. In an interlinked series of deep penetration and encirclement operations over the next several months, the Red Army recaptured Kharkov, cleared German troops out of the Donbass, and established bridgeheads west of the Dnepr River. These bold river crossings prevented the Germans from consolidating a defensive line on river, and in November the Ukrainian capital of Kiev was recaptured. In winter 1943–1944 the Red Army conducted a further series of major offensives that recaptured southern Ukraine and Soviet Moldova. Red Army advances were supported by well-organized guerrilla forces that were integrated into Soviet planning. Operating behind German lines, partisan bands included Red Army soldiers cut off during earlier retreats together with local peasants and Jews escaping the *Shoah*. Partisans gathered vital intelligence and waged a relentless campaign against German supply lines by attacking truck convoys, sabotaging train tracks, and ambushing isolated units.

The military crisis fueled an accelerated drive to complete the extermination of European Jewry. In a nationally broadcast speech from the Berlin Sportpalast in February 1943, Propaganda Minister Joseph Goebbels called on the German people to wage "total war" against the Jewish-Bolshevik danger, and anti-Semitism was further inflamed by propaganda blaming Allied bombing on Jews. In early 1943, German authorities pushed to empty the ghettos of the General Government. Hundreds of thousands of Jews had already been transported to the extermination camps in summer and fall 1942, but moves to deport the remaining Jews from the Warsaw Ghetto in April 1943 triggered the largest single act of resistance to the *Shoah*. Largely equipped with weapons captured from the Germans, fighters of the ŻOB (Jewish Combat Organization) and the ŻZW (Jewish Military League) rose in revolt. Taking over the ghetto, Jewish fighters and their civilian supporters resisted SS counterattacks for an entire month. Over 13 000 Jews were killed as the Ghetto Rebellion was crushed, and 50 000 more were transported to the Treblinka death camp. The Jewish ghetto was razed to the ground.

Strategic Choices in the Pacific and Wars for National Liberation in Southeast Asia

In summer 1943, American planners reduced the projected size of the US Army from the 215 divisions envisioned in the 1941 Victory Program to just 90. This "ninety division gamble" was justified by mounting evidence that the Soviet Union would bear the brunt of land combat against Germany. Victory in Europe would therefore rely on American matériel distributed via Lend-Lease rather than on American combat soldiers. Material abundance also shaped American decision making in the Pacific. Following the victories at Midway and Guadalcanal, planners proposed two broad lines of advance. The first, championed by Pacific Ocean Areas commander Admiral Chester Nimitz, involved an advance across the Central Pacific towards the Philippines, Taiwan, and mainland China, capturing Japanese island outposts on the way. This advance would be a US Navy affair, based on the new *Essex*-class aircraft carriers and fast battleships then being completed in American shipyards. The second line of attack, advocated from Australia by General Douglas MacArthur, led to the Philippines via a combined land/sea advance through the Solomon Islands and along the coast of New Guinea, capturing the major Japanese base at Rabaul on the way. MacArthur's South West Pacific Area advance would be led by the army and supported by Australian forces.

The abundance of resources allowed the Joint Chiefs of Staff to resolve this debate in April 1943 by agreeing to pursue *both* proposals. Anglo-American summit conferences in Washington in May (*Trident*) and in Quebec in August (*Quadrant*) approved this two-pronged offensive, underscoring the Combined Chiefs' 1942 decision to grant Washington control of the Pacific War. In addition, the Combined Chiefs hoped to reopen the Burma Road into China by a

British-led advance into Burma organized by the new South East Asia Command (SEAC) under British admiral Lord Louis Mountbatten. This proposed campaign was envisioned as a subordinate element of a broader Pacific strategy run by Washington. Churchill waged an extended but unsuccessful campaign in favor of a British-led operation to capture the northern tip of Sumatra, a position that he hoped would serve as a base for reestablishing imperial rule in Malaya, Singapore, and the Netherlands East Indies. The alternative, Churchill feared, was that Washington would demand a "dominating say" in these areas, including taking "full profit from their produce, especially oil."[2]

During 1943, American forces began moving forward on both lines. MacArthur's campaign in the Solomons and New Guinea made slow but steady progress against fierce Japanese resistance. American and Australian ground troops were backed by effective airpower, while their supporting naval forces scored a series of victories over the Japanese navy. As the offensive progressed, MacArthur increasingly sidelined Australian forces, revealing that for the American commander the close alliance with Australia was an unequal and short-term affair. Nimitz's offensive got underway later as new warships became available, and in November US Marines captured Tarawa in the Gilbert Islands after a bloody battle. Photographs of American casualties caused alarm in the United States, and some concluded that the attack had been a terrible mistake, but strategically Tarawa led to the capture of Kwajalein and Eniwetok in the Marshall Islands in early 1944. American commanders quickly realized that they could use naval mobility and airpower to neutralize the major Japanese naval bases at Truk and Rabaul without having to capture them. American aircraft bombed Rabaul in November 1943, and in February 1944 aircraft from a nine-carrier taskforce attacked Truk, destroying 40 ships and 270 aircraft and forcing the Japanese to abandon it as a major base.

Tokyo struggled to shape a response to these American advances. Tōjō had already concluded that Japan was in danger of losing the war, and he contemplated suing for peace with the help of the neutral USSR. In the militarized world of the Japanese government, however, it was impossible to discuss these doubts openly. Instead, Tōjō and his senior commanders decided to go onto the offensive. This was easier said than done. American air and naval power made it difficult to reinforce Japan's island outposts, and many poorly trained pilots were lost attempting the long transoceanic flights required just to reach the warzones. Moreover, as Admiral Yamamoto had concluded before his death in an aerial ambush in April 1943, the battle fleet had to be conserved to prevent the Americans from seizing the Marianas Islands and basing strategic bombers there. Tokyo also feared American strategic bombers based in China, and there they did have the resources for an offensive response. In late 1943, planning began for *Ichigō*, a major offensive slated for April 1944 with the goal of driving US bombers out of China and opening a land route to Indochina. This new route would allow raw materials to be shipped from the Co-Prosperity Sphere to Japan by train rather than through sea lanes increasingly infested with American submarines.

Japan also tried to strengthen its diplomatic position by giving its Co-Prosperity Sphere greater political substance. On August 1, 1943 Tokyo recognized the establishment of the independent State of Burma under Ba Maw's leadership in the hope of boosting Burmese support for the Japanese war effort. In November political leaders from across Southeast Asia traveled to Tokyo for the first Greater East Asia Conference. Along with Prime Minister Tōjō, participants included Wan Waithayakon, the Oxford-educated foreign minister of Thailand; president José Laurel of the Philippines; Burmese leader Ba Maw; Reorganized National Government of China head Wang Jingwei; and a representative from Manchukuo. The charismatic *Azad Hind* (Free India) leader Subhas Chandra Bose attended as an observer. Bose had spent the previous 18 months building support for *Azad Hind* among the expatriate Indian communities of Southeast Asia, and the Indian National Army (INA) now included new contingents recruited from Tamil-speaking rubber workers as well as an all-female regiment. In contrast to Britain's Indian Army, which carefully segregated soldiers from different ethnic and religious groups, the INA promoted their integration. In December 1943, Tokyo recognized the growing strength of *Azad Hind* by giving Bose's provisional government control of the Andaman and Nicobar Islands in the Bay of Bengal.

Despite Tokyo's lofty appeal to pan-Asian solidarity, however, there was little that either the Greater East Asia Conference or the establishment of nominally independent states in Burma, India, and the Philippines could do to bolster Japan's war effort beyond providing it with useful propaganda. Moreover, while Ba Maw and Bose had committed their limited military forces to the Japanese, throughout much of Southeast Asia initial popular support for Japan had soured. As the rapacious reality of Japanese rule became increasingly apparent, Tokyo found itself confronting militant nationalist movements in Malaya and Indochina. The shattering of European and American colonial rule had transformed politics across the region, and while business and landlord elites often collaborated with their new Japanese overlords, peasant-based guerrilla movements tended to gravitate towards communism and radical nationalism, combining opposition to the Japanese with radical land reform programs.

During 1943 Aung San, the defense minister in the new State of Burma and leader of the Burmese National Army, began to forge links with Burmese communist leader Thakin Soe and other opponents of the Japanese rule. The following year Aung San split with Ba Maw to join the communists in the Anti-Fascist Organization (later the Anti-Fascist People's Freedom League), which launched a broad uprising against the Japanese occupation forces in 1945. Meanwhile, in Malaya the 8000-strong communist-led Malayan People's

Anti-Japanese Army conducted guerrilla attacks on Japanese forces using weapons supplied by the British Special Operations Executive (SOE). Moscow-trained communist Ho Chi Minh's League for the Independence of Vietnam – or Viet Minh – fought both French and Japanese occupiers in Indochina. Claiming 400 000 members in 1944, Viet Minh successes against the Japanese secured the limited support of the American Office of Strategic Services (OSS).

Communists also played a major role in the resistance to the Japanese occupation of the Philippines. In Luzon, the largest island in the archipelago and home of Manila, the peasant-based Hukbalahap (People's Anti-Japanese Army) combined guerrilla warfare against the Japanese with anti-landlord militancy. The intersection of class and national struggles was fueled by the fact that many wealthy Filipinos aligned themselves with the collaborationist government of José Laurel and worked with the Japanese occupation. By 1944 the Hukbalahap fielded guerrilla squadrons composed of around 10 000 fighters – both women and men – and they disrupted Japanese and Filipino government control across much of central Luzon. The Philippines were also home to numerous non-communist insurgencies, including the *americanistas* led by army officer Ramon Magsaysay (later president of the Philippines) and composed of Filipino and American soldiers who carried on fighting after the official surrender in 1942. Organized under the direction of the US Army in Australia, these forces helped to prepare the American invasion of the Philippines in October 1944.

Japan's occupation of Korea also encountered increasing resistance as the demands of war intensified Tokyo's economic exploitation of the peninsula. As news of the 200 000 Korean women forced into sexual slavery as "comfort women" and of the thousands transported to work as forced laborers in Japan circulated in Korea, it further deepened opposition to the Japanese occupation. Guerrilla attacks on Japanese forces took place across the country, but fierce Japanese repression forced many Korean insurgents to operate from Manchukuo, where they joined forces with the Chinese Communist Party. As Japanese repression intensified some guerrilla fighters, including future North Korean leader Kim Il-sung, escaped to the USSR, where they received political and military training.

The Transformation of British-Ruled India

The military threat to India receded in summer 1942 following the Japanese defeats at the Coral Sea and Midway. The British rulers used the reprieve to push back against the Indian National Congress (INC) by crushing the popular "Quit India" campaign. Launched in August 1942, "Quit India" mobilized mass street demonstrations that spilled over into attacks on police stations and other local institutions of British rule. In response, British officials imprisoned Gandhi and other INC leaders along with thousands of rank-and-file Congress members. Hundreds more were shot as British troops dispersed street protests. In the name of opposing all diversions from the struggle against fascism, the small but influential Indian Communist Party backed London's actions. For the rest of the war, there was little public protest against British rule in India, but nationalist sentiment continued to expand in both elite and popular circles. At the same time, the All-India Muslim League, led by lawyer Muhammad Ali Jinnah, was promoted by the British as a counterweight to the INC, and for the first time the idea of partitioning the subcontinent by creating a pro-British Muslim state of Pakistan began to gain traction.

Indian businessmen, many of them INC supporters, took advantage of British orders for war matériel to make huge profits. The colony's industrial base expanded as Indian capitalists used imported machine tools to develop a manufacturing sector, and textile, coal, and steel production all grew. Reforms enacted by London in 1935 allowed Indian-born financiers to form a majority on the board of the Reserve Bank of India, and in February 1943 they appointed Cambridge-trained economist Chintaman Deshmukh as governor. In January 1944, a group of Indian businessmen published the Bombay Plan, a detailed scheme for state-led postwar industrialization inspired by the New Deal and the Soviet Union's Five-Year Plans. This expansive plan for national economic development rested on a profound shift in the economic relationship between Britain and India. In an unprecedented – and in London's view outrageous – inversion, Britain was increasingly indebted to its Indian colony, owing £1.3 billion by 1945. This money was effectively frozen as a positive "sterling balance" in an Indian government account in London, and access to it became a major point of contention. Nevertheless, its existence demonstrated the growing strength of the Indian economy and of Indian-owned business.

While India's industry boomed, war disrupted food production and distribution across much of the subcontinent. In the northeastern province of Bengal (now divided between India and Bangladesh), the loss of rice imports from Burma combined with inflation and speculative hoarding to produce a devastating famine. The crisis was exacerbated by the willful inactivity of the British government, which rejected pleas from colonial officials to ship food to Bengal. At least two million people died from starvation and famine-related disease; they were as much victims of the war as those killed in combat or by bombing. Another 1.5 million peasants sold their land to buy food, becoming landless workers in Calcutta and other industrial centers. The British government's callous indifference to the famine further inflamed nationalist sentiment.

Britain expanded its Indian Army tenfold during the war, reaching beyond the traditional Muslim and Sikh "martial races" to recruit Hindus into the 2.5 million-strong force. Many of these volunteer soldiers were motivated more by the prospect of a secure job and technical training than by pro-British sentiment.

Training struggled to keep pace with recruitment, and the Japanese easily defeated an offensive by inexperienced Indian soldiers in the coastal Arakan region of Burma in early 1943. The Indian Army was not ready to launch another major offensive into Burma until 1944, by which time the British had begun commissioning Indian officers in significant numbers. While these new units were being trained, existing Indian Army formations continued to serve with British-Imperial armies in the Middle East, North Africa, and Italy. Military service overseas exposed Indian soldiers to new ideas and experiences, and for many it reinforced a growing sense of national identity; as British Indian Army commander Claude Auchinleck noted ruefully in 1945, "every Indian officer worth his salt is today a nationalist."[3]

China and the Cairo Conference

Three Chinese governments contended for power during the war, each with its own vision of a modern Chinese nation-state: Chiang Kai-shek's Nationalist/ Guomindang government in Chongqing; Mao Zedong's Chinese Communist Party (CCP) in Yan'an; and Wang Jingwei's Reorganized National Government in Nanjing. On the international stage, Chiang projected Nationalist China as a liberal-democratic state struggling against Japanese militarism. In early 1943, Chiang's wife Soong Mei-ling made a barnstorming tour of the United States, addressing Congress to ask for increased military aid and receiving enthusiastic public welcomes in several cities. Behind this democratic façade, however, Chiang's regime was becoming increasingly dictatorial as the secret police – the Military Investigation and Statistics Bureau (MSB) – used informers and enforcers to crush political dissent.

Despite Washington's support for Chiang, some American officials in Chongqing, including General Stilwell and Ambassador Clarence Gauss, were alarmed by the regime's corruption, political illiberalism, and military incompetence. Others, like General Chennault, remained enthusiastic supporters of Chiang and advocated basing a large American bomber force in the country. American intelligence agencies also took sides, with the OSS joining Chiang's detractors while naval intelligence chief Admiral Milton Miles worked closely with the MSB in the Sino-American Cooperation Organization. During late 1943, Chiang's American critics became convinced of the need to develop links with the Communists as a counterbalance to the Guomindang's corruption and inefficiency, and after months of negotiation the Dixie Mission departed for Yan'an in July 1944.

The Dixie Mission's American officers were impressed by the discipline, sobriety, and sense of purpose that they found in the Communist capital, especially in contrast to the chaos and corruption in Chongqing. Unlike the

Guomindang, the emerging Communist regime enjoyed significant popular support, won by promoting land reforms favoring poor peasants in its base areas. CCP agrarian policies abandoned Soviet-style collectivization, favoring instead a broad leveling out of peasant property that undercut the predominance of big landowners and wealthy peasants, expanded the middle peasantry, and gave land to landless laborers. At the same time, the Communists had their own security apparatus, dedicated to enforcing the burgeoning cult of personality around Mao Zedong by purging suspected political opponents.

Washington's strained relations with Chiang, the difficulty of launching a British-Imperial counteroffensive in Burma, and the centrality of the Pacific to American war planning all contributed to a lack of strategic drive in the China–Burma–India (CBI) theater – so much so that many joked that the initials stood for Confused Beyond Imagination. The Americans were happy to designate it a British-led theater, readily agreeing to Mountbatten's appointment to the new Southeast Asia Command. But American strategists did want to expand the flow of supplies to Chongqing and, given the limitations of the air route over the Hump, that required a land offensive to reopen the Burma Road. These conflicting pressures came to a head when Anglo-American leaders talked with Chiang in Cairo in November 1943 on their way to meet Stalin in Tehran. Soviet leaders did not attend for fear of jeopardizing their neutrality pact with Tokyo.

Chiang's visit to Cairo was the product of American efforts to boost China's diplomatic status, and it was a political coup for the Generalissimo. But despite the smiling propaganda photos of Chiang and Soong Mei-ling with Churchill and Roosevelt, confusion abounded. Chiang agreed to American proposals to use Chinese troops for an offensive into northern Burma, but he insisted that British-led forces mount diversionary landings on the Burmese coast, code-named Operation *Buccaneer*. Churchill was not persuaded – he continued to hanker after an invasion of Sumatra – but Roosevelt privately assured Chiang that *Buccaneer* would go ahead. Chiang flew home well pleased with his foray into top-level diplomacy, but his achievement was short-lived. At the Tehran Conference the following week Allied leaders pledged to invade France in summer 1944, and it soon became clear that they did not have enough landing craft to conduct major amphibious operations in Europe and the Indian Ocean simultaneously. Much to Churchill's relief, *Buccaneer* was canceled.

This decision forced Roosevelt to break his promise to Chiang, who responded by canceling Chinese participation in the invasion of Burma. There was a deep tension at work here. Roosevelt was promoting China as one of the "four policemen" responsible for the postwar world order, and it was hard to organize effective action in Southeast Asia without it, but at the same time none of the allies treated Chiang as an equal. American planners pressed ahead with efforts to base a strategic bomber force in China, but none of their plans involved the commitment of substantial American ground forces. These tensions intersected with Washington's concerns about the viability of the Chongqing government and underscored the desire to develop links with the Communists; after Cairo, Chiang's status in American eyes slid rapidly downhill.

War, Popular Revolt, and Allied Politics in Italy

At their fourth summit conference (*Trident*) in Washington in May 1943, Allied leaders agreed that the upcoming invasion of Sicily would open a campaign to knock Italy out of the war. The scale of these operations, however, would be limited by preparations for the invasion of France, now slated for May 1944. In contrast to the earlier summit conference where Roosevelt had disagreed with his military chiefs by favoring extended Mediterranean operations, at *Trident* the Americans presented a united front in favor of a cross-Channel invasion. By this time Washington was well on the way to securing the postwar dominance of the Mediterranean that Roosevelt wanted, and he took a firm stand against Churchill's plans for operations in the eastern Mediterranean. Washington's ability to impose its strategic approach – after some heated off-the-record arguments – signaled a clear shift in the power dynamics within the Anglo-American alliance. Henceforth, Washington would call the shots.

Appointed supreme commander of all Allied forces in the Mediterranean in February 1943, General Eisenhower had a talent for forging Anglo-American cooperation. Under his leadership a team of British and American officers planned the invasion of Sicily from Allied Forces Headquarters (AFHQ) in Algiers. The invasion began on July 10, 1943 with a large and complicated amphibious operation that saw the first use of large tank landing ships (LSTs) capable of unloading vehicles directly onto a beach. The British-Imperial Eighth Army (General Montgomery) and the American Seventh Army (General George Patton) landed in southern Sicily, and while German defenders fought fiercely, Italian resistance quickly crumbled. Worn down by years of fighting in North Africa, the British advanced slowly, leaving Patton to stage a dramatic armored breakout that captured the Sicilian capital of Palermo before leading the final charge into Messina. Despite overwhelming Allied air and naval power, however, the Germans were able to evacuate most of their men and heavy equipment to the Italian mainland.

The Allied landing in Sicily had dramatic political consequences. Large sections of the Italian elite had already concluded that they had lost the war, but they recognized that there was no possibility of a negotiated peace as long as Mussolini remained in power. The Fascist Grand Council removed Mussolini from office on July 24, and King Victor Emmanuel III appointed former army chief of staff Pietro Badoglio as prime minister. Marshal Badoglio had led the

Italian invasion of Ethiopia in 1935 – for which he was made Duke of Addis Ababa – before overseeing the military buildup of the late 1930s. His appointment represented an attempt to create a kind of Fascism lite, preserving as much of the social and political character of the regime as possible but removing its most overt Fascist trappings in order to allow negotiations with the Allies.

In industrial northern Italy, workers responded to the ouster of Mussolini by organizing strikes and protest marches to demand an immediate end to the war. The Badoglio government countered by declaring martial law, and over the following weeks there were bloody clashes between soldiers and striking workers. In a move ostensibly designed to pressure Badoglio into surrendering, London launched bombing attacks on Milan and Turin that caused heavy damage and forced the population to seek safety in the countryside. Allied bombing and Italian government repression combined to break the momentum of the workers' protests. On the diplomatic front Badoglio played for time, declaring loyalty to the Axis but opening secret talks with the Allies. Despite their pledge to avoid compromise peace deals, the Allies agreed surrender terms with the new Italian government on September 3. British forces had already begun landing in southern Italy, and on September 9 the American Fifth Army landed at Salerno just south of Naples.

Under the terms of the armistice, Italy became a kind of semi-ally, or "co-belligerent." This arrangement had several advantages for the Allies. Anglo-American planners had anticipated setting up Allied Military Governments (AMGOT) at local, regional, and national levels as they advanced into Italy. Run by Allied civil affairs officers working with Italian elites, military governments would supply the food and medical supplies necessary to avoid famine and disease while heading off political unrest and demands for radical social change. But military governments are necessarily temporary arrangements, and the Allies needed a reliable Italian partner that could take over the long-term administration of the country. The Badoglio government was just what they were looking for. As the Anglo-American armies advanced they did set up military governments in front-line areas, but they then quickly handed the governance of areas behind the combat zone over to the Badoglio government. In turn, the government was supervised by an Allied Control Commission (ACC). All military governments imply a radical denial of domestic sovereignty, but this arrangement limited the period of direct Allied rule by quickly handing political power back to a seemingly legitimate Italian government.

This arrangement was soon under fire from several directions. Berlin took advantage of the time lag between the ouster of Mussolini and the conclusion of the armistice to rush German troops into Italy, transforming the military situation in the peninsula. Meanwhile, many Italians were disgusted by the Badoglio government, and led by a resurgent Italian Communist Party (PCI) and other radical parties they took to the streets to express their opposition to living under a reformed version of fascism. The political situation was further complicated by the daring German rescue of Mussolini from captivity in September 1943. Evacuated to northern Italy, Mussolini established the Italian Social Republic (RSI) based in the resort town of Salò. Under the German occupation of northern Italy, the RSI enjoyed little power even within its own nominal territory, but it did raise four divisions to fight alongside the Germans and its paramilitary Black Brigades conducted brutal counterinsurgency operations against leftist Partisans.

The arrival of 16 German divisions in Italy during Operation *Achse* (Axis) created a powerful army under defensive strategist Field Marshal Albert Kesselring. Twenty thousand Italian soldiers were killed during the German invasion, and over 500 000 more were shipped to Germany as forced laborers. Kesselring's troops forced the king and Badoglio to flee Rome before taking up strong defensive positions south of the capital. When American troops landed at Salerno, they found themselves facing crack *Wehrmacht* armored units. Only massive Allied air and naval support enabled the landing force to hold on the beachhead, and on October 1 Allied troops finally entered Naples. The capture of Naples gave the Allies the port facilities necessary for a large-scale military buildup, but the near-success of the German counterattack at Salerno previewed the hard struggle that lay ahead. Allied armies advanced north of Naples, but soon ran into a network of defensive lines running through mountainous terrain and along fast-flowing rivers, epitomized by the German bastion around the mountaintop abbey at Monte Cassino. Despite their overwhelming superiority in firepower, the Allied advance ground to a halt in a series of poorly planned and bloody battles, and there was no further progress on this front until summer 1944.

Military deadlock dashed Allied hopes that a rapid advance on Rome would bring a quick end to the fighting, and it intensified the Allies' mounting political difficulties. When Allied troops entered Naples, they found that the city had already freed itself from German occupation through an uprising of its citizens. After student protests against the Germans in early September, Neapolitan workers launched a four-day insurrection – the *Quattro giornate di Napoli* – at the end of the month. As parties long suppressed by the Fascists began to function openly, Naples was awash with political literature and buzzed to a constant round of rallies and meetings. Six parties including the well-organized PCI formed the Committee of National Liberation (CLN), a broad anti-fascist alliance led by liberal philosopher Benedetto Croce. To many Italians, Badoglio was little better than Mussolini, and the CLN combined anti-fascist protests with agitation against the monarchy and for a democratic government. Some went further, seeing the *Quattro giornate* as a prelude to a socialist revolution in Italy.

These developments made a strong impression on Allied officers in Italy and at AFHQ Algiers. Some were sympathetic to the CLN and saw that Allied support for the king and Badoglio went against the wishes of a majority of the Italian people. They feared that clashes between Allied forces and Italian anti-fascists would follow, with dire consequences for the image of an alliance pledged to restore democracy. Thinking back to 1917–1918, some also understood that the social dislocation produced by war could create the conditions for social revolution and that the *Quattro giornate* might herald a much bigger uprising. Eisenhower and his advisers at AFHQ concluded that a radical shift was necessary, and they advocated either "broadening" the Badoglio government or replacing it entirely with a liberal/anti-fascist coalition. Washington quickly embraced these proposals, and by early 1944 American policymakers were pushing for a liberal-democratic government in Italy. London had a different reaction. Churchill defended the "King/Badoglio show" as the best option available and vetoed efforts by Washington and AFHQ to overturn it.[4] The political divide between London and Washington was deepening.

Chetniks and Partisans in Yugoslavia

Across the Adriatic Sea in Yugoslavia, the war was also giving rise to a profound political transformation. After the German occupation of Yugoslavia in 1941 many Serbian landlord and business elites backed Milan Nedić's collaborationist Government of National Salvation. Others, like Colonel Draža Mihailović, remained loyal to the government-in-exile of King Peter II. Mihailović and other former Yugoslav army officers organized bands of "Chetnik" fighters and began making guerrilla attacks on German forces. German reprisals were swift and bloody, and several thousand civilians were executed in retaliation for small-scale guerrilla raids. Jews and Romani were particularly targeted, and by late 1941 almost all Jewish men in Serbia had been killed. The severity of the German response convinced Mihailović that armed resistance was futile and that his Chetnik forces should be conserved pending an Allied invasion of the Balkans. The Chetniks were not a disciplined and homogeneous force, and their common Serbian nationalism allowed Mihailović and other Chetnik leaders to maintain ties with the Nedić regime. Some Chetniks went further, joining German attacks on Communist-led Partisans.

In summer 1941, the Yugoslav Communist Party (CPY) launched its own force of "Partisan" guerrilla fighters. By this time the USSR was at war with Germany, and – in contrast to the situation in France the previous year – Moscow urged Communists to engage in armed resistance to the Nazi occupation. The CPY was well equipped for this task. It was a disciplined organization, some of its members had gained military experience in the Spanish Civil War, and it was led by a cohesive team around the charismatic figure of Josip Broz, known simply as Tito. Tito came from a peasant family in Croatia, and he had joined the

Communists during the Russian Revolution before receiving political training in Moscow in the 1930s. Although schooled in Stalinist politics, Tito was a tough-minded and independent leader who did not follow Moscow's orders unquestioningly.

In contrast to the Chetniks' Serbian nationalism, the Partisans advocated a multi-ethnic Yugoslavia in which all of the country's national and religious groups would enjoy equal rights. This non-sectarian approach was combined with support for land reform and the creation of democratic assemblies at local level. Land reform and opposition to the German occupation were easily intertwined because many landlords were collaborating with the occupiers. In this, the CPY's practice paralleled that of the Chinese Communist Party, and it allowed the Partisans to carve out substantial liberated zones where they began to carry out land reform and establish rudimentary health care and public education. Heavy and persistent German attacks, often conducted with Chetnik support, meant that the borders of these liberated zones were frequently in flux, but they inspired peasant resistance across the country. Peasant support provided volunteer fighters of both sexes in such numbers that by 1943 the Partisans were able to field regular military formations.

It was difficult for the Allies to get accurate information about the situation in Yugoslavia, and with Peter II and the government-in-exile installed in London, British and American leaders initially gave Mihailović their backing. By early 1943 Allied doubts about the Chetniks were growing, and Churchill had two special missions parachuted into Yugoslavia to get a more accurate picture of the situation on the ground. Their reports confirmed that the Partisans were doing most of the fighting and that some Chetniks were collaborating with the Germans. On this basis, London decided to ditch Mihailović and to begin supplying weapons and equipment to the Partisans. The British still hoped that King Peter would lead the postwar government, but they recognized that the military strength of the Partisans enabled them to tie down German troops that might otherwise have been deployed in Italy. The decision to support the Partisans never sat well with Washington, where officials did not share Churchill's admiration for Tito. Nevertheless, when Allied leaders met in Tehran, they approved London's proposal to begin arms shipments to the Partisans.

The Tehran Conference

Churchill, Roosevelt, and Stalin held their first wartime meeting in Tehran in November 1943. Unlike the Anglo-American summits, the Tehran Conference was not dedicated to military strategizing but focused instead on the shape of the postwar world. Stalin did prod his Western allies to set a firm date for the invasion of France and to name its supreme commander, but the discussion focused primarily on political matters. In global terms, the conference marked the unmistakable emergence of a bipolar world, unevenly divided between United States' predominance in the capitalist world and Soviet control over much of Eastern Europe. This new reality implied the final dissolution of Britain's global predominance. Over the preceding months, the shifting balance within the Anglo-American alliance had become increasingly evident as Washington's massive economic and military power strengthened its voice at London's expense. Churchill and other British leaders had hoped that London's long experience of global power would allow them to continue punching above their weight by bending American policymakers to their will. At Tehran, confident American leaders showed that this hope was entirely unfounded.

Anglo-American leaders arrived in Tehran concerned – as ever – about Soviet intentions. But the content of their concern had changed, with earlier fears of a Soviet collapse giving way to alarm that a great deal of Europe might end up under Soviet control. In July 1943, Moscow's creation of a National Committee for a Free Germany made up of exiled German Communists and captured *Wehrmacht* officers showed that it, too, was thinking about a postwar Germany under Soviet control. Likewise, developments in Italy and Yugoslavia raised the prospect of Communist forces challenging for political power, while the underground French Communist Party was playing an increasingly important role in the growing French Resistance. This all contributed to a gnawing fear that a revolutionary crisis like that of 1917–1919 could reoccur.

Roosevelt's solution was to strike a grand bargain with Stalin based on dividing Europe into spheres of influence. Since Moscow was not directly involved in the war in Asia, it was assumed that there would be no need for a parallel postwar division there. Under this arrangement, Washington would recognize Moscow's predominance in Eastern Europe and accept its argument that the USSR needed a physical barrier against future German attacks. The borders of Poland would be shifted to the west, ceding territory to the USSR in the east and gaining it from Germany. Germany itself would be partitioned and deindustrialized. For its part, Moscow would accept American hegemony in Western Europe, and Soviet leaders would prevent local Communist parties from leading anti-capitalist revolts there. Stalin's enthusiasm for this accord underscores the fact that while Moscow wanted to strengthen its strategic position in Eastern Europe, it did not seek the widespread export of its brand of "communism." In fact, the ruling bureaucracy in the USSR felt threatened by the prospect of popular revolutionary upsurges that could easily escape its iron control. In May 1943, they signaled their support for "peaceful coexistence" with the West by dissolving the Comintern, the international organization pledged – in theory – to the worldwide overthrow of capitalism.

As the outline of a new bipolar world order took shape at Tehran, Roosevelt cemented his relationship with Stalin by cracking jokes at Churchill's expense.

There was a serious reality behind these barbs. The British were now clearly the junior partners in the West, and Roosevelt and Stalin joined forces to block Churchill's plans for extended campaigning in the eastern Mediterranean. To many postwar critics, Roosevelt seemed overly keen to make concessions to Stalin, in particular by his willingness to redraw the boundaries of Poland. In fact, within the framework of alliance politics he did not have a great deal of choice. After Kursk, it was clear that the Red Army would end up controlling much of Eastern Europe: the task facing Roosevelt was to limit this westward advance while securing American hegemony in Western Europe, and from this point of view the Americans were successful at Tehran.

The Soviets acted quickly to uphold their side of the deal. In March 1944, Italian Communist Party leader Palmiro Togliatti returned to Italy from exile in Moscow. Briefed by Stalin on the political framework established at Tehran, Togliatti was instructed to persuade the PCI to drop its campaign against Badoglio and to join his government instead, thereby legitimizing both it and the Allied occupation. This dramatic flip shocked party members, many of whom wanted the PCI to launch a revolutionary seizure of power. The enormous prestige of the USSR helped Togliatti to convince a special party congress in Salerno to follow the new line, and this "Salerno Switch" persuaded other anti-fascists to moderate their criticism of Badoglio. These actions, a direct product of the spheres of influence sketched out in Tehran, tamped down the political crisis that had been brewing in Italy since the Allied invasion and opened the road to the formation of a liberal capitalist government.

Notes

1. Franklin D. Roosevelt, quoted in Stoler, M.A. (2000). *Allies and Adversaries: The Joint Chiefs of Staff, the Grand Alliance, and U.S. Strategy in World War II*, 136. Chapel Hill: University of North Carolina Press.
2. Churchill memorandum, February 29, 1944, quoted in Bell, C.M. (2013). *Churchill and Sea Power*, 295. New York: Oxford University Press.
3. Claude Auchinleck, quoted in Callahan (2008), 41.
4. Winston Churchill, quoted in Buchanan (2014), 143.

References

Buchanan, A. (2014). *American Grand Strategy in the Mediterranean During World War II*. New York: Cambridge University Press.
Callahan, R.A. (2008). Winston Churchill, two armies, and military transformation. *Global War Studies* 5 (4): 36–42.

Further Reading

Agarossi, E. (2006). *A Nation Collapses: The Italian Surrender of September 1943.* Cambridge: Cambridge University Press.

Citino, R.M. (2012). *The Wehrmacht Retreats: Fighting a Lost War, 1943.* Lawrence, KS: University Press of Kansas.

Ellwood, D.W. (1985). *Italy 1943–1945.* New York: Holmes & Meier.

Johnson, C. (1962). *Peasant Nationalism and Communist China: The Emergence of Communist China, 1937–1945.* Palo Alto: Stanford University Press.

Kahn, Y. (2015). *The Raj at War: A People's History of India's Second World War.* London: Bodley Head.

Overy, R. (2013). *The Bombing War: Europe, 1939–1945.* New York: Penguin.

Raghavan, S. (2016). *India's War: World War II and the Making of Modern Asia.* New York: Basic Books.

Roberts, G. (2006). *Stalin's Wars: From World War to Cold War, 1939–1953.* New Haven: Yale University Press.

Roberts, W.R. (1973). *Tito, Mihailovic, and the Allies, 1941–1945.* New Brunswick, NJ: Rutgers University Press.

Showalter, D.E. (2013). *Armor and Blood: The Battle of Kursk, the Turning Point of World War II.* New York: Random House.

Stargardt, N. (2017). *The German War: A Nation Under Arms, 1939–1945.* New York: Basic Books.

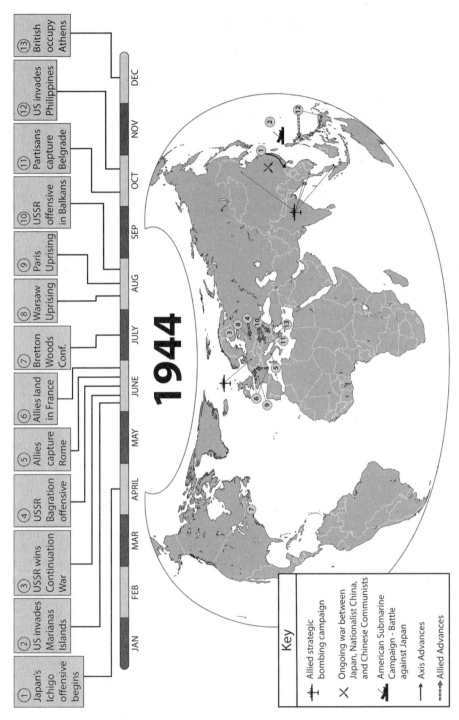

1944

| 1 | Japan's Ichigo offensive begins | 2 | US invades Marianas Islands | 3 | USSR wins Continuation War | 4 | USSR Bagration offensive | 5 | Allies capture Rome | 6 | Allies land in France | 7 | Bretton Woods Conf. | 8 | Warsaw Uprising | 9 | Paris Uprising | 10 | USSR offensive in Balkans | 11 | Partisans capture Belgrade | 12 | US invades Philippines | 13 | British occupy Athens |

JAN   FEB   MAR   APRIL   MAY   JUNE   JULY   AUG   SEP   OCT   NOV   DEC

Key

⊥ Allied strategic bombing campaign

✕ Ongoing war between Japan, Nationalist China, and Chinese Communists

⚓ American Submarine Campaign – Battle against Japan

→ Axis Advances

===▶ Allied Advances

Map: 1944.

8

1944: The Allies March Towards Victory

World War and Latin America

When the 25 000 men of the Brazilian Expeditionary Force (BEF) arrived in Naples in July 1944, they were quickly integrated into the American-led Fifth Army. Organized like a regular American division, equipped with American weapons, and wearing American uniforms, the BEF took part in attacks on the German Gothic Line in winter 1944–1945. The following spring, the Brazilian troops participated in the final Allied breakthrough into northern Italy. In the final weeks of the war the BEF captured thousands of Axis soldiers as German resistance collapsed, entering Turin on May 2. In addition to these ground troops, a Brazilian fighter squadron flying American P-47 aircraft flew with the US Army Air Force, attacking transportation targets across northern Italy.

Brazil's participation in the war was the product of deepening collaboration between Washington and the dictatorial regime of Brazilian president Getúlio Vargas registered by the May 1942 Brazil–United States Political-Military Agreement. Brazil had broken diplomatic ties with the Axis countries in January 1942, and after Brazilian merchant ships were sunk by German U-boats it declared war in August. Brazilian warships joined US Navy anti-submarine patrols, and airbases in northern Brazil developed by Pan Am were further expanded by military engineers to support trans-Atlantic supply routes to Africa. President Roosevelt visited Vargas on his way home from the Casablanca Conference in January 1943, and in exchange for Lend-Lease arms the Brazilian leader promised to send soldiers to fight in Europe; they were the only Latin American ground troops to serve overseas during the war (Figure 8.1).

World War II in Global Perspective, 1931–1953: A Short History, First Edition. Andrew N. Buchanan.
© 2019 John Wiley & Sons, Inc. Published 2019 by John Wiley & Sons, Inc.

Figure 8.1 Italian civilians greet members of the Brazilian Expeditionary Force in the Italian town of Massarossa, September 1944. (*Source*: Wikimedia. Photo credit: Durval Jr.)

At first glance, Vargas's *Estado Novo* (New State) seems an unlikely US ally. Vargas had come to power through a military coup in 1930, and in his first years he relied on the fascist Integralist Party of Plíno Salgado to break up the influential Brazilian Communist Party. Vargas turned against the Integralists after he had consolidated his personal dictatorship with the establishment of the *Estado Novo* in 1937, but his regime continued to be based on corporatist ideas borrowed from Italian Fascism. Brazil developed close economic ties with both Germany and Italy – Germany was a top importer of Brazilian cotton and coffee, and German bankers helped to reorganize Brazilian banking and finance – and both Berlin and Rome cultivated political and military relationships with the *Estado Novo*. As war loomed, however, it was clear that British naval power would make it difficult to maintain close ties with the European Axis, and Brazil began to move into Washington's orbit. A visit to Brazil by newly appointed US Army Chief of Staff George C. Marshall in May 1939 consolidated this evolution and opened the door to expanded wartime cooperation. While American opinion formers presented Brazil as a new ally in the defense of democracy, the blunt fact was that the dictatorial and distinctly undemocratic character of the *Estado Novo* was no barrier to its integration into American war planning.

American military aid changed the balance of power within Latin America, enabling Brazil to surpass Argentina as the region's predominant military force. The alliance with Washington also brought economic benefits. America's wartime demand for rubber stimulated production in Amazonia – using the forced labor of "rubber soldiers" – and American capital funded the giant state-owned Volta Redonda plant, the first major steel mill in Latin America. US businesses profited from the relationship, taking advantage of the opportunity to push aside their German and British competitors. Likewise, other national elites in Latin America took similar advantage of wartime conditions to situate themselves firmly within the framework of US economic predominance. This wartime extension of the Good Neighbor policy gave American business a significant degree of control over Colombian platinum, Chilean copper, and other critical raw materials. American officials worked with Latin American governments to restructure their financial and banking sectors, and these "reforms" further strengthened their integration into American financial networks.

War also reset relations between Mexico and the United States that had been strained since the 1938 nationalization of American oil assets by President Lázaro Cárdenas's Party of the Mexican Revolution (PRM). With war boosting the demand for oil, American companies resumed trading with Mexico's state-owned oil industry, driving double-digit growth in key industrial sectors. New president Manuel Ávila Camacho sought closer political relations with the United States, and after German U-boats sank two Mexican oil tankers in May 1942 he declared war on the Axis. In 1944 a Mexican fighter squadron – *Escuadrón 201* – joined American forces fighting in the Philippines. *Escuadrón 201*'s integration into the US Air Force was not easy, and pilot Reynaldo Gallardo recalled how racist taunts over the intercom led to a knock-down fight after the squadron landed.

Mexico's modest military contribution was popular back home, and the relationship with the United States that it symbolized gave Camacho the political leverage to consolidate the dominance of the increasingly conservative PRM – tellingly renamed the Institutional Revolutionary Party (PRI) in 1946. Under the PRI's long postwar rule, Mexico functioned as a junior partner of the United States, and the influx of American military trainers and equipment accelerated the professionalization and depoliticization of the Mexican army. As we saw in Chapter 6, the war also forged new relationships between American farmers and Mexican migrant workers, with around 150 000 *braceros* traveling to work in the United States during the war. The *braceros* program established new patterns of labor migration, and after the war hundreds of thousands of Mexicans worked in the United States, some on short-term contracts and others moving permanently.

The expansion of US economic influence in Central and South America was accompanied by the consolidation of American political leadership. Washington pressed for regional unity by working to resolve conflicts like the 1941 border war between Ecuador and Peru, and State Department Coordinator of Inter-American Affairs Nelson Rockefeller promoted American technical know-how as the key to economic modernization. With wartime conditions reinforcing US economic predominance, American diplomats encouraged national governments, many led by military dictators, to position themselves as loyal allies. Rightist *caudillos* – military strongmen – with close ties to Washington included Rafael Trujillo in the Dominican Republic and Fulgencio Batista in Cuba. At Washington's bidding, six Central American countries plus Cuba and the Dominican Republic declared war on the Axis in December 1941, thereby becoming founding members of the United Nations alliance. Mexico and Brazil followed suit in 1942. While closely tied to the United States, other Latin American countries remained neutral until early 1945, when at Washington's urging they declared war in order to secure places at the founding conference of the United Nations organization.

The extension of American hegemony in Latin America was contested by nationalist forces, although – given Moscow's alliance with Washington – communist criticism of US policy was muted. The 1942 agreement to permit the construction of an American military base on Ecuador's Galapagos Islands provoked an anti-base protest movement that contributed to the overthrow of the Carlos Arroyo del Río dictatorship in 1944. Nevertheless, the new government balked at ejecting US military bases, and they remained operational until closed by Washington in 1946.

Argentina also pushed back against America's growing predominance in Latin America. Argentinian elites, many of them large landowners who raised beef for export to Britain, viewed themselves as the natural leaders of South America, and their status was boosted by close economic and diplomatic relations with Britain. Some Argentine leaders – like their contemporaries throughout the region – were attracted to fascism, but their predominant political characteristics were their desire to preserve Argentinian neutrality and to resist American domination. During the war, neutralism was reinforced by large-scale industrial development undertaken to compensate for a sharp decline in British imports.

Argentinian leaders feared that American support for Brazil would enable Rio to undercut their claims to regional leadership. They also faced a relentless American campaign to force them to abandon neutrality, break relations with the Axis, and accept Washington's regional hegemony. In 1943 a military coup toppled the neutralist government of Ramón Castillo and installed a junta led by army officers including General Juan Perón. The new government hoped to carve out a major role for Argentina in a US-dominated postwar world, signaling this desire by arguing for pan-American military cooperation and promising to break relations with the Axis. This cut little ice in Washington, where concern about Argentina's regional influence continued to mount. By 1944

Argentina had accumulated over £1 billion through wartime beef exports to Britain, and British businesses were poised to move back into Argentina's domestic market as wartime trade restrictions eased. This prospect was unacceptable to Washington, which feared Britain would use its special relationship with Argentina as a bridgehead to rebuild its trade throughout the southern cone of Latin America. American threats to cut Lend-Lease aid forced the British to back off, while Washington intensified its campaign against "fascist" Argentina.

Washington's campaign hardened anti-American sentiment in Argentina. In early 1944 Juan Perón emerged as the leading figure in the Argentinian government. Perón planned to build on Argentina's wartime industrialization to create a strong capitalist state that would be the leading power in the continent's southern cone. He buttressed his pragmatic nationalism with populist anti-American demagogy and used wage raises and rent cuts to appeal to the large and well-organized Argentinian working class. This alarmed American policymakers, who denounced Perón as a fascist – a remarkable claim in the light of America's warm relationship with Vargas. Argentina was pointedly not invited to the Bretton Woods conference in July 1944, and Buenos Aires' last-minute declaration of war on the Axis in March 1945 did little to moderate Washington's opposition to Perónism, which continued well into the postwar period.

The consolidation of American predominance in Latin America and the marginalization of British and German interests was one of the major – if frequently overlooked – consequences of World War II. It was formalized at the Inter-American Conference on the Problems of War and Peace held in Mexico City in March 1945. Orchestrated by Nelson Rockefeller and the US State Department, the conference produced the Act of Chapultepec, a continental defense pact that solidified American regional predominance and furnished Washington with a powerful voting bloc at the founding conference of the United Nations later in the year. Although a signatory to the Act of Chapultepec, Argentina was not fully integrated into this continental bloc until Perón was toppled by a military coup in 1955. Endorsed by Washington, the coup marked the end of Argentina's attempt to pursue an independent course in Latin America.

The Neutral Countries

During 1943–1944, the growing strength of the United Nations forced the neutral governments in Spain, Turkey, Portugal, Switzerland, and Sweden to modify their relations with both warring alliances.

Early in the war, the Allies used economic incentives to prevent Francisco Franco's enthusiasm for Nazi Germany from turning into formal membership of the Axis alliance. This was a controversial policy in the United States, where many viewed supplying Franco's Spain with oil as a betrayal of the anti-fascist

principles that framed the American war effort. Whatever its ideological difficulties, this policy of appeasement was successful: Spain did not join the Axis,
and it did not try to disrupt the Allied invasion of North Africa in 1942. In 1943,
Madrid responded to the changing military situation by dropping its pro-Axis
"non-belligerency" in favor of formal neutrality. It also withdrew the volunteer
Blue Division from the *Ostfront*. At the same time, Washington distanced itself
from its earlier policy by becoming sharply critical of Franco, suspending oil
shipments to Spain in January 1944 in an effort to force Madrid to stop exporting tungsten ore to Germany. Tungsten was a critical element to the manufacture of military-grade steels. In April Madrid finally agreed to curtail tungsten
exports, but by that time Allied bombing and control of the seas made it a moot
point. In any case, Washington's campaign was largely a piece of political theater
designed to burnish its liberal credentials, and at no time did American policymakers advocate Franco's overthrow.

Blocking the export of strategic minerals to Germany also figured in Allied
relations with Turkey, a major supplier of chromite – essential to the production
of stainless steel – to Germany. At the height of Axis advances in the Mediterranean
in 1941 Turkey had edged away from neutrality by signing a non-aggression pact
with Germany. As the war swung in the Allies' favor, however, London stepped up
pressure on Ankara to abandon neutrality and join the war. After the Casablanca
Conference in January 1943 Churchill made a long and dangerous journey to
Turkey to meet President İsmet İnönü in person, but despite being promised
large quantities of weapons, Ankara concluded that the threat of German
invasion from Bulgaria outweighed the benefits of joining the Allies. American
planners were less keen on wooing Ankara than their British allies out of concern
that Turkish belligerency might reinforce Churchill's arguments for extended
operations in the eastern Mediterranean. Allied pressure finally forced Turkey to
suspend chromite exports to Germany in April 1944, and Ankara declared war on
Germany in February 1945, just in time to secure a seat at the founding conference
of the United Nations. As Washington consolidated its predominance in the
Mediterranean after the war, Turkey became increasingly important to America's
military and diplomatic position in West Asia.

The shifting military balance impelled other neutral countries to turn towards
the Allies. At the start of the war, the conservative Portuguese dictator António
de Oliveira Salazar was openly sympathetic to the Axis, but the country's exposed
geographical position and the vulnerability of its African colonies prompted
caution, and Lisbon declared itself neutral. The 1939 Iberian Pact stressed the
neutrality of Portugal and Spain but, while Salazar shared Franco's pro-Axis
views, he was suspicious of Madrid's desire to dominate the peninsula. As the
war went on Salazar leaned more towards the Allies, permitting Washington to
build airbases in the Azores in 1943. Airfields on this strategic archipelago
strengthened Allied anti-U-boat patrols in the mid-Atlantic and allowed the

opening of a new trans-Atlantic air route: by mid-1944 over 1900 American aircraft had flown to Europe via Lajes Field. Like Spain, Portugal supplied Germany with tungsten until a threatened Allied trade embargo ended the trade in June 1944. At the same time, American diplomats conducted a charm offensive to boost Washington's influence in Lisbon, and this effort, conducted at London's expense, eased Portugal into the US-led postwar order.

As a small landlocked state embedded in Western Europe, Switzerland had long been a "professional neutral." In summer 1940 it was surrounded by Axis and Axis-occupied states, and Bern responded by loudly asserting its neutrality while the Swiss army fortified a defensive bastion in the Alps. In June 1940, *Luftwaffe* violations of Swiss airspace resulted in confused aerial dogfights in which both sides flew German-built Messerschmitt fighters. Despite these defensive military measures, Swiss businesses continued to enjoy close ties with Nazi Germany. Swiss banks gave Germany access to foreign currency in exchange for gold looted from European Jews, and Swiss factories supplied Germany with precision military equipment. In exchange, Germany supplied Switzerland with essential shipments of coal and iron ore. Although small in absolute terms, Swiss financial and industrial services met critical German needs. As the fortunes of war shifted Switzerland tacked towards the Allies, although its geographical position and economic dependence on Germany limited its room for maneuver. Swiss demands that German gold display "impeccable provenance" did little to slow its flow into Swiss accounts, which continued into 1945. Despite these ties to Germany, however, the Allies benefited from the ambiguity of Bern's position – the Office of Strategic Services maintained a key post there – and they were reluctant to criticize Switzerland publicly. As a result, Switzerland emerged from the war with its reputation for integrity and neutrality largely intact.

Sweden also had a long history of neutrality, but like Switzerland it had close economic ties to Germany. In 1940, high-grade Swedish iron ore accounted for nearly 40% of German steel production, and Swedish ball bearings played an important role in German armaments production. The German occupations of Denmark and Norway in April 1940 allowed Berlin to intensify its efforts to integrate Sweden into its new European order. A strong Swedish military helped to deter a German invasion, but the willingness of Swedish elites to cooperate with Berlin made direct military conquest unnecessary, despite the fact that Swedish public opinion generally favored the Allies. Swedish exports to Germany continued at a high level until summer 1944, and Sweden also allowed German troops to cross its territory by train. As the war turned in the Allies' favor, Washington stepped up pressure on Stockholm by threatening to end American oil shipments; Sweden halted the transit of German troops in summer 1943 and trade with Germany finally ended in late 1944. Nevertheless, while the blast furnaces of the Ruhr were never wholly dependent on the mines of Lapland, Swedish trade was both critical to the German war effort and highly profitable for Swedish elites.

Allied Advances: The Red Army Rolls On

During the summer and fall of 1944, the Soviet Red Army launched a series of offensives against German forces and their battered Romanian allies that took it deep into Poland and the northern Balkans. Campaigning began in early June, when Red Army attacks on Finnish forces north of Leningrad forced Helsinki to surrender, ending the "Continuation War." Under the Moscow Armistice, Finland accepted the imposition of heavy financial reparations and the loss of some territory but, in a sign that Moscow was willing to limit its territorial demands, the country remained independent and unoccupied.

In late June Soviet forces launched a major strategic offensive aimed at exposed German positions in Soviet Byelorussia (Belarus) and eastern Poland. Operation *Bagration* – named after a Russian general in the war against Napoleon – is considered by many military historians to be the "most impressive ground operation of the war."[1] Masking their preparations with sophisticated deception operations, Red Army forces utterly destroyed the 25-division-strong Army Group Center in less than two weeks. Over 400 000 Germans were killed or captured, many in a giant encirclement battle around Minsk, and in mid-July 50 000 German prisoners led by their senior officers were marched through the streets of Moscow in a triumphal parade reminiscent of Imperial Rome.

During *Bagration*, the Red Army displayed its mastery of huge blitzkrieg-style operations. Initial Soviet breakthroughs were followed by an exploitation phase during which fast-moving armored forces drove deep into German rear areas, cutting supply lines, disrupting communication, and sowing panic and confusion. Red Army mobility was enhanced by the widespread use of rugged American-built General Motors and Studebaker trucks supplied under Lend-Lease, and American-made radios strengthened command and control across vast battlespaces. Soviet forces also benefited from the actions of thousands of partisans whose attacks on German lines of communication shut down the flow of supplies to Army Group Center. On the other side, the position of the demotorized and often largely tank-less German defenders was made worse by Army High Command (OKH) orders to turn cities into *Feste Plätze* or fortified strongpoints to be held at all costs. Poorly prepared and impossible to supply, these so-called "fortresses" further limited German mobility and often became death-traps for the infantry divisions trapped inside them.

In a cascading series of "consecutive operations" the Red Army cleared German forces out of Soviet Byelorussia and advanced to the Vistula River in central Poland. There the advance finally halted as exhaustion, logistical overstretch, and mechanical breakdowns overcame Soviet armored spearheads. As the Red Army approached the Polish capital of Warsaw (situated on the west bank of the Vistula) in early August, the Polish government-in-exile in London instructed its underground Home Army (AK) to launch an uprising in the city. The exiled government hoped that a rising in Warsaw would underscore its claim to postwar leadership. This was an urgent matter. Moscow had broken relations with the government-in-exile in April 1943 after it demanded an investigation into the Soviet massacre of Polish officers at Katyń in 1940, and it had formed the nucleus of an alternative Polish government. The Polish Committee for National Liberation – known as the Lublin Committee after the first Polish city captured by the Red Army – was composed of communists and other left-wingers, and Soviet leaders intended that it would be beholden to them rather than to the Western Allies. In July the divide between the government-in-exile and the Lublin Committee deepened after London-based leader Władysław Sikorski, who favored an accommodation between the two organizations, was killed in a plane crash.

In Warsaw, bitter fighting raged throughout August and September as AK fighters battled German army, SS, and paramilitary police forces. Sixteen thousand AK fighters and 150 000 civilians were killed as Warsaw was razed to the ground; 700 000 more were evicted from the ruined city. Halted on the east bank of the Vistula and recovering from a ferocious German armored counterattack in early August, the Red Army did not intervene in the fighting. Soviet units were exhausted after their long advance – some had covered 450 miles in six weeks – and the river crossing would have been difficult even for fresh troops. Nevertheless, Moscow made no effort to support the insurgents, and it only allowed British and American aircraft to drop limited quantities of supplies to them: clearly, the destruction of AK weakened the government-in-exile's claim to leadership and served Stalin's political purposes.

The next Soviet attack began in late August against German and Romanian forces on the Dnestr River at the southern end of the front. The Red Army enjoyed an overwhelming superiority in tanks and heavy artillery, and the offensive made rapid progress. As the Romanian defenses crumbled, King Michael I joined with the Romanian Communist Party to launch a coup against the Antonescu dictatorship. As in Italy, key sections of the Romanian elite recognized that drastic action was necessary to salvage their power and position. Antonescu was arrested, and on August 25 a new national government declared war on Germany. A formal armistice was signed in early September, and Moscow recognized Romania as a co-belligerent, the same status accorded to the Badoglio government in Italy. Many Romanian units simply switched sides and began fighting alongside their former enemies. German forces were left surrounded and isolated, and 300 000 German soldiers were killed or captured.

The Red Army victory in Romania opened Bulgaria and Hungary to attack. The approach of Soviet troops precipitated a political crisis in Bulgaria, where the Fatherland Front (FF) seized power in early September. The FF was a diverse bloc of anti-Axis forces that stretched from the ultra-nationalist army officers in the Zveno organization to the Bulgarian Communist Party. Zveno leader Kimon Georgiev formed a new government, declared war on Germany, and sent three Bulgarian corps to join the Red Army advance on Yugoslavia. Soviet and Romanian forces also rolled into Hungary. Here, royal regent Admiral Miklós Horthy twice attempted to lead Hungary out of the Axis, but a significant section of the ruling elite remained loyal to Germany. When Horthy accepted Soviet armistice terms he was removed by the SS and replaced by Hungary's homegrown fascist movement, the Arrow-Cross. A confused struggle followed, with some Hungarian units fighting alongside the Germans while others joined the Soviet–Romanian invasion force. The Red Army fought its way to Budapest in late December but had to beat back determined SS counterattacks before finally capturing the city in February 1945.

In Yugoslavia, a rapid expansion of Partisan activity in 1944 vindicated the Tehran Conference decision to back Tito. As the territory under Partisan control expanded so did recruitment, and by mid-1944 there were over 300 000 fighters under arms. They included 20 000 former Italian soldiers who threw their lot in with the Partisans after Italy surrendered. Partisan forces faced a series of ferocious German offensives, including one in May 1944 that nearly captured Tito before American aircraft arrived in the nick of time to evacuate him to the British-controlled island of Vis. Despite these difficulties, Allied equipment allowed the Partisans to begin organizing large-scale operations involving division-strength formations. The transition from guerrilla force to regular army was not easy, but it allowed the Yugoslav Communists to lay the basis for a postwar national army even before the fighting ended. In June 1944, the Allies' newly formed Balkan Air Force began supporting the Partisans, flying from bases in Italy to deliver supplies, evacuate wounded Partisans, and provide tactical air support.

Soviet and Bulgarian forces crossed into Yugoslavia, joining the Partisans in a coordinated offensive that captured Belgrade in mid-October. In the only such bottom-up revolution in wartime Europe, Tito quickly established Belgrade as the capital of the new Socialist Federal Republic of Yugoslavia. London and Washington both hoped that Tito would include leaders of King Peter's government-in-exile in the new government, while Moscow was concerned that social revolution in Yugoslavia would deepen political instability throughout the Balkans and also favored a coalition government. Some leaders of the royal government-in-exile did join the new regime, but it soon became clear that Tito had no interest in sharing power with the old Yugoslav elite, and in November 1945 an overwhelming popular vote for the newly formed People's Front led to the abolition of the monarchy and the formal establishment of a federal republic.

Allied Advances: Italy and France

In January 1944 the American Fifth Army tried to break the deadlock in Italy, using Allied naval power to outflank German defenses by landing troops at Anzio, just south of Rome. This bold move failed when German counterattacks kept the Allies bottled up in the beachhead after coming close to throwing them back into the sea. The military stalemate was finally broken by a new Allied offensive in May. At the start of Operation *Diadem* Polish troops of General Władysław Anders's II Corps finally captured Monte Cassino, while North African light infantry in de Gaulle's French Expeditionary Corps (CEF) advanced through the mountains and British and Canadian tanks pushed into the Liri Valley. As the German front collapsed American troops broke out of the Anzio beachhead, but instead of cutting off the retreating Germans they turned north into Rome, entering the city on June 4. It is likely that American commander Mark Clark had already secured President Roosevelt's approval for this dramatic violation of the Allied battle plan during a secret visit to Washington before the attack. Significantly, Clark's success placed Rome under sole US control for several days.

American control of Rome opened a window within which a political coup could take place, and American officials quickly facilitated the ouster of Badoglio and his replacement by a left-liberal government led by socialist Ivanoe Bonomi. Bonomi's cabinet contained leaders of the anti-fascist alliance including Communist leader Palmiro Togliatti. Churchill was outraged by the removal of Badoglio but despite protesting to Roosevelt he could do nothing to reverse it. Over the following months London was forced to acquiesce to a further series of American initiatives designed to liberalize the Allied military occupation and to begin rebuilding the Italian economy. Not surprisingly, these measures also strengthened Washington's influence with the new government in Rome, where Communist participation smoothed relations between Allied troops and leftist guerrillas in German-occupied northern Italy.

Retreating German forces regrouped north of Florence, setting up new defensive positions across the peninsula known as the Gothic Line. In late 1944, Allied armies attacked the Gothic Line without success, and another winter of military deadlock followed. Allied forces in Italy were weakened by the withdrawal of seven divisions, including the entire CEF, for the Operation *Dragoon* landings in southern France. Churchill bitterly opposed this move, arguing in a flight of military fancy for an advance from Italy into northern Yugoslavia and Austria. The growing predominance of Washington within the Anglo-American alliance ensured that the Americans prevailed in this argument, and *Dragoon* went ahead in August. The redeployment of the CEF was partially offset by the arrival in Italy of the Brazilian Expeditionary Force, the predominantly African American 92nd Infantry Division, and specialist US mountain troops, but these forces could not reverse the loss of offensive momentum. Meanwhile, to the north of the Gothic Line the struggle between Communist-led Partisans and the paramilitary forces of Mussolini's Italian Social Republic escalated over the winter of 1944–1945 into a brutal civil war.

Just two days after the Americans entered Rome, Allied troops launched Operation *Overlord*, their long-awaited cross-Channel attack, on June 6, 1944. Awaiting them in Normandy was a thin shell of German defenses garrisoned in part by overage conscripts, men recovering from wounds, and "eastern battalions" composed of volunteers from occupied Eastern Europe and recruits rounded up from prisoner of war camps. The presence of large numbers of Polish, Ukrainian, Russian, and Mongolian "Hiwis" – so many that the Allies began producing multilingual propaganda leaflets – flatly contradicts the image of the *Wehrmacht* as an all-German organization. One soldier, Korean Yang Kyougjong, had been drafted in turn into the Japanese, Soviet, and German armies before being captured by American paratroopers in Normandy.

To get ashore in France the Allies utilized the amphibious landing techniques developed in the Mediterranean over the previous two years. These were based on the integration of airpower, naval gunfire, and paratroop drops with beach landings employing hundreds of landing craft and specialized armored vehicles. Despite their overwhelming material resources and firepower, however, Allied forces faced a hard fight to secure the beachhead against fierce German counterattacks. As both sides fed reinforcements into the battle, the Allies' material and logistical superiority became fully evident: Free French resistance fighters sabotaged German supply lines, Allied bombers pounded railroads across northern France, and roving aircraft savaged German road convoys, making it nearly impossible to move critical armored divisions into the battlespace during daylight. On the Allied side, prefabricated "Mulberry" harbors and large tank landing ships allowed men and equipment to be unloaded into the beachhead, while air superiority meant that these efforts were not disrupted by the *Luftwaffe*. In just two weeks the Allies moved 94000 vehicles, 245000 tons of equipment, and 620000 soldiers across the Normandy beaches.

Two weeks after D-Day, Berlin was shaken by a major political crisis after a bomb placed in a briefing room narrowly failed to kill Hitler. The bomb attack was launched by a conspiratorial group of senior army officers who had concluded that the war was lost and that they had to remove Hitler in order to begin peace talks with the Allies. The plotters were products of the old aristocratic officer corps, conservative nationalists who still hoped to preserve German conquests in the East. Unlike the opposition to Mussolini, which unfolded *within* the top echelons of the Fascist Party, the German conspirators did not include any of the central cadre of the Nazi Party. The failure to assassinate Hitler derailed a planned military coup in Berlin, allowing the Nazi security apparatus to react with speed and brutality. Over 7000 alleged conspirators were rounded up and nearly 5000 were executed. Some, like Erwin Rommel, chose suicide over a public trial and execution. The bloody defeat of the coup solidified the Nazi regime and ensured that no further challenge emerged from within the German ruling classes; despite their misgivings about Hitler the bulk of the officer corps remained deeply committed to a vision of Greater Germany premised on military conquest and racial supremacy. Unlike in Italy, Romania, and Bulgaria, there would be no escape from a war to the bitter end.

As Nazi leaders were dealing with the attempted coup, American troops began to break out of the Normandy beachhead. Supported by the deployment of heavy strategic bombers against German frontline positions, the American advance triggered a generalized *Wehrmacht* collapse in northern France. As German forces retreated towards the Rhine they were pursued by the fast-moving tanks of General Patton's newly formed Third Army. Under General Eisenhower's leadership, four Allied armies (one British, one Canadian, and two American) advanced on a broad front, entering Paris in late August followed by Brussels and the key port of Antwerp in early September. With French railroads wrecked by Allied bombing, nearly 6000 trucks and their largely African American drivers supported the advance by running the Red Ball Express, a round-the-clock trucking operation that moved over 12000 tons of supplies every day from Cherbourg to forward supply dumps. In November, the broad Allied front was extended by American and French armies that had advanced up the Rhône valley following the Operation *Dragoon* landings on the French Riviera in August.

Despite British opposition, Operation *Dragoon* was a major success. French troops quickly secured the major ports of Marseilles and Toulon, while American forces swung north up the Rhône Valley, chasing the Germans out of southern France. The landings reintroduced a large French-led army to France, giving the new government in Paris its own armed forces. Their role was critical to the establishment of political stability. In Marseilles, French troops arrived in time to both support and control a popular insurrection led by Communists and trade unionists, and throughout the south local bands of Free French fighters were either disarmed or incorporated into the army. The quick repair of the docks at Marseilles and Toulon eased the Allies' logistical problems, and until the reopening of Antwerp in November nearly half of all Allied supplies arrived in France through these southern ports.

Despite the all-out efforts of dockworkers and Red Ball Express truckers, exhaustion, mechanical breakdowns, and fuel shortages began to slow the Allied armies. The German army succeeded in extricating itself from France, and it regrouped in the defensive positions of the *Westwall* on Germany's frontier. Delays in getting the port of Antwerp operational further slowed the Allied advance, and the dramatic failure of British airborne forces to secure the bridge over the Rhine at Arnhem in September ensured that Allied armies would not cross this key river in 1944. Allied hopes for a quick end to the war were dashed. In the northern Netherlands, German reprisals after a strike by Dutch railroad workers led to the collapse of food distribution and widespread famine during the "Hunger Winter" of 1944–1945. In the central part of the front bloody American offensives in the Huertgen Forest and at Metz completed operations for the year, and Allied armies settled down for winter.

Berlin had different ideas. Undetected by Allied intelligence 20 German divisions, including elite SS formations equipped with the latest super-heavy tanks, were assembled opposite the thinly defended front in the Ardennes. As in 1940, Allied commanders assumed that no major attack could be made over this difficult terrain. When the German blow fell in mid-December, American frontline units were quickly overrun in the opening stages of what the Allies soon called the "Battle of the Bulge," and once again German tanks were driving forward. German planners entertained the naïve hope that a shattering blow would divide the Allies, disrupt their logistical base, and force them to begin peace talks, thus allowing Berlin to concentrate its forces against the Red Army. In fact, the Americans recovered quickly. Clearing skies enabled Allied ground attack aircraft to operate freely, and as German tanks exhausted their meager fuel supplies the offensive stalled. By late January the front had been stabilized. The fighting in the "bulge" brought a new level of savagery to the fighting in Western Europe, with both sides routinely executing prisoners. Despite the failure of the German attack, however, the Battle of the Bulge forced the Allies to postpone their spring offensive by six weeks: that delay would have major political consequences.

General Charles de Gaulle and the Revival of France

The Allied invasion of France posed point-blank the question of what political setup would follow the German occupation. In Italy the Allies established direct military rule in frontline areas and then gradually handed power over to a recognized Italian government. Unlike Italy, however, France was a defeated ally rather than a former enemy, and it was appropriate that political authority pass directly to a new French government without passing through the radical denial of sovereignty inherent in military government. Nevertheless, the Allies still wanted to determine *which* Frenchmen should govern. The obvious candidate was Charles de Gaulle's Free French movement, but Washington remained deeply hostile to the general's vision of a strong postwar France, envisaging instead a relatively weak and subordinate state. This political divergence underlay the notoriously bad relationship between Roosevelt and de Gaulle.

Despite Washington's hostility, the Free French could not be shunted aside easily. Colonial administrator Félix Éboué – the first person of African descent to hold high office in the empire – had rallied the colony of Chad for de Gaulle in 1940, and despite the failure of an Anglo-Free French attack on Dakar in September 1940, Éboué's bridgehead allowed the Free French to build a substantial base of support in West and Equatorial Africa. As we have seen, the Free French also gained control of Syria (July 1941) and Madagascar (May 1942) following British-led invasions, and in mid-1943 they seized the French Caribbean island of Martinique, evicting the Vichy governor and seizing the French gold reserves deposited there.

After the *Torch* landings in North Africa in 1942 Washington promoted first Admiral Darlan and then General Giraud in an effort to marginalize de Gaulle, but the growing popularity of the Free French in France's African colonies and later in occupied France meant that de Gaulle could not be excluded. Under Allied pressure, de Gaulle and Giraud were formally reconciled at the Casablanca conference in January 1943, and in June the two generals became co-leaders of the newly formed *Comité français de Libération nationale* (CFLN). The CFLN attracted support from a broad political spectrum ranging from the French Communist Party (PCF) to influential conservative businessmen and army officers. During 1943 the CFLN emerged as the authoritative leader of the growing resistance movements within France thanks to daring undercover work by de Gaulle's lieutenants. In a sign of his increasing support among colonial administrators, the CFLN organized a conference of imperial officials in Brazzaville, French Equatorial Africa, in January 1944. With his eyes on the postwar world, de Gaulle outlined plans to reinvigorate the French Empire while promising political reforms that would give French colonial subjects new rights.

These political gains meant that there was a strong case for recognizing the CFLN as the French government-in-exile. Nevertheless, Washington balked at this step, and its hostility to de Gaulle intensified after he sidelined Giraud and assumed sole leadership of the movement in late 1943. Matters were further complicated by Roosevelt's pledge to Giraud at Casablanca that the United States would arm and equip 11 French divisions. By summer 1944, these troops – mostly Arab and African soldiers with French officers – were armed, trained, and ready for action at bases in North Africa, but with Giraud gone most were commanded by officers loyal to de Gaulle.

American hostility to the CFLN complicated Allied planning for *Overlord*. Washington still hoped to avoid a de Gaulle government and planners toyed with alternatives that included establishing military governance or even restoring Pétain. These issues were not resolved before the D-Day landings, although General Eisenhower did establish effective military collaboration with French resistance fighters in Normandy. At the same time, the Resistance launched an uprising on the Vercors Plateau in southern France that established a short-lived liberated zone before being crushed by a bloody German offensive. Over 600 *maquisard* fighters and 200 French civilians were killed.

With Allied troops established in Normandy, de Gaulle seized the political initiative. Arriving in the beachhead for a one-day visit on June 14, de Gaulle was welcomed into Bayeux by enthusiastic crowds. Speaking from the balcony of the town hall, he proclaimed Bayeux the temporary capital of a new Provisional Government of the French Republic, and he appointed an aide to head its local administration. Shocked at being outmaneuvered, the Allies did not formally recognize de Gaulle's new government, but Anglo-American military leaders quickly saw the practical benefits of working with a French leadership that had broad popular support. Allied planners had intended to bypass Paris as their armies headed east after the retreating Germans, but on August 14 Parisian workers and squads of Resistance fighters launched an uprising against German occupation forces in the city. Troubled by the prospect of a Communist-led insurrection in the French capital, the Allies appealed to de Gaulle, who promptly ordered General Philippe Leclerc's 2nd Armored Division – the only French military formation in the Normandy landings – to head directly for Paris. Leclerc's tanks, led by a detachment of Spanish Republicans, entered Paris to a tumultuous reception on August 24, and two days later de Gaulle led a jubilant parade down the Champs-Élysées.

Riding a powerful wave of popular enthusiasm that combined nationalism and social reformism, de Gaulle moved his government to Paris and formed a "national unanimity" cabinet with the support of the communists, socialists, and the conservative Popular Republican Movement. The new government granted women the right to vote and began to reform health care and labor laws. Communist leader Maurice Thorez returned from exile in the USSR in November 1944, but despite being the largest party the PCF received only two cabinet slots. During late 1944 the Resistance – much of it led by the PCF – was gradually disarmed, and many of its fighters were inducted into the regular army. Their recruitment "whitened" the French army as Arab and African soldiers were sent back to the colonies; after their homelands became independent countries in the 1960s, the French government suspended their military pensions.

The collapse of the occupation triggered an outburst of violent retribution – *épuration sauvage* – against those accused of collaborating with the Germans. Nearly 10 000 members of Vichy's *milice* (militia) were executed, often with little legal process, and women denounced for having had relationships with German soldiers were publicly humiliated by having their heads shaved. As the new government became established it prosecuted alleged collaborators in the courts – *épuration légale* – and a further 770 people were executed. The *épuration sauvage* was part of a broader breakdown of social order in which the presence of relatively well-paid Allied soldiers helped to create a sprawling black market and rampant criminality. Military supplies of food, fuel, and cigarettes were widely available – at a price – and for American GIs on leave Paris and other French towns became wartime wonderlands of sex and alcohol. Literally thousands of men failed to rejoin their units, sliding instead into an underworld of petty criminals, prostitutes, and deserters. Others went a step further, joining like-minded and heavily armed deserters from every army in organized gangs that made a good living by hijacking army vehicles, robbing bars, and running prostitutes.

In contrast to the contentious situation in France, issues of political power and national sovereignty in Belgium seemed relatively straightforward. During the war the Allies recognized the Belgian government-in-exile in London as the legitimate political authority, and it returned to Brussels when British troops entered the city in September 1944. Catholic Party politician and exiled leader Hubert Pierlot became prime minister. King Leopold III had remained in Belgium during the occupation and was widely viewed as a collaborator, so his brother Charles took over as regent, neatly sidestepping an immediate crisis over the future of the monarchy. Nevertheless, the new government faced other pressing problems. Unlike de Gaulle's CFLN, the Belgian government-in-exile was not identified with the domestic resistance movement, and Pierlot's return prompted no national rejoicing. Instead, Belgian workers seized the moment to press for sweeping social and economic reforms. Pierlot included members of the fast-growing Belgian Communist Party (PCB-KPB) in his national unity government, but soon clashed with them over plans to disarm leftist resistance groups. The PCB-KPB ministers resigned, precipitating a crisis that deepened as coal miners and other workers struck to protest ongoing shortages of food and fuel. In February 1945, moderate socialist Achille van Acker replaced Pierlot as prime minister, and reforms in health care, housing, and workplace conditions combined with an improving economy to help dissipate working-class protest.

War and Politics in Italy and Greece

In July 1944, top State Department official James Dunn noted that with the formation of Bonomi's "anti-fascist, pro-United Nations and democratic" government, Italy was entering the "post-war period."[2] Without minimizing the hard fighting that lay ahead, Dunn understood that the "postwar" order was taking shape during the war itself and that "war" and "postwar" were not discrete conditions but points on a continuum. As the postwar order emerged in Italy, American aid, applied first to immediate relief and then to the reconstruction of the Italian economy, helped to forge close ties between Washington and Rome.

As in France, war dislocated the basic social and economic structures of Italian life. Food distribution collapsed, and civilians in Allied-controlled areas were expected to live on rations yielding just 615 calories per day – less than half of their calorific intake under German occupation. In the cities, many people survived by turning to a black market supplied with huge quantities of military goods stolen from ports and supply depots. Italian gangs worked closely with Allied military personnel, entire truckloads of supplies were commandeered for private sale, and up to one-third of all military supplies arriving in Naples disappeared onto the black market. Spiraling inflation worsened civilian hardship, and some women survived by selling sex for cans of army rations. Bands of Allied deserters preyed on Italian civilians, and the notorious Lane Gang – led by young US Army private Werner Schmiedel – engaged in robbery, extortion, and murder in alliance with Italian gangsters. Across broad swaths of southern Italy, government authority collapsed in the face of what officials referred to as "banditism." At the same time, many American soldiers posted behind the frontlines had time to form ongoing relationships with Italian women or to follow the advice of pocket-sized army-issue guidebooks by engaging in tourism during their off-duty hours.

Alarmed by widespread food riots during which protestors displayed Communist Party banners, American officials recognized the importance of increasing food rations. In a statement issued in September 1944 from the president's country residence at Hyde Park, Roosevelt and Churchill promised a "New Deal" for Italy that included increased food supplies, the civilianization of the Allied occupation, and more funding for economic reconstruction. Behind the façade of Allied unity, the British continued to try to block key measures designed to raise the living standards of the Italian people. British leaders lacked the resources to match American largesse, and they were bitterly aware that Washington's actions – like its unilateral decision to increase the bread ration in October 1944 – bought it political influence in a country that London had long viewed as part of its sphere of interest.

The aid mobilized by American government agencies was augmented by the work of charities like American Relief for Italy, which alone distributed $37 million of supplies. Increasingly, Washington's efforts were supported by the work of the United Nations Relief and Rehabilitation Administration (UNRRA). Founded in November 1943 by 44 allied governments, UNRRA was the first civilian agency of the United Nations. Despite its multilateral veneer, UNRRA was largely funded by the United States, which also provided its headquarters, most of its staff, and its director general, New York politician Herbert Lehman. Led by Britain and Yugoslavia, some member states opposed providing UNRRA aid to former enemies, but at Washington's insistence the organization began operating in Italy in November 1944.

In Italy, as in France and Belgium, the transition from war to postwar was carried through with the help of local Communist parties acting in accordance with the division of Europe into Soviet- and American-led spheres. This division was further consolidated when Churchill and American ambassador William Averell Harriman met with Stalin in October 1944. In the light of the Red Army's advance into the Balkans, it was agreed that the USSR would dominate postwar Romania, Bulgaria, and Hungary. Given that neither the Allies nor Moscow had control over Tito, influence in Yugoslavia would be split fifty-fifty, while London regarded Greece as critical to its interests in the eastern Mediterranean and insisted that it (together with the United States) be assigned predominance there. This division required that Moscow rein in the Communist Party of Greece (KKE).

After the Axis conquest of Greece in 1941, King George II fled to British-ruled Cairo and then to London, and his government-in-exile had little direct contact with events in the country. Within Greece, the KKE helped to form the five-party National Liberation Front (EAM) and its guerrilla army (ELAS). While the KKE had an influential voice, it did not control these broadly based alliances with decentralized command structures. After the collapse of Fascist Italy in 1943, captured Italian weapons and a number of Italian volunteer fighters helped EAM/ELAS to establish extensive liberated zones in the mountainous uplands. Local EAM committees effectively governed around two-thirds of the country, and in March 1944 they were unified into the Political Committee of National Liberation, popularly known as the Mountain Government. The monarchist government-in-exile refused to collaborate with this popular new administration, and in April British soldiers forcibly suppressed demonstrations in favor of unity between the two governments by Greek troops serving with Allied forces in Egypt. Twenty thousand Greek soldiers spent the rest of the war in British prison camps.

In the light of the division of the Balkans outlined at Tehran, Moscow instructed the KKE to recognize the authority of the government-in-exile in exchange for limited EAM representation in a new Government of National Unity. With Soviet troops moving into the Balkans in summer 1944 the Germans began a hasty withdrawal from Greece, and in much of the country EAM/ELAS established political control as the Germans pulled out. The Allies acted quickly to block EAM's advance, and with American logistical support British paratroopers seized Athens in early October in the carefully planned Operation *Manna*. The government-in-exile returned with the British forces. At first EAM supporters welcomed the British as fellow anti-fascist fighters, but relations quickly soured as it became clear that London aimed to minimize EAM participation in the new Greek government.

The crisis came to a head in December 1944 when the new government provocatively demanded that ELAS fighters – or *andartes* – disarm, and after EAM ministers resigned in protest Greek police opened fire on a massive protest rally, killing 24 people and wounding many more. The massacre triggered a month of fighting as ELAS *andartes* battled British soldiers, Greek police, and monarchist militias. With the military outcome still undecided, Churchill visited Athens in person in late December to broker a settlement. With British soldiers and ELAS fighters exchanging shots in the background, KKE leaders greeted Churchill as "our great ally" and began to hammer out a compromise deal.[3] As agreed by Stalin at his meeting with Churchill the previous October, Moscow put its weight behind British efforts to secure a pro-Western government in Greece.

Under the February 1945 Varkiza Agreement, ELAS agreed to withdraw from Athens and to disarm its fighters; in exchange EAM was promised an end to political violence, elections for a constituent assembly, and a plebiscite on the monarchy. In fact, as the *andartes* disarmed the Varkiza Agreement opened the door to a wave of rightist – or "white" – terror in which tens of thousands of EAM/ELAS members were murdered or imprisoned. A full-scale civil war followed (1946–1949) in which Britain and (after 1947) the United States intervened to support the conservative-monarchist regime that ruled Greece until 1974. True to its word, Moscow did not criticize Britain's actions in 1944–1945. In contrast to Yugoslavia, where Tito refused to subordinate the Partisan movement to Moscow's diplomatic interests, the KKE split under the intense pressure. Some communists, together with many of the non-communist members of EAM/ELAS, wanted to resist British efforts to reestablish the monarchy, but a majority followed Moscow's directive to avoid conflict with British troops and Greek monarchists by disarming. The price they paid for their loyalty to Moscow was high indeed.

American Advances in the Pacific and Japan's *Ichigō* Offensive in China

During 1944 the US Navy launched a concerted drive into the Central Pacific with an unprecedented concentration of naval firepower: Task Force 58, the flotilla that spearheaded the invasion of the Marianas Islands, comprised seven battleships, 15 aircraft carriers, and nearly 900 aircraft, and it was just one of several such forces. A large and efficient "fleet train" of oilers and cargo ships supported the warships, extending their range and endurance by using new techniques to resupply them at sea. This armada, together with the Marine and Army units it transported, was directed at the islands of Guam, Saipan, and Tinian in the Marianas archipelago. American commanders wanted these small islands because from there the giant new B-29 bomber could reach Japan, and their capture would enable the launch of a sustained strategic bombing campaign.

As American commanders anticipated, Japan's First Mobile Fleet attempted to block the landings. On paper, this was an impressive force of six battleships, nine carriers, and 800 carrier- and land-based aircraft. But the numbers conceal the fact that while American pilots had been gaining combat experience, the Japanese had lost many of their experienced naval aviators and were having great difficulty training replacements. As a result, the June 19–20 Battle of the Philippine Sea was a one-sided slaughter, known to American pilots as the Great

Marianas Turkey Shoot. Onshore, Marine and Army units faced a brutal struggle against determined Japanese defenders, but even before the fighting was over Navy Seabees were at work building landing strips for the B-29 bombers of the Twentieth Air Force.

After the Marianas, the US Navy headed for the Philippines, where its task forces converged with General MacArthur's advance along the coast of New Guinea. Some Navy commanders saw this offensive as a diversion from a direct advance on Japan via Taiwan, but as well as reestablishing American control over the Philippines the attack did force a decisive engagement with Japan's still-powerful battleship force. Fought in late October 1944 in the complex waterways of the Philippine archipelago, the sprawling three-day Battle of Leyte Gulf destroyed the Imperial Japanese Navy as a fighting force. Although decisive, the battle was not entirely one-sided, and but for a critical loss of nerve Japanese battleships might have wreaked havoc on the American landing force. Again, the outcome of battle was decided by a *combination* of material strength, leadership, and luck. The land campaign in the Philippines was equally hard fought, and fighting was still continuing when Japan surrendered in August 1945; by that time, tens of thousands of Filipino civilians had been killed.

By the end of 1943 it was clear to Allied planners that the war against Japan would be won by American forces in the Pacific, and not by American, Chinese, and British-Imperial armies fighting on the Asian mainland. From a purely military standpoint this made a great deal of sense, as the crushing naval victories in the Philippine Sea and at Leyte Gulf demonstrated. From a political view-point, however, the situation was more problematic. Military progress in China was vital if the Nationalist government in Chongqing was to emerge victorious in the intertwined struggles against *both* the Japanese and the incipient Communist regime in Yan'an. Moreover, Roosevelt still hoped to establish China as one of the world's four postwar "policemen." The problem was that Washington lacked the military means to bring this about. When Roosevelt's promise to launch a major amphibious operation in Burma unraveled just weeks after the Cairo conference, Washington pledged to base a large force of B-29 strategic bombers in China instead. This, too, turned out to be a weak reed.

In early 1944, workers at the new Boeing plant in Wichita, Kansas were struggling to get production of the B-29 rolling. With development costs of $3 billion, the B-29 was the most expensive weapons system of the war, and its advanced technology tested even America's prodigious productive capacity. The B-29's pressurized crew cabin, remote-controlled defensive armament, and powerful radial engines were all challenging new designs, and the first aircraft off the production lines had to be stripped down and rebuilt in freezing winter conditions. While this "Battle of Wichita" was unfolding, tens of thousands of workers were breaking rocks by hand to build the four airfields – two in India and two in China – that would house the big bombers. This combination of technological sophistication in the United States and hard manual labor in Asia enabled the first B-29s to fly out to China via the South Atlantic transport route in April 1944.

The Twentieth Air Force began operations in June, attacking railyards in Bangkok, steel mills in Yawata on the southern Japanese island of Kyūshū, and the Shōwa industrial complex in Manchukuo. Despite these raids, it soon became clear that the difficulty of supplying the bombers with fuel and munitions flown in over the "Hump" from India made it impossible to wage a high-tempo bombing campaign from China. By late 1944 these difficulties, together with the threat posed by Japan's *Ichigō* offensive, prompted the withdrawal of the B-29s from China. Most went to airbases in the newly conquered Marianas Islands, while others remained in India to attack Singapore, Saigon, and other targets in Southeast Asia. Before they left China, the bombers struck Japanese supply bases in Hankou in central China in a raid that gave the Twentieth Air Force's new commander General Curtis LeMay a chance for a "little experimental work with incendiaries."[4] Hankou's wooden buildings burned for three days, destroying 50% of the city, and tens of thousands of civilians died in the fires; for LeMay, it augured well for bombing attacks on Japan's wooden cities.

The withdrawal of the B-29s from China was accelerated by Operation *Ichigō*, Japan's last and largest land offensive. Running from April to December 1944 and involving over 500 000 soldiers, *Ichigō* saw Japanese troops advance deep into southern China against determined but often poorly organized Guomindang resistance. Their goal was to open a land route to Indochina, connecting the Co-Prosperity Sphere to Korea and then, via a short sea crossing, to Japan. In theory, this route created the possibility of supplying Japanese industry with critical raw materials while avoiding sea lanes increasingly infested with American submarines. In the course of the offensive Japanese troops also seized the rich agricultural provinces of Henan and Hunan, compelled the evacuation of the American bomber bases, and killed over 500 000 Chinese civilians.

Alongside *Ichigō*, the Japanese Burma Area Army launched Operation *U-Gō*, a new drive against British-Imperial and Chinese forces in northern Burma. *U-Gō* aimed to disrupt Allied preparations for an offensive into Burma and to halt work on the Ledo Road. This major construction project, carried out largely by segregated African American engineering units, was designed to reopen a land route from India into China by linking into sections of the old Burma Road that were still under Chinese control. The 84 000 Japanese troops committed to *U-Gō* were joined by 12 000 members of *Azad Hind*'s Indian National Army (INA). Subhas Chandra Bose hoped that once his troops crossed into India they would rekindle the "Quit India" movement and provoke a generalized uprising against British rule. Organized into regular brigades named after Gandhi and other longtime nationalist leaders, the men and women of the

INA advanced confident that the road would take them, as Bose's slogan put it, "Chalo Delhi – Onward to Delhi!"[5]

As the Japanese and INA forces advanced, British commander William Slim's Fourteenth Army fell back across the Indian border to the towns of Kohima and Imphal, where it fought two bitter defensive battles. Sustained by Allied air-power, the defenders weathered ferocious Japanese and INA assaults before counterattacking. Japanese and INA troops were exhausted, out of supplies, and desperately hungry, and by June 1944 Japanese forces in northern Burma had been virtually destroyed along with much of the INA. Bose's surviving troops, including the women's regiment, conducted an arduous but disciplined retreat into Thailand. Slim's victory demonstrated that two years of rebuilding and intense training had produced an Indian Army capable of undertaking major offensive operations. The eviction of the Japanese from northern Burma allowed the completion of the Ledo Road, and the first truck convoy left India for Chongqing in January 1945.

In addition to the military blows it dealt to the Nationalist armies, *Ichigo* deepened the political rift between Chongqing and Washington. The reversal of the promises made to Chiang in Cairo demonstrated that the Americans did not view Chinese leaders as equals, a point underscored by General Stilwell's harsh criticism of the Chinese military. Not without justification, Chiang argued that his army's ability to resist *Ichigo* was compromised by the fact that their best units were in Burma supporting the construction of the Ledo Road. This new clash enflamed long-standing antagonisms between American officials and the Guomindang, and in September Roosevelt demanded that Chiang appoint Stilwell as leader of the entire Chinese army. Chiang countered this unvarnished assault on Chinese sovereignty by demanding Stilwell's removal, and faced with a complete rupture in Sino-American relations Roosevelt backed down, recalling Stilwell in October.

Stilwell's replacement, General Albert Wedemeyer, was more sympathetic to Chiang, and his arrival overlapped with the replacement of US ambassador Clarence Gauss by Patrick Hurley, Roosevelt's personal representative in China. Initially, Hurley continued the Stilwell–Gauss policy of building bridges to the Communists, visiting Mao in Yan'an and proposing that the Chinese Communist Party (CCP) join the Guomindang in a coalition government. Chiang refused to participate in this plan, and as Wedemeyer and Hurley took their distance from the CCP, relations between Washington and Chongqing rebounded from their low point under Stilwell.

Despite their reenergized alliance with Chiang, neither the Americans nor the Nationalists could ignore the Communists, who by late 1944 claimed one million members and fielded an army of 900 000. Although they had not engaged in large-scale operations since the Hundred Regiments campaign in 1940, Communist forces had successfully beaten off both Japanese and

Guomindang attacks on their base areas. Moreover, the area under Communist control continued to expand as their land reform policy won new peasant adherents. In line with other Communist leaders around the world, Mao accepted Moscow's insistence on collaboration with pro-capitalist forces and expressed support both for Stilwell's plan to integrate CCP units into a new national army and for Hurley's proposed coalition government. In this, Mao proved much more receptive to Washington's proposals than Chiang, the schemes' intended beneficiary.

With CCP influence continuing to grow, with the Japanese and their Chinese allies strengthening their position through the *Ichigō* offensive, and with the obvious weaknesses of the Nationalist government looming large, Washington began to face the prospect that the war with Japan could be won in the Pacific while major military and political issues in China remained unresolved. Moreover, the limitations posed by the "ninety division gamble" and by the existing global deployment of US forces effectively precluded the possibility of getting American "boots on the ground" in China in the near future. In effect, the Americans were now increasingly confronted with the consequences of relying on British-Imperial forces to prosecute the war in Burma and of relying on air forces to create an American presence in China. The results of this dilemma would soon be felt.

Notes

1. Murray, W. and Millett, A.R. (2000). *A War to Be Won: Fighting the Second World War*, 450. Cambridge, MA: Harvard University Press.
2. James Dunn, quoted in Buchanan, A. (2014). *American Grand Strategy in the Mediterranean During World War II*, 191. New York: Cambridge University Press.
3. Churchill, W. (1953). *The Second World War*, Vol. VI, 276. Boston: Houghton Mifflin.
4. Curtis LeMay, quoted in Cohn, R.H. (ed.) (1988). *Strategic Air Warfare: An Interview with Four Generals*, 57. Washington, DC: Office of Air Force History.
5. Bose, S. (2011). *His Majesty's Opponent: Subhas Chandra Bose and India's Struggle Against Empire*, 271–272. Cambridge, MA: Harvard University Press.

Further Reading

Atkinson, R. (2013). *The Guns at Last Light: The War in Western Europe, 1944–1945*. New York: Henry Holt.

Beevor, A. (2015). *Ardennes 1944: The Battle of the Bulge*. New York: Penguin.

Bratzel, J.F. and Leonard, T.M. (2007). *Latin America During World War II*. Lanham, MD: Rowman & Littlefield.

Citino, R.M. (2017). *The Wehrmacht's Last Stand: The German Campaigns of 1944–1945*. Lawrence, KS: University Press of Kansas.

Footitt, H. (2004). *War and Liberation in France: Living with the Liberators.* New York: Palgrave Macmillan.

Gamboa, E. (2000). *Mexican Labor and World War II: Braceros in the Pacific Northwest, 1942–1947.* Seattle: University of Washington Press.

Gildea, R. (2015). *Fighters in the Shadows: A New History of the French Resistance.* Cambridge, MA: Harvard University Press.

Glass, C. (2013). *The Deserters: A Hidden History of World War II.* New York: Penguin.

Jones, H. (2014). *The War Has Brought Peace to Mexico: World War II and the Consolidation of the Post-Revolutionary State.* Albuquerque: University of New Mexico Press.

Kochanski, H. (2012). *The Eagle Unbowed: Poland and the Poles in the Second World War.* Cambridge, MA: Harvard University Press.

Kolko, G. [1968](1990). *The Politics of War: The World and United States Foreign Policy, 1943–1945.* New York: Pantheon.

Leitz, C. (2001). *Sympathy for the Devil: Neutral Europe and Nazi Germany in World War II.* New York: New York University Pess.

Lewis, N. (2005). *Naples '44: A World War II Diary of Occupied Italy.* New York: Carroll & Graf.

Maguire, G.E. (1995). *Anglo-American Policy Towards the Free French.* New York: Palgrave Macmillan.

McCann, F.D. Jr. (1973). *The Brazilian–American Alliance, 1937–1945.* Princeton: Princeton University Press.

Miller, J.E. (1986). *The United States and Italy, 1940–1950.* Chapel Hill: University of North Carolina Press.

Roberts, M.L. (2013). *What Soldiers Do: Sex and the American GI in World War II France.* Chicago: Chicago University Press.

Robertson, C.L. (2011). *When Roosevelt Planned to Govern France.* Amherst: University of Massachusetts Press.

Wittner, L.S. (1982). *American Intervention in Greece, 1943–1949.* New York: Columbia University Press.

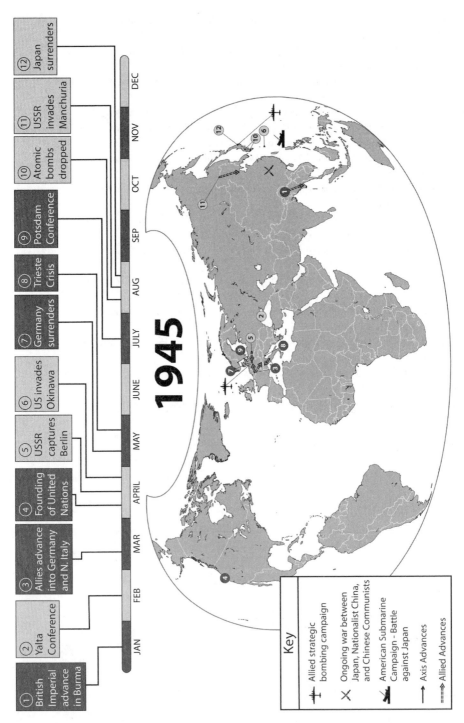

| JAN | FEB | MAR | APRIL | MAY | JUNE | JULY | AUG | SEP | OCT | NOV | DEC |

1. British Imperial advance in Burma
2. Yalta Conference
3. Allies advance into Germany and N. Italy
4. Founding of United Nations
5. USSR captures Berlin
6. US invades Okinawa
7. Germany surrenders
8. Trieste Crisis
9. Potsdam Conference
10. Atomic bombs dropped
11. USSR invades Manchuria
12. Japan surrenders

1945

Key

✈ Allied strategic bombing campaign

✕ Ongoing war between Japan, Nationalist China, and Chinese Communists

⚓ American Submarine Campaign - Battle against Japan

→ Axis Advances

⇒ Allied Advances

Map: 1945.

9

1945: The War Ends, Fighting Continues

A New World Economic Order

Just weeks after the Allied invasion of France in summer 1944, representatives from 44 countries met in the picturesque American mountain resort of Bretton Woods, New Hampshire. All were signatories of the United Nations declaration, and in addition to the major Allied powers delegates represented the nations of the Americas (except Argentina); the British Dominions (including India); and the governments-in-exile of Belgium, Holland, Greece, Norway, Yugoslavia, and the Philippines. Egypt, Iran, Iraq, and Syria were represented, as were South Africa, Ethiopia, and Liberia, the only nation-states in sub-Saharan Africa. Washington pointedly refused to invite Argentina, punishing Buenos Aires for its resistance to American regional hegemony. The conference registered America's global preponderance, and under its leadership delegates restructured the world economy in ways that facilitated the long postwar expansion of capitalism. American business – and the American government – were already getting ready for the ending of wartime trade regulations, and free trade was central to the new economic order.

During the war, most trade between Allied countries flowed through highly regulated channels. In addition to the $50 billion of war matériel distributed by the US government under Lend-Lease, Washington participated in various regional schemes that managed the circulation of American goods. In Cairo, American officials joined British officers in the Middle East Supply Center, and in Algiers they participated in the North African Economic Board. These committees of military officers, diplomats, and businessmen managed the distribution of food, fuel, and clothing on the assumption that modest

World War II in Global Perspective, 1931–1953: A Short History, First Edition. Andrew N. Buchanan.
© 2019 John Wiley & Sons, Inc. Published 2019 by John Wiley & Sons, Inc.

material incentives would avert the danger of economic dislocation producing political unrest. Most of the goods came from the United States, and their circulation helped to project an image of American benevolence throughout the Arab world while simultaneously creating new markets for American products.

As the world's major manufacturing power – and therefore the one with the most to gain from the unrestricted circulation of goods – advocacy of free trade had been central to American policy since the turn of the century. Free trade was central to President Wilson's vision of a post-World War I world order, but it was shouldered aside in the 1930s as the Great Depression prompted a worldwide retreat into autarky, protectionism, and "Imperial Preference." By 1944, however, America's growing economic and military power gave it the authority to insist that free markets should be the principal feature of the postwar world economy. Washington's insistence on free trade provoked conflict with London and Paris, which wanted to maintain preferential trade relations with their colonies. Their position was undercut by the fact that France was not yet reestablished as a major power and by Britain's wartime economic dependency on the United States. These unequal relationships were underscored in 1945 when Washington used the promise of loans for postwar reconstruction to cajole both London and Paris into full compliance with the system of free trade established at Bretton Woods.

The Bretton Woods Conference initiated a series of talks on lowering or removing import tariffs that culminated in the 1949 General Agreement on Tariffs and Trade, the forerunner of today's World Trade Organization. The conference also registered America's economic predominance by adopting the dollar as the main medium of global trade. Delegates effectively reestablished the gold standard by making the dollar convertible to gold at a fixed rate of $35 per ounce and by pegging other currencies to the dollar. The British pound held sway for several more years within the "sterling area" of the old British Empire, but the global supremacy of the dollar was now incontestable as Wall Street replaced the City of London as the premier center of global finance.

The conference underpinned this system by setting up the International Monetary Fund (IMF). The IMF was designed to maintain the stability of foreign exchange markets by making loans to countries whose trade imbalances would otherwise have forced them to devalue their currency. The IMF could make loans conditional on recipients agreeing to restructure their domestic economies in ways that were beneficial to local elites and their American backers. Member states were assigned voting rights in proportion to their contribution to IMF coffers, giving Washington a decisive say in Fund affairs. Delegates rejected a rival British plan that was the brainchild of economist John Maynard Keynes. It would have smoothed currency fluctuations with loans from an international bank that could issue its own currency, or "bancor," but whatever its other merits Keynes's plan would have blocked the emergence of the dollar as the world's reserve currency, and that alone made it unacceptable to American negotiators.

Bretton Woods also structured American economic relations with the independent states and colonies in what would soon be referred to as the "Third World." Washington's push for worldwide free trade built on its use of bilateral trade agreements to lower tariffs throughout Latin America. These moves were tied to a drive to restructure banking and finance in several Latin American countries in ways that facilitated the free flow of goods and capital. Washington saw economic development in Latin America and throughout the colonial world as critical to America's own postwar prosperity. As senior advisers explained, by creating new markets for American goods the economic advancement of the "Balkan peasant, of the Hindu and Moslem in India [and] of the Chinese [would] contribute in the long run to both the economic and political security of the United States."[1] Many Third World leaders bought into this vision and cooperated with Washington to bring it about, often seeking American loans for key state-led industrialization projects.

Washington ensured that these Third World perspectives were represented at Bretton Woods, not least because they helped to undermine the old imperial systems defended by Britain and France. China had the second-largest delegation, and 19 of the 44 countries represented were from Latin America. These delegates provided Washington with a reliable voting bloc, and they helped to craft the International Bank for Reconstruction and Development (IBRD), the second major institution established at Bretton Woods and a component of the new World Bank. Again, the IBRD was largely funded and controlled by the United States. Initially geared towards financing reconstruction in Europe – its first major loan was to France – the bank's focus soon shifted towards infrastructural development in the Third World. This shift connected American officials, bankers, and businessmen to major modernization projects, underscoring Washington's internationalist claim to be acting in the interests of worldwide economic development. In fact, the conditions placed on World Bank loans gave Washington considerable political leverage, and the 1947 French loan was made conditional on the removal of Communist ministers from government.

Immediately after Bretton Woods, a special American trade delegation led by diplomat William Culbertson swung through the Mediterranean and Middle East. It reviewed American trade in this critical region and made proposals for its postwar development. Culbertson concluded that the North African Economic Board and the Middle East Supply Center had outlived their usefulness and should be wound up as part of a rapid return to "normal" commercial activity. Culbertson emphasized that his pro-free trade conclusions applied to Italy and France as well as to the various colonies and independent states in the region. With American businessmen keen to move into these markets, the State Department quickly concurred with Culbertson's report, signifying its support for an end to regulated wartime trade.

The Bretton Woods Conference was followed in November 1944 by the Chicago Convention on International Civil Aviation. Here, too, Washington used its wartime predominance to secure postwar free trade. American delegates argued that civil aircraft should be able to overfly any territory as they shipped goods and passengers around the world. American diplomats presented this "open skies" policy in internationalist terms, arguing that the air was a "highway given by nature to all men."[2] Behind this globalist rhetoric, the United States was the only country with the operating experience, transport aircraft, trained pilots, and network of bases necessary to take advantage of the "open skies." This fact was not lost on London, which viewed "open skies" as a euphemism for "American-dominated skies" and which sought to defend its own flagship airline from American competition. Washington, backed by the Latin American nations already integrated into US air transportation networks and by Australia, Canada, and New Zealand, easily defeated the British challenge. In the tense years of the Cold War Washington dropped the grandiose globalism of the Chicago Convention, but by this time the predominance of American civil aviation was already firmly established.

The Yalta Conference

A Soviet delegation participated in the Bretton Woods Conference, and Moscow hoped that the multilateral economic institutions established there would structure an ongoing relationship between the capitalist world and the socialized economy of the Soviet Union. In particular, Moscow hoped to secure American loans for postwar reconstruction. These hopes were reinforced by the fact that Harry Dexter White, the lead American negotiator at Bretton Woods, was supplying Moscow with information on American plans. White was not a Communist, but he envisaged a postwar order based on continued collaboration between the USSR and the United States. Despite the illusions of White and other New Deal liberals, Washington had no interest in long-term "peaceful coexistence" with a state in which private capital had been abolished, and as the end of the war approached many American policymakers became increasingly hostile to the USSR and to the extension of Soviet power into Eastern Europe.

Soviet military strength framed discussion on the political shape of the postwar settlement when Churchill, Roosevelt, and Stalin met in the Crimean resort of Yalta in February 1945. Along with its desire for ongoing peaceful coexistence with America, the Soviet government wanted to strengthen its defensive position by dominating Eastern Europe. Moscow's negotiating position was reinforced by the military situation, which in early 1945 saw Marshal Zhukov's armies poised within 50 miles of Berlin while Anglo-American forces were still reeling from the Battle of the Bulge. This favorable military balance gave weight to Moscow's political proposals, particularly with regard to Poland.

The conference agreed that Poland should be shifted bodily westward, awarding territory in eastern Poland to the USSR while giving it a chunk of Germany. Allied leaders also agreed that the Soviet-sponsored Lublin Committee would form the basis of the new Polish government, requiring only that this setup be legitimized by elections.

The Allies' long-term plans for Germany remained rather vague, but there was broad agreement on the idea of setting up a weak, demilitarized, and at least partly deindustrialized state. In the short term, the conference agreed that Germany would be split into four occupation zones administered by American, British, French, and Soviet authorities. The French occupation zone was carved out of territory initially allocated to Britain and the United States. The city of Berlin – situated deep in the Soviet zone – would likewise be partitioned four ways. The conference set up a four-nation Allied Control Commission to oversee the military occupation of Germany and to prosecute senior Nazis, while an Allied Reparations Committee would determine the compensation owed by Germany for wartime destruction. With regard to Asia, Soviet leaders reiterated their promise to join the war against Japan three months after victory in Europe; in exchange, they demanded territorial and economic concessions that would be legitimized by a new Sino-Soviet treaty. On broader international questions, the Big Three approved plans for the founding conference of the new United Nations organization to be held in San Francisco in April 1945.

Moscow achieved its main goals at Yalta, securing Anglo-American approval for Soviet predominance in Poland and Eastern Europe and for the creation of a weak – if eventually reunified – Germany. After the war, President Roosevelt, who was ill throughout the conference and died shortly afterwards, was accused of having capitulated to the Soviets. In fact, Roosevelt's "appeasement" of Stalin at Yalta simply reflected the military situation on the ground in Europe and, more broadly, the geopolitical consequences of Washington's decision to wage a war in which the USSR would do most of the actual fighting. In early 1945, Anglo-American forces had no realistic chance of imposing a more pro-Western solution in Poland or Eastern Europe.

Roosevelt stopped over on his way back from Yalta for a meeting with King Ibn Saud of Saudi Arabia. Saudi Arabia had emerged as a nation-state in 1932, and it was soon clear to American engineers that it possessed massive oil reserves. In a 1933 deal backed by the US government, Standard Oil of California (SoCal) – later a key component of the postwar ARAMCO (Arabian American Oil Company) consortium – was granted exclusive rights to Saudi oil. During the war, the United States relied primarily on its own domestically produced oil, but American oilmen had already set their sights on dominating postwar production worldwide. For this reason, the oil-rich Middle East loomed large in American geopolitical thinking for the first time, and the development of relations with the Saudis became central to American plans for the entire region.

In another demonstration of Washington's use of military aid to gain political leverage, the government in Riyadh was made eligible to receive Lend-Lease supplies in 1943. Roosevelt's meeting with Ibn Saud cemented this deepening US–Saudi relationship. It laid the basis for an expanded American military presence in the region, while from Saudi Arabia well-funded American companies would be able to challenge British control of oilfields in Iraq and Kuwait. This threat to British power in the Middle East had already become a major source of tension between London and Washington, and it was only temporarily relieved by the 1944 Anglo-American Petroleum Agreement. Roosevelt jokingly reassured Churchill that America was not making "sheep's eyes at your oilfields in Iraq or Iran," but he could not dispel British fears that in the Middle East, as elsewhere, British economic interests were being shouldered aside by powerful American companies whose advance was backed by Washington.[3]

The End in Europe

In the weeks after Yalta, the military situation in Europe changed dramatically. On March 7, American forces dashed across a bridge over the Rhine that the Germans had failed to demolish, and soon American armored units were charging deep into Germany. To the north, British and Canadian armies advanced into Holland and northern Germany. In April American forces encircled the Ruhr industrial region in a giant blitzkrieg-style operation, capturing over 300 000 German prisoners. As Allied armies advanced the strategic bombing campaign continued, with bombers based in Britain and southern Italy ranging freely across the Reich attacking oil supplies and transportation hubs. Under this battering, the economic and social structures of German society began to disintegrate. Roads throughout the country were jammed with refugees fleeing the bombing and the advancing Allied armies, and thousands were killed – along with local residents and prisoners of war – when Allied bombers attacked the historic city of Dresden in February. An estimated 25 000 people died in the resulting firestorm.

As Allied armies advanced into central Germany and swung southwards towards Austria and Czechoslovakia, the German military lost the capacity for organized large-scale resistance. Some units, particularly elite SS formations, continued to fight fiercely, but others quickly surrendered as Allied troops approached. Desperate commanders pushed the old men and young boys of the *Volkssturm* home defense militia into the front lines, where they suffered predictably heavy casualties. With the end in sight American commanders were reluctant to risk taking heavy casualties, and they often responded to modest local resistance with heavy artillery barrages and air attacks that increased physical devastation and civilian deaths.

The Red Army, now supported by two Polish armies, launched a new drive on Berlin in mid-April. Some of the Poles had been captured by the Red Army during the invasion of Poland in 1939 and later joined their captors in the war against Germany. After heavy fighting, the attackers broke through German defenses on the Oder River and advanced on Berlin, while Allied bombers pummeled the city. By late April, Berlin was surrounded. As Soviet troops fought their way forward, Hitler named Admiral Karl Dönitz as head of state before committing suicide on April 30. Two days later, Soviet soldiers raised the red flag over the battered Reichstag. After making a final attempt to secure a separate peace with the Western Allies, Dönitz surrendered to Eisenhower on May 7 and then to all three Allies the following day. American and Soviet troops had already met at Torgau on the Elbe River on April 25; their historic handshake signaled both the military defeat of Germany and its coming partition.

Most German troops quickly laid down their arms, but some units battling the Soviets in Czechoslovakia and Croatia fought on, hoping to surrender to the Americans instead. In parts of central Germany, American troops overran the partition line decided at Yalta by as much as 200 miles, and some of them remained in position for several months before finally turning the territory over to the Soviets. In Norway, a small British airborne force arrived in Oslo to take the surrender of the 400 000-strong German garrison, bringing the king and the government-in-exile with them. In the far north, retreating German troops devastated the countryside as the Red Army briefly entered Norway to link up with local resistance forces before withdrawing in September 1945.

The death-agony of the Third Reich saw some of the most ferocious fighting of the war. More than 80 000 Soviet and Polish soldiers were killed in the final assault on Berlin. Encouraged by official propaganda, Red Army soldiers sought revenge for the suffering of the Soviet people: surrendering German soldiers were often shot, there was widespread looting, and hundreds of thousands of German women were raped. Moscow made no attempt to encourage a working-class uprising against the Nazis. Instead, and in line with the Russian nationalism at the heart of Soviet policy, Moscow stressed a crude "anti-Hitlerite" ideology that viewed all Germans as Nazis. As a result, the Red Army appeared in Germany not as a liberator, but as a terrible instrument of Russian vengeance and anti-woman violence.

The final crisis of the Reich also witnessed the last brutal spasms of the *Shoah* as Berlin blamed military catastrophe and Allied "terror bombing" on a world-wide Jewish conspiracy. Having already emptied the ghettos of the General Government, anti-Semitic violence flowed in new directions as nearly half a million Hungarian Jews were deported to Auschwitz by the newly installed Arrow-Cross government. The shipment of French Jews to Auschwitz had begun in summer 1942 with the enthusiastic support of the Vichy's paramilitary *milice* and it, too, accelerated in 1943–1944. By the time the last train left France in July 1944, 75 000 Jews had been shipped off to their deaths. In summer 1944 the apparatus of mass extermination began to disintegrate as Soviet troops overran the death camp at Majdanek in eastern Poland. From then on, allied armies liberated camp after horrific camp. The arrival of American, British, and Soviet troops and their attendant news media brought the full horror of the *Shoah* to international attention for the first time. But still it was not over. As the Allies advanced, camp guards evacuated inmates by means of brutal forced marches, often in harsh weather and without food or shelter. At least 250 000 Jews and tens of thousands of prisoners of war died on these death marches in the final months of the war.

In spring 1945, Allied armies in Italy finally broke through the Gothic Line into northern Italy, where a civil war between anti-fascist partisans and the paramilitary forces of Mussolini's Italian Social Republic was raging. As Allied troops advanced they found that partisan uprisings and mass strikes had already driven the Germans out of Bologna, Turin, Milan, and other industrial cities. As the German occupation collapsed, popular local governments emerged under the leadership of the Communist Party and other radical forces. The full benefit to the Allies of Bonomi's anti-fascist government now became clear. In December 1944, Rome had persuaded the partisans to place themselves under Allied military command, and now as Allied troops arrived the guerrillas turned their guns – and much of their political power – over to Allied officials in a series of carefully orchestrated ceremonies (Figure 9.1). As promised at Tehran, Moscow

Figure 9.1 Italian partisans turn their weapons over to the Allied occupation forces in an elaborate ceremony in Verona's Roman amphitheater, April 25, 1945. Here armed partisans march into the stadium behind signs announcing their home towns and villages before dumping their guns into American military trucks. (*Source:* James C. Hare.)

used its influence to ensure that the Allies did not have to contend with a Communist-led revolutionary upsurge in northern Italy.

The Trieste Crisis and the Potsdam Conference

In the final days of the war, Allied commanders in Italy sent New Zealand troops racing towards the city of Trieste on the Adriatic coast. Their mission was to establish a pro-Western military presence in the city, which had been the site of conflict between Italy and Yugoslavia since the dissolution of the Habsburg Empire in 1918. On April 30, Italian and Slovenian anti-fascists launched an uprising against the German occupation forces in Trieste, and Yugoslav Partisans entered the city the following day. The New Zealanders arrived on May 2 to accept the surrender of the German garrison, and they and the Partisans established an uneasy joint occupation. The British government had previously agreed that Trieste should be part of Yugoslavia, but both London and Washington now wanted to keep it out of Tito's hands. After a 40-day standoff, Yugoslav forces withdrew from Trieste in early June. Tito wanted to stay, but Stalin made it clear that he was not going to "begin World War Three" by backing the Yugoslavs in an armed confrontation with Allied troops.[4] Deprived of Soviet support, Tito had little choice but to back down. Yugoslavia did gain part of the surrounding Julian March, but Trieste itself remained under Allied military rule until it was turned over to Italy in 1954.

The Trieste crisis helped to shape the last wartime summit conference, held in the Berlin suburb of Potsdam July 16 to August 2. The clear lesson of the Trieste crisis was that Moscow's desire for continued cooperation with the West meant that when faced with determined opposition it would back down rather than risk conflict. This conclusion sat well with the American administration of Harry S. Truman, who became president after Roosevelt's death on April 12. Truman was keen to push back against the expansion of Soviet influence in Eastern Europe, and this newly confrontational approach was underpinned by the dramatic change in the military situation in the five months since Yalta. In that time, the Red Army had battled its way into Berlin and secured control of Hungary and Czechoslovakia, but Allied armies had sprinted deep into central Germany and western Austria. Just six days before he died, President Roosevelt told Churchill that these advances would enable the Allies to take a "tougher" approach to Stalin.[5]

It is impossible to say how Roosevelt's approach to the USSR might have evolved had he lived longer, but the adoption of a "tougher" stance would have been in line with the views of many of his key advisers. Truman set the tone of his presidency with a stinging dressing-down of Soviet Foreign Minister Vyacheslav Molotov for Moscow's failure to organize elections in Poland.

At Potsdam, Truman's hard line was reinforced by the first successful test of a nuclear weapon at Los Alamos, New Mexico, on July 16. When Truman told Stalin that the Americans now possessed a weapon of unprecedented power, the Russian leader urged its rapid use against Japan, but the potential effect of this new bomb on relations between Moscow and Washington was plain to see.

Given the increasingly confrontational character of US–Soviet relations, Potsdam accomplished little beyond ratifying the new borders of Poland and the four-way partition of Germany already agreed in principle at Yalta. The conference also set up a Council of Foreign Ministers (CFM) composed of representatives of the Big Three plus China and France and charged with drafting peace treaties with the former Axis powers. As well as highlighting mounting tensions between America and the Soviet Union, Potsdam showcased the declining influence of Britain, leading one wit to describe it as a meeting of the "Big Two-and-a-Half." British leaders were shocked by Washington's decision to terminate Lend-Lease as soon as the fighting in Europe ended, and the Americans further underscored Britain's second-rank status by rejecting London's attempt to have a greater say in the direction of Allied strategy in the Pacific.

Britain's changing status was symbolized at Potsdam by the replacement of veteran war leader Winston Churchill by the uncharismatic Clement Attlee, leader of the Labour Party. British elections do not follow a fixed schedule, and after the Labour Party quit the wartime coalition in early 1945, Churchill dissolved the government and held a general election fought along party lines. While many working-class Britons respected Churchill's wartime leadership, they remembered his tough anti-trade union stance in the 1920s and did not trust him with the peace. British workers, like those throughout Europe, hoped that victory over Nazi Germany would usher in a more just world, and the massive upwelling of support for the Labour Party was a moderate British expression of the mass working-class rebellions in Italy and France. The program of Attlee's Labour Party appealed to these egalitarian aspirations, promising socialized medicine, expanded public education and housing, and the nationalization of key industries. Some of these measures had been contained in the National Government's 1942 Beveridge Report and in the 1944 Education Act, but many did not believe that Churchill's Conservative Party could be trusted to implement them.

Labour received particularly strong support from serving soldiers, who were able to vote in camps around the world. Their wartime experiences had convinced many of the need for sweeping social change, and some had participated in political discussion groups and in the "forces parliaments" that met on several overseas bases. Five hundred soldiers packed a meeting of one such "parliament" in a Cairo night club, where they voted to nationalize the banks and build four million homes for working people before being shut down by the top brass. The July 5 election produced a landslide victory for Labour, and Attlee replaced a shocked Churchill as prime minister in the middle of the Potsdam Conference.

Strategic Bombing and the War in the Pacific

At Potsdam, Stalin informed his Western allies that forces in the Japanese government who wanted to explore a negotiated peace had asked Moscow to serve as an intermediary. In reply, the American, British, and Chinese governments issued a strongly worded declaration reaffirming their demand that Tokyo surrender unconditionally. The Potsdam Declaration made no mention of the atomic bomb, but it threatened that unless Japan surrendered it would face "prompt and utter destruction."[6] The statement also spelled out that Japan would be subject to Allied military occupation, the loss of its colonies, and the imposition of sweeping economic and political reforms.

After the failure to launch a sustained strategic bombing campaign against Japan from bases in China, most of Twentieth Air Force's B-29 bombers had moved to newly constructed airfields in the Marianas Islands in late 1944. From there bombers could attack targets throughout Japan, but their initial attempts at high-level precision bombing were disrupted by bad weather and high winds and produced minimal damage. Desperate for results that would justify the enormous cost of the B-29 program, General Curtis LeMay adopted new tactics, loading the big airplanes with incendiary bombs and sending them on low-level nighttime raids on Japan's highly flammable cities. The results were devastating. On the night of March 9–10, 334 B-29s dropped 1665 tons of incendiary bombs on Tokyo, kindling a gigantic firestorm that claimed over 80 000 lives and destroyed 250 000 houses and 22 major factories. It is difficult to comprehend the sheer scale of the slaughter: 80 000 deaths in one city in one single night of bombing. After Tokyo, LeMay's bombers began systematically working their way through a list of Japan's key industrial centers.

By the end of March, the bombers had used up all the available incendiary bombs, but the degradation of Japan's air defenses enabled them to launch daylight raids with high explosives instead. Sixty-seven Japanese cities were attacked, and many – including Nagoya, Osaka, and Kobe – suffered over 50% destruction. Some, like the aluminum-producing city of Toyama, were effectively obliterated. Well over 300 000 Japanese civilians were killed in the bombing, and while overall casualties were less than in Germany, they were inflicted over a much shorter time frame. Millions of civilians, many of them children, were evacuated into the country, and others fled without waiting for official approval. In just five months, American bombing completely dislocated Japan's industrial economy. Meanwhile, US submarines operating in Japan's maritime trade routes had blocked the import of critical raw materials. Japan's capacity to wage a modern industrial war was effectively ended.

While heavy bombers blasted Japan's cities, American naval forces were advancing on the Home Islands. In mid-February Marines launched a bloody month-long struggle to capture the tiny island of Iwo Jima, and from April to

June a joint Army/Marine task force conquered the island of Okinawa, just 350 miles from southern Japan. Over 100 000 Okinawan civilians were killed in the fighting. In both battles, American forces deployed overwhelming firepower, with the American fleet at Okinawa containing 40 aircraft carriers and hundreds of escorts and support ships. Despite the scale of the American attack, well-fortified Japanese defenders inflicted heavy casualties on the invaders, and at Okinawa, *kamikaze* suicide aircraft sank 36 American ships and damaged 360 more. *Kamikaze* methods were clearly unsustainable in the long term, but they offered an effective way to utilize dedicated but poorly trained pilots and they terrified Allied planners and navy crewmen alike.

American military engineers quickly turned Okinawa into a giant construction site, building airbases and supply dumps in preparation for the invasion of Japan. The American plan was for a two-phase offensive, landing on the southern island of Kyūshū in November 1945 before attacking Honshū – including Tokyo – in March 1946. These were to be massive operations involving troops, equipment, and airplanes redeployed from Europe, and American commanders reluctantly agreed to include a British-led Commonwealth Corps and a British-Imperial force of long-range bombers. Nevertheless, the experience of Iwo Jima and Okinawa convinced some American commanders that the invasion of Japan would result in very substantial American casualties. Their estimated casualty figures are often cited to justify the use of atomic weapons against Japan. In fact, the use of atomic bombs was motivated primarily by strategic and geopolitical concerns and not primarily by a desire to avoid American casualties.

Geopolitics in Asia and the Atomic Bombing of Japan

The ultimate center of Washington's geopolitical interest in Asia was not Japan but China, and the defeat of Japan was essentially a step towards the establishment of American predominance on the Asian mainland and in the vast Chinese market. With Japan on the verge of defeat, however, it was now clear that the war would end with nearly two million Japanese soldiers still undefeated in China and with large sections of the country under Communist Party control. Washington's relations with Chiang Kai-shek had improved after Stilwell's recall, but the Nationalist government still faced major political and military challenges. In contrast to Europe, where powerful Anglo-American ground forces occupied big chunks of Germany, America only had a small military presence in China, and this weakness limited its political leverage. And, as it had promised at Potsdam, the USSR was poised to enter the war in Asia three months after its victory in Europe.

The only significant Allied advance in mainland Asia in 1945 was the British-Imperial drive into Burma, launched in late 1944 after the final Japanese push towards India had been defeated. General William Slim's Fourteenth Army contained 13 infantry divisions, including eight from India, two from British West Africa, one from British East Africa, and only two from Britain itself. This multinational force was supported by six Chinese divisions and by Aung San's Burmese National Army. Imperial forces were well trained for jungle warfare, supported by overwhelming airpower, and backed by a sophisticated logistical system that utilized aerial resupply and casualty evacuation from newly constructed airstrips. In contrast, Japan's Burma Area Army was hungry, exhausted, and poorly equipped. In March 1945, the Fourteenth Army captured Mandalay in central Burma, and in May it entered the capital, Rangoon. Meanwhile, an Australian corps landed in Borneo, where it linked up with nationalist guerrillas who opposed Japanese rule but who did not favor the return of their former British and Dutch masters.

Although significant, these advances did not directly challenge Japan's grip on China. General Wedemeyer, Stilwell's replacement as Chiang's chief of staff, spent spring 1945 preparing a major offensive from Burma into southern China, but the war ended before it could be launched. Like Stilwell before him, Wedemeyer urged Washington to broker a settlement between the Guomindang and the Communists. His proposal reflected an appreciation of the growing strength of the CCP and it aimed to control Mao by bringing him – with Moscow's backing – into a common government. Other American officials, including Ambassador Hurley, disagreed with Wedemeyer. They rejected any coalition with the Communists and argued instead for expanding American efforts to build up the Nationalist regime. In contrast to Europe, however, where Washington's powerful military presence enabled it to push back against the USSR, it had no such leverage in China. The massively powerful American naval forces critical to the victory over Japan were of limited use in the vast landmass of China.

The difficult situation facing the Americans in China seemed likely to get worse when the long-promised Soviet intervention happened. At Yalta, Stalin secured promises of territorial and economic concessions in China as a reward for joining the war against Japan. He also assured Roosevelt that the Soviet troops would not back the CCP against the Guomindang, and in the August 1945 Sino-Soviet Treaty of Friendship and Alliance Moscow recognized the Nationalist regime as the legitimate government of China. This approach reflected the importance Moscow placed on securing postwar "peaceful coexistence" with Washington, even if it meant reining in the CCP. In the context of sharpening tensions in Europe, however, Moscow's promises did not reassure American policymakers, and Washington decided to bring the war in the Pacific to a rapid conclusion by using its new atomic bombs to shock Tokyo into surrender.

A great deal has been written about the "decision" to use the atomic bomb, but the only real discussion at the time was *when* and *where* to use this devastating new weapon, not *whether* to use it. Among senior American commanders only Admiral William Leahy, the unofficial head of the Joint Chiefs of Staff, expressed serious doubts about using the bomb, and his concerns reflected his conviction that naval blockade and bombing had already brought Japan to its knees. Moreover, with one aircraft now able to accomplish the work of hundreds, atomic bombs effectively *extended* the ongoing assault on Japan's cities; from the viewpoint of the civilian victims, it was surely impossible to see any significant moral difference between conventional and nuclear bombing. Some commentators have claimed that the use of the atomic bomb was motivated by racist attitudes towards the Japanese, and that the bomb would not have been used against Germans. It is certainly true that American propaganda used racist imagery to fuel what historian John Dower describes as a "war without mercy," but there is no evidence to suggest that the atom bomb would *not* have been used against Germany if it had been developed in time.

On August 6, 1945, a B-29 bomber named *Enola Gay* after the pilot's mother dropped an atomic bomb on the industrial city of Hiroshima. Around 100 000 people died in the explosion and the resulting firestorm, and about 70% of Hiroshima was leveled.

Three days later, the Soviet Union declared war on Japan. Over 1.5 million Soviet soldiers and 5500 tanks poured into Manchukuo. In a giant encirclement operation, the Red Army's Trans-Baikal Front advanced through the deserts of Mongolia and over the Greater Khingan mountains. The best units of Japan's Kwantung Army had been transferred to reinforce Japanese forces in the Pacific, and the remainder disintegrated in the face of the Soviet onslaught. By the time the offensive halted on August 20 the Japanese puppet states of Manchukuo and Mengkiang (Inner Mongolia) had been totally smashed, leaving the Red Army in complete control of Manchuria. Despite protests from local Chinese Communists, the behavior of Soviet troops in Manchuria was hardly less brutal than in Germany, and Soviet engineers quickly began stripping Manchuria of industrial plant. In late August, Soviet troops rolled into the northern part of Japanese-occupied Korea, finally halting on the 38th Parallel in compliance with the division of the peninsula proposed by Washington. No Koreans were consulted by either Great Power.

Just hours after the Red Army invaded Manchuria, an American bomber dropped a second atomic bomb on the port city of Nagasaki, killing an estimated 40 000 people. As in Hiroshima, the presence of large numbers of poorly documented forced laborers from Korea and the Co-Prosperity Sphere makes it impossible to give a precise casualty figure. After the second atomic bomb, and with the Soviet invasion of Manchuria unfolding with shocking speed, a substantial pro-surrender faction emerged within the Japanese government. After long hours of discussion Emperor Hirohito intervened in favor of those seeking peace, insisting only that he retain his position as head of the Japanese state.

As in Italy, the monarch played a critical role in forcing political and military elites to recognize that they had lost the war. American leaders responded favorably, agreeing that the emperor could remain but insisting that he be subject to the supreme commander of the American occupation forces, General Douglas MacArthur. After beating off an attempted coup by the pro-war faction, Tokyo agreed to these terms on August 15.

The formal surrender took place on September 2, 1945 under the mighty guns of the battleship USS *Missouri*, anchored with other American warships in Tokyo Bay. Underscoring Japan's humiliation, the American flag flown by Commodore Matthew Perry's flagship when it entered Tokyo Bay in 1853 was on prominent display. Yet for all the contemporary bluster – and constant repetition by historians – what took place on the deck of the *Missouri* was *not* an unconditional surrender. American leaders had in fact agreed to Tokyo's one key condition – the maintenance of the monarchy – despite Hirohito's direct involvement in all of the major strategic decisions of the war. The preservation of the monarchy certainly had symbolic and religious significance, but it also provided a critical rallying point around which a new political order could be constructed. In the end, as in Italy, a conditional surrender suited both parties.

The Ragged End of the War in Asia

In the weeks following the ceremony on the *Missouri* Japanese troops throughout the former Co-Prosperity Sphere surrendered to representatives of the Allied powers. In China, MacArthur insisted that Japanese soldiers surrender only to the Nationalists, and many remained under arms as Guomindang officials enlisted them to fight the Communists. Their experience was replicated throughout Southeast Asia as Allied forces employed tens of thousands of "Japanese Surrendered Personnel" – a category invented specifically to circumvent international prohibitions on the use of prisoners of war for military operations – to battle Nationalist insurgencies. In Malaya, Singapore, the Netherlands East Indies, and Hong Kong British detachments arrived to accept the Japanese surrender and to begin the task of reimposing colonial rule. In many places, American and British-Imperial troops confronted what the *New York Times* referred to as the "fires of nationalism," and the newspaper conceded that the Allies' stated support for national self-determination made their opposition to its realization an uncomfortable "paradox."[7] As we shall see in the next chapter, American policymakers were inclined to see communism and popular nationalism as much the same thing, and they pushed back forcefully against both.

The ragged character of the end of the war in Asia stood in sharp contrast to the end of the fighting in Europe. In Europe, most space was directly occupied by one or another of the Allied armies, while throughout much of Asia and the

Pacific over 3.5 million undefeated Japanese soldiers were still in control of extensive territory. In Europe – with the exception of Greece – the division established at Tehran and implemented with the help of national Communist parties avoided major clashes between Allied armies and local resistance movements. Soviet influence over nationalist movements in Asia was weaker, and anti-colonial militants were often unwilling to subordinate their struggles to Moscow's search for postwar coexistence with the United States. These factors ensured continued political and military instability as popular nationalist forces – often citing the Atlantic Charter – seized the moment to demand complete national independence. At the same time, the weakness of the Guomindang regime allowed the CCP, its popularity boosted by its land reform program, to strengthen its position.

Washington's efforts to get control of the situation in China were hindered by the relative lack of American "boots on the ground." When the war ended, there were 60 000 US soldiers in China, many assigned to transport and logistical tasks. Washington rushed two Marine divisions (about 50 000 men) to North China to secure key cities and transport hubs until Nationalist troops arrived from the south on US transport aircraft. But, as the Japanese had found out, control of "points and lines" did not grant control of the countryside, which was where the Communists were based. That would require many more men but, in one of the most remarkable chapters of the war, Washington's attempt to increase its military presence in China was derailed by American soldiers themselves.

In late 1945 and early 1946, American military bases in the Pacific saw large demonstrations and protest meetings as servicemen and women protested plans to send them into China and Southeast Asia and demanded their immediate demobilization (Figure 9.2). In Manila, over 12 000 soldiers jammed the bombed-out Hall of Congress to hear speakers denounce American aggression in China and Indonesia, and enlisted men on Guam staged a hunger strike. In a display of global connectivity and solidarity, American soldiers around the world voiced support for the protests in the Pacific, while friends and family in the US bombarded Congress with letters and telegrams. In Paris, soldiers drafted an "Enlisted Man's Magna Carta" demanding an end to class divisions in the military. Many of these soldiers had been trade union activists during the great strikes of the 1930s, and their leaders were often non-commissioned officers who had experience as union shop stewards. The results were dramatic. Protests speeded demobilization, and the military shrank from 12 million in 1945 to 3 million by summer 1946 and 1.5 million the following year. This demobilization effectively precluded any large-scale US military interventions in the immediate postwar period. Most soldiers simply felt that they had done their job and should be allowed to go home, but many were also motivated by arguments against US intervention, and most still saw communists and anti-colonial resistance fighters as valiant allies rather than as deadly enemies.

Figure 9.2   American soldiers march on the Western Pacific Headquarters in Manila demanding their immediate demobilization, January 6, 1946. (*Source*: National Archive and Records Administration, College Park. Image in File RG 319-CE-124-SC (Philippines).)

With no viable military option, American policymakers tried to blunt the Communist challenge in China by promoting the establishment of a Guomindang–CCP coalition government. Truman entrusted this critical diplomatic mission to General George Marshall, Washington's top wartime planner. Marshall arrived in China in December 1945 and quickly negotiated the formation of a coalition government. Prompted by Moscow, CCP leaders agreed to participate, hailing the coalition as a "great victory for China's democratic revolution."[8] The agreement also inspired Nationalist leaders who wanted to pursue social reform – a Chinese version of Britain's Beveridge Report was discussed – and Washington hoped that the coalition might simultaneously tame the Communists and liberalize the Nationalists. For his part, Mao was prepared for a protracted period of "non-military mass work" within a unified capitalist nation-state. In practice, however, it was impossible to square the peasant-based land reform championed by the CCP with the interests of the landlord elite represented by the Guomindang. By March 1946, the putative coalition began to unravel as Chiang's Nationalists took advantage of the withdrawal of the Red Army from Manchuria to attack CCP-led forces there. A new Chinese civil war was beginning.

197

Notes

1. Alvin Hansen and Charles Kindleberger, *Foreign Affairs*, April 1942, quoted in Helleiner (2014), 126.
2. Conference chair and leader of the US delegation Adolf Berle, quoted in Van Vleck, J. (2013). *Empire of the Air: Aviation and the American Ascendancy*, 184. Cambridge, MA: Harvard University Press.
3. Roosevelt to Churchill, Telegraph R-485, May 3, 1944, in Churchill, W. (1984). *Churchill and Roosevelt: The Complete Correspondence*, Vol. III (ed. W. Kimball), 14. London: Collins.
4. Joseph Stalin, quoted in DiNardo (Summer 1997), 378.
5. Franklin D. Roosevelt, quoted in Stoler (2005), 200.
6. Text of the July 26, 1945 Potsdam Declaration quoted in Stoler (2005), 208.
7. "Abroad," *New York Times*, November 25, 1945, 69.
8. CCP Central Committee statement, quoted in Offner (2002), 322–323.

References

DiNardo, R.S. (Summer 1997). Glimpse of an old world order? Reconsidering the Trieste crisis of 1945. *Diplomatic History* 21 (3): 365–381.

Helleiner, E. (2014). *Forgotten Foundations of Bretton Woods: International Development and the Making of the Postwar Order*. Ithaca: Cornell University Press.

Offner, A.A. (2002). *Another Such Victory: President Truman and the Cold War, 1945–1953*. Stanford: Stanford University Press.

Stoler, M.A. (2005). *Allies in War: Britain and America Against the Axis Power*. London: Hodder Arnold.

Further Reading

Biddle, T.D. (April 2008). Dresden 1945: reality, history, and memory. *Journal of Military History* 72 (2)): 413–449.

Brogi, A. (2011). *Confronting America: The Cold War Between the United States and Communists in France and Spain*. Chapel Hill: University of North Carolina Press.

Cummings, B. (2010). *The Korean War: A History*. New York: Modern Library.

DeNovo, J.A. (1977). The Culbertson Economic Mission and Anglo-American tensions in the Middle East, 1944–1945. *Journal of American History* 63 (4): 913–936.

Dower, J. (1987). *War Without Mercy: Race and Power in the Pacific War*. New York: Pantheon.

Garcia, D.E. (September 2010). Class and brass: demobilization, working-class politics and American foreign policy between World War and Cold War. *Diplomatic History* 34 (4): 681–698.

La Faber, W. (December 1975). Roosevelt, Churchill and Indochina, 1942–1945. *The American Historical Review* 80 (5): 1277–1295.

Lanzona, V.A. (2009). *Amazons of the Huk Rebellion: Gender, Sex, and Revolution in the Philippines*. Madison: University of Wisconsin.

Little, D. (2004). *American Orientalism: The United States and the Middle East, Since 1945*. Chapel Hill: University of North Carolina Press.

Searle, T.R. (January 2002). 'It made a lot of sense to kill skilled workers': the firebombing of Tokyo in March 1945. *Journal of Military History* 66 (1): 103–133.

Wittner, L.S. (1982). *American Intervention in Greece, 1943–1949*. New York: Columbia University Press.

10

War and Postwar, 1945–1953

The Human Cost

On the day that Germany surrendered, 5000 Arabs and Berbers took to the streets of Sétif to celebrate. The crowd in this town in French-ruled Algeria included many veterans of the French army, some recently returned from Europe, and they carried the flags of the victorious Allies. They also carried banners calling for the independence of Algeria and for the release of nationalist leaders imprisoned by the French authorities. When colonial policemen tried to seize the banners, they triggered a riot that left over 100 French settlers, or *pieds-noirs*, dead. The French response was swift and brutal. Police and *pied-noir* vigilantes killed several thousand Arab and Berber civilians, while French aircraft bombed remote settlements and a warship shelled coastal villages. The Sétif Massacre was the moment at which many Algerians understood that despite their contribution to the French war effort, and despite de Gaulle's promises at Brazzaville, Paris had no intention of treating its colonial subjects as equals. A full-scale anti-colonial rebellion did not break out in Algeria until 1954, but its origins lay in World War II: France had been on the winning side, but war had simultaneously accentuated and shaken the bonds of empire.

It is not possible to give a full account of the human cost of World War II. Casualty figures are notoriously unreliable. On top of the obvious difficulties of keeping accurate records on sprawling battlefields, body counts were often manipulated for political reasons. Since the overthrow of the Soviet Union, for example, Russian scholars have revised Soviet casualty estimates *upwards*, to a total of 27 million, 17 million of them civilians. Despite these difficulties, there

World War II in Global Perspective, 1931–1953: A Short History, First Edition. Andrew N. Buchanan.
© 2019 John Wiley & Sons, Inc. Published 2019 by John Wiley & Sons, Inc.

is broad agreement on a global total of about 60 million deaths. Of these, around 21 million were soldiers – including five million prisoners of war who never returned home – and the rest civilians, including the victims of military repression and state-sponsored genocide. Six million Jews were killed in the *Shoah*, accounting for around two-thirds of the Jewish population of prewar Europe, and two million civilians worldwide died when their homes were bombed. Even this unimaginable slaughter underestimates the true toll. If war-induced famine and disease are included – and they surely must be – then millions of victims in India, China, and elsewhere swell the total to around 80 million, or nearly 4% of the prewar world population. In contrast to World War I, where a majority of the war's 17 million dead were soldiers, the predominance of civilian deaths in World War II speaks to the erasure of the long-standing distinction between soldiers and civilians and to the war's "total" character.

The deaths are just a beginning. In Europe alone, 50 million people were forced from their homes and 16 million of them became "displaced persons" or simply "DPs," the bureaucratic name for the refugees, forced laborers, and concentration camp inmates who ended the war outside of their homelands. In China, over 90 million people became refugees *within* their own country, while three million Japanese fled into the countryside to avoid the incendiary bombs raining on their cities. Some refugees later returned home, struggling to rebuild shattered lives and bombed-out houses. Others tried to carve out new lives elsewhere. Thousands of European Jews set course for Palestine, the "national home" promised them by the British government, but to which it now denied them entry.

Refugees everywhere battled powerful political forces over which they had no control. The Allies incarcerated millions of DPs in dilapidated camps, many run by the United Nations Relief and Rehabilitation Agency. Some remained there for years. British and American officials shipped more than two million former Soviet prisoners of war back to the USSR, where suspicious Stalinist officials sent many to labor camps in the *Gulag*, some for life. Members of nationalities distrusted by Moscow received particularly harsh treatment, like the 230 000 Crimean Tartars forcibly relocated from their homeland to Soviet republics in the east. British officials sent 45 000 Cossacks, many of whom had fought for Germany, back to face their fate in the USSR. Over 100 000 Polish soldiers, many of whom had fought with British-Imperial forces in Italy, chose to settle in Britain rather than return to Soviet-dominated Poland. Meanwhile, under the division of Europe established at Potsdam, 12 million ethnic Germans were expelled from Soviet-dominated Eastern Europe and resettled in Germany. Given that these *Volksdeutsche* were on the losing side, their forced migration and the suffering it entailed are often overlooked, but they were no less real.

These horrific statistics register the most intense spasm of death, destruction, and dispossession in world history. But this human suffering, and the shattered homes, factories, farms, and infrastructure that accompanied it, were not – and could not be – spread evenly. Of Poland's 34 million prewar inhabitants, six million were dead and 10 million had been deported or had fled by the time the fighting, partition, and waves of anti-Semitic and anti-Slav fury were done. In the Soviet Union, total wartime deaths accounted for nearly 14% of the prewar population. In contrast, the United States suffered over 407 000 military casualties and 12 000 civilian deaths, most of them merchant seamen lost in the North Atlantic. In addition, a Japanese balloon bomb killed six unlucky picnickers in the mountains of Oregon. They were the only civilian casualties in the continental United States during the entire war, although there is surely a case for including the 86 000 Americans killed in industrial accidents, many as a result of speeded-up production and lowered safety standards. Taken together, however, these American casualties amounted to just 0.32% of the prewar population: these numbers do not belittle the human cost of these deaths to the families and communities that bore them, but they do help to put them into global perspective.

In addition to its human cost, the war brought environmental destruction on a massive scale. Battles and bombing destroyed farmland and smashed cities, and in the most intensely contested spaces destruction was layered upon destruction; the Soviet city of Kharkov was captured and recaptured four times, while Berlin was blasted from the air before being smashed by Soviet artillery. In many German cities, the rubble was piled up in man-made mountains or *Schuttberge*, and cities across the world bore the scars of war for decades. In addition to the destruction, wartime *con*struction also had major environmental consequences, as powerful bulldozers and gangs of forced laborers drove roads and railways through jungle and over deserts, built sprawling bases from the Arctic to the Galapagos Islands, and turned coral atolls into airfields. Urgent efforts to acquire raw materials drove an expansion of mining operations from the Chilean copper mines to the uranium beds of the Belgian Congo. These physical effects were accompanied by a widespread transformation of agriculture: in the United States, unprecedented mechanization and the large-scale use of chemical fertilizers and pesticides boosted productivity, while in parts of colonial Africa peasant farming gave way to state-sponsored monocultures.

Why Did the Allies Win?

At one level, it is easy to explain why the Allies won: the Axis powers were simply overwhelmed by a tsunami of Allied war matériel. By 1945, the total gross domestic product of the Allied countries was around five times that of the Axis – a stunning figure that reflects both the growth of Allied – particularly American – production and the collapse of the Axis economies under the weight of Allied bombing and military defeat. To be effective, matériel has to be transported from factory to fighting front, and here, too, the Allies excelled. Allied engineers and construction workers built global supply chains whose aerial and oceanic webs, railroad tracks, and supply bases connected farms and factories in the American Midwest to combat soldiers in Kursk, Chongqing, and on tiny Pacific atolls. This all required planning, organization, and the commitment of significant resources, and the logistical "tail" (non-combatant support troops) in the Allied armies was always far bigger than that of their Axis opponents.

But wars are not won simply by having the most stuff in the right places, and while material superiority often underpins battlefield success, it does not predetermine it. Fighting quality – an elusive combination of leadership, training, experience, and good equipment – is also needed, and here the Allied advantage was much less clear-cut. Early in the war, the fighting quality of German and Japanese forces was clearly superior, as their dramatic victories against seemingly powerful opponents in China, Southeast Asia, Poland, and France demonstrated. Axis strategy rested on leveraging their superior fighting quality to offset their relative material weakness, and it required quick and decisive victories. Allied forces developed their fighting quality over time and through experience, and by the end of the war the Red Army was conducting massive blitzkrieg-style "deep operations" while the US Navy had developed the techniques of air-sea warfare virtually from scratch. In contrast to the Axis powers, which often substituted drive and daring for careful logistical preparation, advances in Allied fighting power rested on the integration of supply and logistics into operational planning: American-supplied trucks were key to the Red Army's mobile operations, and without its supportive fleet train the operations of the Pacific Fleet would have been impossible.

Fighting quality is intertwined with an even more abstract quality, perhaps best described as "will." This intangible element combines top-level political and military leadership with broader factors, including popular political commitment, nationalism, resilience, and fear of defeat. The determination of the Soviet people to fight on in the face of the stunning defeats suffered during *Barbarossa* demonstrated collective will, as did the willingness of the British people to face large-scale bombing after the disaster at Dunkirk. Will is easily mythologized as national exceptionalism, but that does not mean that it should be discounted. The effects of its absence – in France in 1940, British-ruled Southeast Asia in 1942, and Italy in 1943 – all underscore its significance. Nor, of course, was will unique to the Allies. In Germany, popular determination to continue fighting was stoked by anti-Semitic propaganda after the intensification of Allied "terror bombing" in summer 1943, and in both Japan and Germany the war was sustained long after defeat had become inevitable.

The outcome of World War II was determined by the complex interplay between economic determinism and contingent factors that included fighting quality and will. Within this matrix, human agency – often expressed in misjudgments, errors of over-projection, and flawed strategic planning – plays a significant role, as does the outcome of individual campaigns and battles. Even major battles are rarely truly decisive, but they can mark critical tipping points at which strategic initiative and momentum pass from one side to another.

The war ended with the complete defeat of the German and Japanese autarkic-colonial projects in both western and eastern Eurasia and with the survival and strengthening of their Soviet and Chinese opponents. Long before these colonizing efforts were defeated, Italy's hopes of establishing a new Roman Empire on the shores of the Mediterranean had already been shattered. A great deal of the fighting and dying was done in these would-be colonial spaces, and the mighty land battles fought in Eastern Europe, the Soviet Union, and China, as well as in the Balkans and Southeast Asia, were critical to the overall outcome of the war. At the same time, much of the material strength that helped to make these victories possible – either by supplying the combatants within Eurasia or by opening additional fronts in Western Europe, the Mediterranean, and the Pacific – was generated *outside* of Eurasia. It came from the African colonies of Britain and France, from British-ruled India, from US-dominated Latin America, from the "White Dominions" of Australia, Canada, New Zealand, and South Africa, and above all from the United States. Several of these countries did engage in major land-based military operations, but theirs was *primarily* a war of naval and air power and of raw material extraction, food production, industrial manufacturing, and transportation.

With the exception of a brief period after the fall of France, the combined output of the Axis powers never came close to challenging American and British-Imperial predominance in these critical economic spheres. The Anglo-American alliance also dominated the air with their strategic bombers and – after Midway and victories in the Atlantic and Mediterranean in 1943 – they exercised increasingly firm control over the world's major waterways. Given Anglo-American predominance in these areas, it is tempting to see them as *the* decisive factors in winning "the war." But that begs the question of *which* war. The United States ended the war in a position of unprecedented global predominance, but its reach did not extend deep into Eurasia, where wars were won by massive and brutal ground battles.

America's Qualified Victory

The United States, the major combatant that suffered the lowest casualties and the least domestic destruction, was the war's single obvious winner. This was clearly true in relationship to the major Axis powers, all three of which were defeated and subjected to military occupations. But America's victory was also evident in relation to the old imperial powers of Britain and France. Britain and the United States fought the war locked into an alliance whose unified command structures led a genuinely and uniquely integrated military effort. Yet over the course of the war the relationship between the two countries shifted decisively in favor of the United States. This changing balance of power was the product of a bloodless war within the war, and despite Churchill's talk of a special bond between the "English-speaking peoples," the Anglo-American alliance was the site of a relentless drive to subordinate Britain to the new global hegemon. Washington's ability to use the war crisis to marginalize its German and British rivals in key Latin American markets was also an important, if often overlooked, aspect of its victory.

But, for all its mighty accomplishments, the American victory was not altogether unqualified. Instead, America's new hegemony was challenged on three fronts: first, by the unanticipated growth of Soviet power; second, by the ongoing crisis in China; and third, by the unpredictable consequences of the weakening of the old imperial order in Africa, the Middle East, and Asia.

At the start of Operation *Barbarossa* in June 1941, many observers expected that Germany's war with the Soviet Union would soon be over. In fact, the USSR not only survived the onslaught but went on to bear the brunt of the land war against Germany and to become a key component of the Grand Alliance. Moscow wanted the alliance to continue into a postwar period of "peaceful coexistence." Some American leaders did believe – despite a complete lack of evidence – that Moscow was bent on spreading communism worldwide, but the American rulers' fundamental problem was that the socialized economy of the USSR was not a place where Americans could invest, sell product, and make profits. Despite the urging of a few hotheads like General Patton, the United States was politically and militarily unable to move directly against the Soviets in 1945, so instead Washington began a protracted military standoff in the hope of weakening the USSR over time. This policy of "containment" shaped the architecture of the global Cold War into the late 1980s.

Despite its crushing victory over Japan, Washington also faced a major challenge in China. Here, America's military weakness on the ground forced Washington to try to broker a coalition government between the Guomindang and the CCP. This was always a fragile proposition, largely because Chiang was firmly opposed to any serious power sharing. Meanwhile, throughout much of the colonial world war had dislocated imperial rule. European colonialism in Southeast Asia was shattered by Japanese invasion, India had effectively been promised independence, and across sub-Saharan Africa wartime mobilizations had created the foundations of modern nation-states. Everywhere, direct imperial rule was tottering. At one level none of this was a problem for American policymakers, who expected economic ties to the United States to replace those to the old imperial powers, but Washington was concerned that anti-colonial movements might chart a revolutionary course to national independence and social transformation.

Washington Organizes Its Hegemony

In the closing stages of the war, the United States began to put in place the structures of its worldwide economic, military, and political predominance. Unlike the old colonial powers, Washington assembled a loose association of conquered enemies and subordinate allies into what has been called an "informal empire." Free of the stigma of direct colonial rule and resting on an American-dominated world economy, this informal empire displayed – and to some extent still displays – great strength and flexibility.

The Bretton Woods Agreement established the institutional framework of a world capitalist economy based on free markets and a dollar-denominated gold standard. With their economic rivals devastated by the war, this provided American manufacturers with virtually unlimited export markets for consumer products, industrial plant, and capital investment. The result was an unprecedented period of sustained economic expansion, making the American "empire," as historian Victoria de Grazia wittily points out, an "emporium."[1] At the same time, domestic demand expanded as wartime rationing ended and millions of returning soldiers took advantage of cheap loans available under the 1944 Servicemen's Readjustment Act, or "GI Bill." American manufacturers converted from producing war matériel to making cars and "consumer durables" like washing machines, refrigerators, and vacuum cleaners. The strong trade unions built during the Depression ensured that capitalist expansion was accompanied by the growth of secure and well-paid working-class jobs. The long economic upswing transformed America into an "affluent society" and a place of unprecedented – if unevenly distributed – prosperity.

Partly in response to GI protests, the American military was quickly demobilized. In another form of transnational migration, tens of thousands of "war brides" traveled to live in the United States with their new soldier husbands. Their migration was eased by the December 1945 "War Brides Act," but marriages also needed the approval of officers, who routinely denied requests by African American soldiers to marry white women. Precise numbers are hard to ascertain, but around 45 000 women came from Britain, 15 000 from Australia, and a significant number from Canada. In the immediate postwar years they were joined by thousands of German, Austrian, Japanese, and Filipina women. Officers often disapproved of relationships between white GIs and Italian women, but nevertheless around 10 000 marriages took place. Around 100 000 women entered the United States under the War Brides Act, and more arrived without benefit of its special exemptions to existing immigration law.

Wartime conscription expired in 1947, and although Selective Service was renewed the following year, relatively few men were actually drafted. But while the size of the military declined, it remained enormously powerful. Planners believed that the United States would remain the only nuclear-armed power for many years, and their anticipated "nuclear monopoly" prompted a global strategy reliant on the long-range bombers of the new Strategic Air Command. At the same time, the US Navy was reshaped around a number of powerful aircraft carrier strike forces, each capable of projecting military power across the world's oceans and into its adjacent land masses, and large fleets – the Sixth in the Mediterranean and the Seventh in the Western Pacific – were permanently based overseas. The US Army shrank dramatically, but it still maintained a strong overseas presence, particularly in occupied Germany, Italy, and Japan. When the wartime military occupations finally ended in the early 1950s, American forces remained under newly negotiated defense treaties.

America's global military presence rested on an extended network of military bases, airfields, and ports. Planning for this postwar "empire of bases" had begun during the war, with the Joint Chiefs of Staff arguing in 1943 that the creation of an "adequate" system of permanent overseas bases was a "primary war aim."[2] Before the war, the United States had a handful of overseas bases, mostly on US-ruled territory; by 1945 it had literally thousands of military outposts worldwide. The number of overseas facilities declined with the postwar demobilization, but many were consolidated into large regional bases designed for long-term occupation. Major facilities were maintained in Iceland, Greenland, and the Azores, in Morocco and Libya, and throughout Latin America. Bases studded Japan (3800 installations!), Germany, Italy, and Britain. In the Pacific, facilities in Okinawa, Guam, and Hawai'i were joined by outposts on the Micronesian islands captured from Japan and governed by Washington under a United Nations mandate. Negotiations with "host" governments to determine the details of America's military presence on foreign soil were often sweetened by economic aid packages and intertwined with deepening diplomatic and business relationships.

Ideological predominance – sometimes referred to as "soft power" – is a slippery concept that lacks the physical materiality of economic and military power. But it is no less real. The United States fought the war under the banner of the liberal internationalism enunciated in the 1941 Atlantic Charter, including support for national self-determination, open markets, international coopera-tion, religious freedom, and postwar disarmament. Much of this had previously been embodied in President Wilson's 14 Points, and it neatly combined American self-interest with high-sounding universal principle. Clearly, free trade was very much in the interests of the United States, and equally clearly American policy-makers did not intend that national self-determination should apply in most of the colonial world in the near future. This practical rejection of self-determination was underscored in 1942 by Washington's decision to underwrite the contin-uation of French colonial rule in North Africa. Despite this hard-edged reality, the liberal *ideas* that framed America's claim to global leadership, so clearly enunciated in Henry Luce's "American Century" editorial in 1941, continued to have considerable worldwide influence.

America's so-called "rules-based" liberal internationalism allowed the ruling elites of other countries to position themselves within an American-dominated world order without having to accept direct subordination to an imperial master. By framing World War II as a simple bipolar struggle between freedom and slavery, American propagandists and opinion-formers created an explanatory device that was easily reshaped to fit the new demands of the Cold War. As tension with the USSR deepened, Soviet "totalitarianism" replaced German and Japanese "militarism" as the primary enemy. The sense of moral superiority that was central to America's wartime liberalism also justified armed interventions into the affairs of "failed" states. In March 1947, the Truman Doctrine proclaimed that the United States had to "support free peoples who are resisting attempted subjugation by armed minorities or by outside pressures."[3] "Support" included direct military involvement in civil wars such as the one raging in Greece, and – of course – Washington determined who was a "free people" and who an "armed minority."

This particularly American mixture of idealism and pragmatism also shaped the formation of the United Nations (UN) as a forum through which Washington could exercise global political leadership. President Roosevelt's initial vision had centered on "four policemen" – Britain, China, the USSR, and the United States – each supervising a regional association. By the end of the war, American policymakers had moved beyond this notion, with its implication of a world divided into imperial or regional blocs, in favor of a world body based on nominally equal nation-states. At the same time Washington had no intention of abandoning its own de facto regional bloc in Latin America, whose economic, military, and diplomatic foundations had been greatly strengthened during the war. Washington encouraged its Latin American allies to join the war in time to be represented at the founding conference of the United Nations in San Francisco in April 1945, and their presence gave Washington a voting bloc that included 20 of the initial 50 member states.

As at Bretton Woods, the smaller nations helped to shape the San Francisco conference, although the main outlines of the new organization had been settled by the great powers at the Dumbarton Oaks conference held in Washington from August to October 1944. The final structure of the new world organization reflected an uneasy compromise between the General Assembly, where all admitted nations had equal representation, and the Security Council, where each of the five permanent members (Roosevelt's "four policemen" plus France) could veto proposals they disagreed with. With its closest allies dominating the Security Council and with a powerful bloc in the General Assembly following its lead, Washington could usually be sure of getting its way, a fact reflected in the decision to base the UN in New York City. Nevertheless, while the UN Charter and the 1948 Universal Declaration of Human Rights cloaked American actions in an aura of justice and international collaboration, under Washington's leadership the UN often walked a fine line. In the accelerating struggle for decolonization, for example, the UN promised to meet the national aspirations of colonized peoples while at the same time defending the imperial interests of key American allies with the argument that the colonies were not yet "ready" for full independence.

The End of Empire in Southeast Asia

In late 1945, Southeast Asia was a "connected arc of protest" as Indonesian revolutionary Tan Malaka's slogan of "one hundred percent *Merdeka* (freedom)!" resonated among nationalists fighting to prevent the reimposition of European colonial rule.[4]

In Indonesia, young radicals prompted Sukarno to use the brief window between the Japanese surrender and the arrival of British-led troops to make a formal proclamation of independence on August 17. This defiant act was quickly followed by the arrival of British-Imperial forces tasked with preparing the return of Dutch rule. Fierce fighting between nationalist *pemuda* guerrillas and British-Imperial troops backed by 35 000 "Japanese Surrendered Personnel" culminated in November in a bloody battle for the city of Surabaya. As many as 15 000 Indonesians were killed in clashes between *pemuda* fighters armed with home-made weapons and heavily armed British-Imperial troops. Despite losing Surabaya, the heroic struggle rallied support for the nationalist cause throughout the Indonesian archipelago. As British-Imperial forces withdrew, the Dutch committed large ground forces in an effort to reestablish colonial rule, violating a preliminary agreement recognizing Indonesian independence and attempting to weaken the nationalists by partitioning the country along ethnic lines. Meanwhile, Sukarno's defeat of an armed challenge from the Indonesian Communist Party won respect in Washington, and under pressure from the UN the Dutch finally recognized Indonesian independence in 1949.

The American invasion of the Philippines in October 1944 opened a bitter struggle with Japanese occupation forces that was still raging at the time Japan surrendered. At the same time, American forces and units of the Philippine Constabulary began counterinsurgency operations against the Communist-led Hukbalahap (People's Anti-Japanese Army). Hukbalahap leader Luis Taruc initially welcomed the arrival of US forces and tried to establish a working relationship with General MacArthur, but American efforts to disarm rebel fighters soon provoked sharp clashes. In February 1945 over 100 guerrillas were massacred by US and Filipino forces. Tensions were exacerbated as wealthy Filipino landlords who had collaborated with the Japanese rallied to the newly returned government-in-exile. When Washington granted the Philippines independence in 1946, Manuel Roxas – a politician described by the Office of

Strategic Services as an "exonerated collaborator" – became the first president of the Third Philippine Republic.[5] Intensified repression of Hukbalahap fighters and their peasant supporters followed as the pro-US government in Manila consolidated its position.

British-Imperial troops reoccupied most of Burma during 1945, reestablishing the structures of British colonial rule and returning prewar governor Sir Reginald Dorman Smith to Rangoon. But it was not so easy to turn the clock back. Advancing British-led troops were aided by a popular uprising led by Aung San's Anti-Fascist People's Freedom League (AFPFL), but after their experience of semi-independence under the Japanese, few Burmese fighters favored the return of British rule. The crisis unfolding in India meant that London could not rely on the Indian Army, and with the AFPFL consolidating its control in the countryside the new Labour government recognized Burmese independence. The Union of Burma was established on January 4, 1948. As in India, the British did not go quietly. Colonial administrators exploited factional divisions among Burmese nationalists and played on justified fears that the minority Chan, Kachin, Karen, and Chin people would face discrimination in the new state. On the left, radical Communists criticized Aung San's deals with the British, prompting the new government to launch a bloody counterinsurgency that culminated in 1962 in the establishment of a military dictatorship.

In Malaya, members of the Communist-led Malay People's Anti-Japanese Army (MPAJA) agreed in early 1944 to operate under the command of the British-led Southeast Asia Command, and in return they received weapons and explosives. The MPAJA welcomed the arrival of British-Imperial forces in September 1945, and the British Military Administration recognized their authority in extensive areas of the country. MPAJA promised to turn over its guns to the British, but many were stockpiled in anticipation of struggles to come. Relations deteriorated after London brokered the formation of the Federation of Malaya in February 1948 in the hope of preserving its influence in the region. As the British battled to repress a rising tide of strikes and mass protests led by rubber plantation workers and tin miners, an armed uprising – or "emergency," as the British called it – broke out. The British responded with a sustained counterinsurgency war that eventually crushed the rebellion, but they were never able to reestablish stable colonial rule and Malaya became an independent member of the British Commonwealth in 1957.

Clashes between Allied forces and local nationalists were particularly sharp in Korea and Indochina. When Soviet and American troops arrived in Korea in summer 1945 they found a nationwide network of nationalists, leftists, and Christian activists organized into Committees for the Preparation of Korean Independence (CPKI). In September 1945, CPKI representatives met in Seoul to establish the People's Republic of Korea (PRK), adopting a radical program that included land reform, the nationalization of key industries, and democratic rights including women's suffrage. In the American occupation zone south of the 38th Parallel, the American Military Government quickly abolished the PRK, but in the north the USSR recognized the government and its leader, Christian nationalist Cho Man-sik. In December, however, Moscow accepted an American proposal for a five-year joint trusteeship over the Korean peninsula pending independence. This negation of Korean sovereignty was unacceptable to Cho and other PRK leaders, and they were purged and replaced by Korean Communists loyal to Moscow. By early 1946, the PRK had been overturned, and in its place client regimes were consolidated on both sides of the 38th Parallel. In the South, Washington presided over the establishment of the Republic of Korea under American-educated anti-communist strongman Syngman Rhee, while in the North Moscow installed anti-Japanese guerrilla leader Kim Il-sung as head of the new Democratic People's Republic of Korea.

The formal end of the war also triggered a political crisis in Indochina. For most of the war, Washington had opposed the restoration of French colonial rule in Indochina as part of its general hostility to the reestablishment of a strong France. Inside Indochina, American OSS agents supported Ho Chi Minh and his Communist-led Viet Minh in their struggle against the Japanese occupation. As tensions with Moscow deepened in early 1945, Roosevelt reversed course and agreed to support the restoration of French rule. At Potsdam, the Allies agreed that Nationalist Chinese forces would enter northern Indochina to receive the surrender of Japanese troops there, while British forces helped restore French rule in the south. The Viet Minh had different ideas, and they responded to the end of the Pacific War by launching a countrywide insurrection known as the "August Revolution." On September 2, Ho proclaimed the establishment of the Democratic Republic of Vietnam (DRV) to large and enthusiastic crowds in Hanoi.

This powerful expression of Vietnamese sovereignty did not halt the British and Chinese invasions, but it did deter the Guomindang from supporting the restoration of French rule in the north. As a result, while the DRV was overturned by British-led troops in the south it continued to function in the north. The revolutionary government there was popular and deeply entrenched: as one OSS agent reported from the northern province of Tonkin in late 1945, "every village flew the Viet Minh flag" and was protected by well-organized local militias that included women and children.[6] The Vietnamese, he concluded, were "prepared to continue their struggle for years." In March 1946, Ho negotiated an agreement with Paris under which the DRV would function as a "free state" within the French Union, the new form of the French Empire. The deal did not last, and its collapse precipitated Vietnam's long war against first France and then the United States – a war that only ended in 1975.

Indian Independence and Anti-Colonialism in Africa

In India, wartime industrialization strengthened business elites tied to the Indian National Congress (INC), while Britain's mobilization of Indian personpower had the unintended consequence of boosting support for Indian independence. The depth of pro-independence sentiment at the end of the war was demonstrated by the mass support for Subhas Chandra Bose's Indian National Army (INA). Fortuitously for the British, Bose himself was killed when the Japanese aircraft carrying him into exile crashed in Taiwan on August 18, but when three INC officers were put on trial in November 1945 for "waging war against the King-Emperor" they were widely seen as Indian patriots. The INC and the Muslim League both campaigned for their release, 10 000 Royal Indian Navy sailors joined strike-mutinies protesting shipboard living conditions and supporting the INA defendants, and there were numerous small-scale mutinies and protests in the Indian Army. With their Indian troops becoming increasingly unreliable, British authorities were alarmed when 50 000 British airmen in India demonstrated to demand immediate demobilization. The three INC officers were found guilty and sentenced to deportation, but continuing protests forced their immediate release.

Under these conditions, the new Labour government in London decided to move quickly to end colonial rule in India. At the same time, however, they hoped to limit the strength and authority of the new state by partitioning the subcontinent along religious lines. The British had long favored India's Muslim minority, which had provided most of the Indian Army's professional soldiers. During the war, British officials played on fears of a Hindu-dominated India to build support for a Muslim state. Britain's exploitation of ethnic and religious divisions – part of their long-standing practice of "divide and rule" – prompted modern India's first mass outbreaks of ethnic cleansing in August 1946 and ensured that independence would be accompanied by partition. The Raj was succeeded by the two new states of India and Pakistan, and ethnic geography ensured that Pakistan was split in two, with East Pakistan later becoming Bangladesh. The process of partition was marked by riots and pogroms as previously integrated populations were violently separated. Some 14.5 million people were forcibly or voluntarily relocated, with Muslims moving to Pakistan while Hindus and Sikhs migrated to India. British policy ensured that national independence was compromised by a fratricidal division whose consequences continue to be felt today.

During the war, imperial administrators in Africa transformed their colonies into centralized polities that resembled nation-states – except, of course, that they lacked sovereignty and independence. After the war, the political consequences of this transformation became evident in the emergence and ultimate triumph of movements for national independence and decolonization. This was a slower process than in Asia, where fighting directly upended colonial rule, but it was nevertheless a direct product of the war. Initially, colonial officials hoped to revitalize the colonies in order to strengthen the metropolitan economies, and in British-ruled Nigeria and Gold Coast (Ghana) new constitutions permitted broader electoral involvement and promoted an educated African elite. France went even further. Its 1946 constitution dissolved the empire and established a multi-ethnic French Union in which – in theory – all citizens enjoyed equal rights. In practice, these schemes could not disguise the basic structural inequalities of colonialism, but they did underscore the fact that the war-weakened imperial powers could not easily control the new social and political realities set in motion by the war.

During the late 1940s Africa was swept by a wave of strikes and demonstrations as workers, middle-class professionals, and peasants all fought for better wages, improved conditions, and greater political rights. In 1947 workers on the Dakar–Niger Railway in French West Africa waged a successful seven-month strike to secure equal rights with French-born workers. Throughout the continent activists linked popular protests against harsh economic conditions to demands for national independence, and in Morocco and elsewhere many framed their demands in the language of the Atlantic Charter. Military veterans, whose outlook had been transformed by service overseas, often helped to lead protest actions and to shape the emergence of anti-colonial movements and parties.

Colonial authorities responded to these developments with intensified repression. In Morocco, leaders of the *Istiqlal* (Independence) Party were denounced as German agents and thousands of their supporters were arrested, while in Madagascar the 1947–1948 revolt against French rule was crushed with the loss of 40 000 lives. Later, the British unleashed ferocious repression against the so-called Mau-Mau rebellion in Kenya (1952–1960), while France waged a brutal war against the Algerian National Liberation Front (1954–1962). Despite these desperate efforts, it became clear that old-style colonial rule could not be maintained, and colonial authorities began to work with moderate nationalist elites to ensure that as colonies moved towards independence they remained tied into world markets as primary commodity producers.

South Africa, too, was transformed by the war as African workers migrated to take jobs in the country's mines or in its booming war industries. The 1948 electoral victory of the Nationalist Party reflected the determination of the white minority to resist the aspirations of the swelling African majority, entrenching racism and white privilege in the legal structure of the apartheid system. Apartheid segregation was backed by London and Washington, which viewed white-ruled South Africa as a key pro-Western bastion in an increasingly volatile region.

214

Nationalism, Oil, and Imperialism in the Middle East

War destabilized economic and political relations throughout the Middle East and North Africa. In Libya, the British-Imperial advance after El Alamein overturned Italian colonial rule and established a British Military Administration. Not surprisingly, Washington rejected plans for a postwar Italian or Soviet trusteeship in Libya, and in January 1952 Libya became an independent monarchy under King Idris as-Senussi. US diplomats had already begun negotiating a "Status of Force Agreement" that allowed them to reactivate the wartime airbase at Wheelus Field as part of Washington's effort to contain alleged Soviet expansionism in the eastern Mediterranean. As elsewhere, American efforts to secure what one diplomat referred to as a "slice of their sovereignty" were sweetened by economic aid to the "host" country, and Wheelus Field itself became a key center of economic activity in an impoverished region.[7] It was a double win for Washington, which gained an important military outpost while strengthening its economic and political influence in the Arab world.

During the war, American officials at the Middle East Supply Center in Cairo promoted domestic industrial development throughout the Middle East. In Egypt, wartime industrialization strengthened local elites and sharpened opposition to British oversight. London still hoped to maintain its economic predominance in the region, but American businessmen were already pushing their British rivals aside in key areas like fertilizer production and power generation. American oil companies were also poised to make further inroads into the Middle East. With State Department backing they tore up the Red Line Agreement limiting access to Iraqi oil in 1946, and by 1948 the American ARAMCO consortium – formed after Washington waived its own anti-trust laws – quickly dominated Middle East production.

While these developments benefited American businessmen and their local collaborators, the war also strengthened anti-colonial and Pan-Arab nationalism. Popular protests fused demands for social and economic justice with calls for national independence. In North Africa, nationalist protests like those in Morocco in 1944 and at Sétif the following year opened a sustained challenge to French rule, while in Cairo striking workers and students took to the streets to demand complete independence from Britain. Initially, the Syrian nationalist government of Shukri al-Quwatli enjoyed the backing of both London and Washington, whose leaders were keen – for their own reasons – to limit French influence, and in June 1945 a British military invasion effectively ended French rule. By 1949 Shukri al-Quwatli had fallen out of favor with Washington for leading the Arab League's attack on Israel and for blocking the construction of the "Tapline" oil pipeline, and he was ousted in a coup backed by the new Central Intelligence Agency (CIA).

Revolutionary change also unfolded in northern Iran, where popular nationalist revolts established new states in Iranian Azerbaijan and the neighboring Kurdish Republic of Mahabad. Both regions had been occupied by the Red Army since the 1941 Soviet–British invasion, and Moscow hoped to use these revolts to pressure Tehran into granting favorable oil contracts. Nevertheless, both were genuine popular revolutions that linked economic and social reforms to cultural and linguistic revivals. Both governments were toppled by Iranian troops in late 1946 after Anglo-American pressure forced the Red Army to withdraw. Despite these counterrevolutionary victories, popular radicalism in Iran – directed in part at wresting control of the Anglo-Iranian Oil Company – continued until an American-backed military coup overthrew the elected government of Mohammed Mossadegh in 1953.

The crisis in British-ruled Palestine was an integral part of these developments. Since the late nineteenth century, European Zionists had advocated the establishment of a separate Jewish state, and in the 1917 Balfour Declaration London agreed to the creation of a Jewish "national home" in Palestine as part of its effort to topple the Ottoman Empire. By 1939, several waves of migration had increased the Jewish community in Palestine (the *Yishuv*) to 325 000, or 3% of the population. After suppressing the 1936–1939 Arab revolt, London feared that a rising Jewish population would further destabilize its rule, and in 1939 immigration was effectively banned. "Illegal" Jewish immigration spiked after 1945 as thousands of Jewish "displaced persons," many of them survivors of the *Shoah*, headed for Palestine. Of the 100 000 people who attempted the journey, over half were turned back by British authorities.

After the war, British rule in Palestine faced mounting opposition from both Arabs and Jews, and in July 1946 the Jewish terrorist group *Irgun* bombed British military headquarters in Jerusalem's King David Hotel. With Palestine sliding towards civil war, London turned its rule over to a United Nations commission. Orchestrated by Washington, the UN proposed to partition Palestine into two ethnic-religious states. This proposal framed the establishment of the state of Israel in May 1948 and secured its rapid recognition by Washington. President Truman's support for Israel is often attributed to his desire to win Jewish votes, but while domestic electoral support was a useful by-product, American backing for Israel was motivated by the desire to create a reliable ally in this newly important region. Ironically, Stalin also hoped to secure Israel as an ally, and Moscow quickly recognized the new state.

The establishment of Israel prompted an assault by a coalition of Arab states, many of whose leaders saw anti-Zionism as a useful means of diverting popular attention away from economic difficulties and political corruption at home. In the 1948–1949 Arab–Israeli War the new Israeli Defense Force defeated the attackers and overran much of the territory assigned to the Palestinian Arabs under the UN partition. In the resulting *Al-Nakba* (catastrophe) over 700 000

Arab Palestinians were driven from their homes. They joined the victims of the British-imposed partition of the Indian subcontinent in the last of the great forced migrations produced by World War II. In Palestine and India, as in Korea and later in Vietnam, externally imposed partitions undercut the possibility for forging unified movements for social change that could bridge ethnic and religious divides.

The Partition of Europe

Much of Germany and Eastern Europe was left in ruins by the war. Millions were on the move, and many more went hungry. Cities were ruined, farmlands untilled, and industry at a standstill; in Germany, thousands of *Trümmerfrauen* or "rubble women" labored to clear millions of tons of debris by hand. The victors also suffered. Much of northern France had twice been a battlefield, and many British cities contained rubble-strewn "bomb sites" well into the 1960s. The British economy was sustained by American loans, and basic foodstuffs like tea, sugar, and eggs were rationed into the 1950s. To help solve postwar labor shortages, British officials encouraged their colonial subjects from the Caribbean and South Asia to move to the "mother country," and these war-prompted migrants began to transform Britain into a multiracial society. Today, the children of the so-called "Windrush generation" – named after the *Empire Windrush*, the ship that brought the first of them to Britain – are still battling British government discrimination.

This continent-wide chaos was gradually overcome within the political framework of the partition of Europe established at the Tehran, Yalta, and Potsdam conferences. The American military maintained a large presence in Britain, and Italy and Germany remained under military occupation until 1947 and 1955. The Red Army likewise stationed large forces in Eastern Europe. Deepening tension between the United States and the USSR, framed by Washington as an effort to "contain" Soviet expansionism, ensured that there was no all-encompassing Versailles-style peace conference. Instead, separate peace treaties with Germany's Axis allies were signed in 1947 as Washington and Moscow consolidated their respective European spheres of influence. The division of Germany was central to this process. Initially, an Allied Control Council presided over a "denazification" effort that included the trials of high-profile Nazi leaders at Nuremberg in late 1945. Despite some glaring legal difficulties – defendants were charged with crimes that had not been defined at the time they were committed – 11 top Nazis were convicted and executed. Others served long prison sentences, and several committed suicide. Tens of thousands of lower-level Nazi officials were banned from holding public office, Nazi publications were outlawed, Nazi symbols were removed from public places, and many Germans were forced to watch films highlighting the horrors of the *Shoah*.

During 1946, the denazification effort ran out of steam. Almost all the administrators in prewar Germany had been NSDAP (Nazi Party) members, and both the Allies and the Soviets needed them to run the country. At the same time, mounting tension between the former allies led to the breakdown of the Allied Control Council, with the occupying powers pursuing their own policies in the areas under their control. In eastern Germany, Moscow advanced the structural assimilation of the region into the Soviet planned economy as industries were nationalized and land confiscated from the Junker aristocracy and distributed to family farmers. Moscow tamped down labor militancy in both parts of Germany, using the revived German Communist Party in the West to calm popular protests against both the removal of industrial plant by the Soviets and the continued presence of former Nazis in the government.

The British and Americans increasingly administered their "bizone" as a single political unit, and in May 1949 they merged it with the French zone to create a new West German state (the Federal Republic of Germany), complete with its own government, currency, and (after 1955) armed forces. Moscow's attempt to derail this process by blocking land access to West Berlin collapsed after an 11-month American-led airlift kept Allied troops and German civilians supplied with food and fuel from June 1948 to May 1949. Forced to accept partition, Moscow established the German Democratic Republic (or "East Germany") in October 1949. The new regime was modeled on the police state in the USSR, and in 1953 the Soviet military was called in to help suppress statewide working-class protests against increased work quotas.

As the partition of Europe was consolidated, the popular radicalism that had marked the closing phases of the war was canalized into electoral politics. As Stalin had promised, Communists in France and Italy smoothed the formation of pro-Western regimes by ensuring that the uprisings in Naples, Marseilles, Paris, and the cities and towns of northern Italy did not turn into a generalized assault on capitalism. As a result, the revolutions of 1917–1919 were not repeated in 1944–1946. For American policymakers, the downside of this welcome development was that it gave Communist leaders seats in the governments of France and Italy, and in May 1947 Washington engineered the expulsion of Communist ministers in both countries. The following year, American officials waged an undercover "political war" to ensure the victory of Alcide De Gasperi's Christian Democrats over the Communists in the Italian general election. This success inspired covert political interventions elsewhere, and in Iran (1953) and Guatemala (1954) the newly formed CIA sponsored military coups that toppled reform-minded government.

The 1947 Truman Doctrine sanctioned American military intervention in the civil war between Greek monarchists and Communists that had resumed in 1946. Deprived of Soviet support – Stalin continued to view the Greek revolt as a dangerous challenge to the agreed division of Europe – the Communist-led forces were defeated in 1949. Greece joined the North Atlantic Treaty Organization (NATO) three years later. The Greek crisis also precipitated a bitter split between Moscow and Belgrade, which urged the USSR to back the Greek Communists. Tito was never willing to subordinate Yugoslav interests to Soviet diplomacy, and as Cold War divisions were consolidated Moscow could not tolerate his outspoken independence. Expelled from the Soviet bloc, Tito became Washington's favorite Communist and the recipient of significant American aid, and he also played a leading role in the new Non-Aligned Movement of postcolonial states.

On the economic front the 1948 European Recovery Program (ERP), better known after its principal author as the Marshall Plan, strengthened the economic foundations of capitalist Western Europe and advanced the partition of the continent. Under the ERP, Washington gave $13 billion to help rebuild shattered European economies. American policymakers believed that a stable and prosperous Western Europe was necessary to resist Soviet expansionism, but they were not blind to the fact that it created a major market for American exports. The ERP also promote greater integration between the economies of Western Europe, culminating in the establishment of the European Coal and Steel Community – the forerunner of today's European Union – in 1951. In Austria, ERP funds boosted economic recovery across the entire country and helped to prevent a German-style partition. In return, Moscow insisted that the 1955 State Treaty established Austria as a neutral state. Washington also offered ERP funds to countries in the Soviet sphere, but the potential political conse-quences of integration into US-dominated markets made their participation unacceptable to Moscow. Instead, the Soviets began to eradicate private capitalism in Eastern Europe and to advance the region's structural assimilation into the Soviet economic system by forming the Council for Mutual Economic Assistance – or Comecon – in 1949.

These developments had political consequences. In February 1948, Czech Communists staged a coup that ended multiparty politics and established one-party rule by the pro-Moscow National Front. Parallel developments took place throughout Eastern Europe as parties loyal to Moscow and backed by the occupying forces of the Red Army consolidated their political control. In the West, partition took on a new military dimension with the formation in 1949 of NATO, an American-led alliance dedicated to "containing" alleged Soviet expansionism. NATO structured a long-term American military presence in West Germany – which formally joined the alliance in 1955 – and throughout Europe and the Mediterranean. Turkey, where American pressure repelled postwar Soviet efforts to secure some control over the straits between the Black Sea and the Mediterranean, joined NATO in 1952.

Military Occupation, War, and Revolution in Asia

In contrast to four-party military occupation of Germany, the 1945–1952 occupation of Japan was an American-dominated affair. Washington's allies were assigned only minor roles, with the Soviet Union occupying South Sakhalin island – which it had invaded in August 1945 – while a 40 000-strong British Commonwealth Occupation Force policed part of western Japan. Most of the 400 000 occupation troops were American, and the Supreme Commander for the Allied Powers (SCAP) was an American proconsul, General Douglas MacArthur. In Japan, even more than in Germany, American officials had an opportunity to remake a nation-state as they saw fit, and MacArthur threw himself into the task. In June 1946, Emperor Hirohito presented a new constitution for approval by the Diet; drafted by American officials, it set up a parliamentary democracy, granted women the vote, and established a range of civil liberties. The new constitution also enshrined the position of the emperor, regarded by both American policymakers and Japanese elites as critical to the maintenance of the social order. In order to distance Hirohito from Tokyo's record of imperial aggression, several leading defendants at the American-organized war crimes trials claimed – entirely implausibly – that the emperor had taken no part in wartime decision making.

As in Germany, the occupation initially had a punitive character. War crimes trials resulted in the conviction of 25 "Class A" defendants and the execution of seven, including Tōjō. Initial American plans envisioned a largely deindustrial-ized state, and officials began dismantling Japan's remaining industrial capacity. In the light of deepening tension with the Soviet Union, however, American policymakers reversed course in 1947 and began promoting the reconstruction of the Japanese economy. Abandoning earlier plans to break up the powerful family-led *zaibatsu* corporations, American officials reorganized these monop-olies into eight major conglomerations known as *keiretsu*, which continued to dominate the postwar Japanese economy.

American-sponsored political reforms went hand-in-hand with efforts to suppress labor radicalism. Many socialist and Communist leaders initially welcomed the Americans as liberators, but the occupation authority's clamp-down on a February 1947 country-wide general strike against low wages made it clear where Washington's interests lay. By vesting power in the hands of a powerful coalition of politicians, bureaucrats, and businessmen, the American occupation enabled Japan to weather a wave of working-class militancy that paralleled postwar labor upsurges elsewhere. And, despite the fact that Article 9 of the new constitution prohibited Tokyo from maintaining military forces, American officials encouraged the formation of an armed police reserve in 1950 and of a "Self-Defense Force" – effectively a combined army, navy, and airforce – in 1954.

America's postwar military occupation allowed it to reconstruct Japan as a loyal ally, economic partner, and military outpost, but it had no such purchase in China. China was itself in a deeply contradictory situation: Chongqing presented itself as a major actor on the world stage, as signified by its membership of the UN Security Council, but at home the Nationalist government faced social and economic breakdown, mass starvation, and a growing Communist-led insurgency. At the same time, as we have seen, there were very few American "boots on the ground" in China, and GI protests in favor of rapid demobilization made it impossible to mount a major military intervention. Washington hoped to resolve these problems in the short term by promoting the establishment of a Nationalist–Communist coalition government, a project that also enjoyed Moscow's support. General Marshall made some progress in brokering an agreement during his mission to China, only to see it collapse when Chiang resumed the offensive against Communist forces in Manchuria in July 1946.

The Nationalist advance into Manchuria coincided with the withdrawal of the Red Army, and within weeks Guomindang forces had captured several major Manchurian cities. In an important symbolic victory, the Nationalists overran the CCP's storied wartime capital of Yan'an in March 1947. Like the Japanese, however, the Nationalists soon found that dominating towns and transport routes did not give them control of the countryside, where an accelerated land reform program was further strengthening support for the Communists. With hopes for a coalition government dashed, Mao defied Moscow and launched a struggle for power.

Extensive campaigning in Manchuria and northern China overstretched the Nationalist military, allowing the Communist-led People's Liberation Army (PLA) under General Lin Biao to launch a devastating series of counterattacks. As their morale crumbled, entire Nationalist units deserted to the Communists, often bringing their tanks and heavy weapons with them. A PLA offensive in September 1948 consolidated CCP control of Manchuria, triggering a broad Nationalist collapse and leading to Communist victories in a series of major battles in late 1948 and early 1949. After the PLA entered Beijing in January 1949, Moscow's pursuit of peaceful coexistence – and its consequent desire to avoid antagonizing Washington – led to a renewed Soviet effort to establish a coalition government based on the partition of China along the line of the Yangtze River. Mao rejected these attempts at foreign intervention and the PLA pushed on, crossing the Yangtze and entering Nanjing in April.

As the CCP extended its control of southern China, Chiang Kai-shek and the remains of the Nationalist army fled mainland China for the island of Taiwan. Others crossed the border into Burma, where they were supported for many years by the CIA, much to the annoyance of the new Burmese government. On October 1, 1949, Mao proclaimed the establishment of the People's Republic of China, while in Taiwan, Chiang continued to rule as president of a much-diminished

Republic of China. Chiang's position was bolstered by a ferocious "white terror" campaign against his Taiwanese political opponents, and martial law remained in force there for the next 38 years.

In its struggle with the Nationalists, the PLA waged a "hybrid" war that combined guerrilla and conventional operations. The key to victory, however, was that Communist military operations rested on a broad popular revolution. As in Yugoslavia, military advances allowed a new state to be built from the bottom up, with land reform, education, and health care organized by Communist cadres in areas controlled by the PLA. In this sense, the question of "who lost China?" that dominated American politics in the early 1950s was misplaced: in fact, a majority of the Chinese people had taken hold of their own country for the first time. From Washington's perspective, however, something vital *had* been "lost," and that was nothing less than the great prize of the war in Asia: despite its crushing victory over Japan, four years later Washington was forced to watch from the sidelines as the vast Chinese market slid from its grasp.

The global war that had emerged in 1941 from a series of regional conflicts now *un*wound into a series of localized struggles, particularly in Asia, where Great Power predominance was weaker. On June 25, 1950, the Korean People's Army (KPA) opened the last chapter in this long world war when it crossed the 38th Parallel into South Korea. North Korean leader Kim Il-sung had long advocated the reunification of Korea by force of arms, convinced that KPA soldiers would be greeted by a popular insurrection in the South. Moscow initially refused to sanction an invasion for fear of provoking a broader conflict with the United States, but emboldened by the successful test of a Soviet atom bomb in 1949 and by the victory of the Chinese Revolution the same year, Stalin finally gave Kim the go-ahead in 1950.

The North Korean advance made rapid progress, capturing Seoul and pushing South Korean and American forces back into a small pocket around the southern port of Pusan. Many South Koreans welcomed the KPA, but 200 000 of them were killed in a bloody reign of terror launched by President Syngman Rhee in response to the North Korean advance. Acting through the United Nations, Washington assembled a powerful military response to the KPA advance. Backed by massive air and naval power, American forces landed at Inchon, just south of Seoul, outflanking and halting the KPA offensive before advancing across the 38th Parallel into the North. A reunification under American and South Korean authority now seemed possible, and US commander Douglas MacArthur fantasized about taking the war into China. The new Communist government in Beijing was unwilling to tolerate an American army on China's border, and in October 1950 the Chinese People's Volunteer Army crossed the Yalu River into Korea, driving the Americans back to the 38th Parallel in a series of bitter winter battles. Despite an American strategic bombing campaign that devastated urban centers and transportation links throughout the North, the ground war deadlocked around the old partition line, where an armistice was finally signed in July 1953. At tremendous cost – nearly one million civilians were killed in the South and 1.5 million in the North – the partition of Korea was maintained.

A Short and Qualified American Century

The war in Korea consolidated the military and geopolitical balance that emerged in Asia after World War II. Washington's air and naval power enabled its land armies to reimpose the partition of the Korean peninsula, while its Seventh Fleet policed Asian waters and blocked Beijing's hopes of crossing the Straits of Taiwan to topple Chiang's Guomindang government. But Washington did not *win* the Korean War. Instead, it was fought to a halt on the 38th Parallel in a stalemate that underscored the difficulty – perhaps even the impossibility – of projecting American military force *into* Asia. Moreover, the deadlock in Korea highlighted the extent to which America's victory in World War II was qualified by the "loss" of China, the strengthening of the Soviet Union, and the destabilizing rise of struggles for national independence and decolonization.

The war ended with the United States as the world's hegemonic power: America stood at the head of a reorganized and revitalized capitalist world-economy, over which it exercised leadership through the "soft power" of its commodity culture and its liberal internationalist ideology as well as through the "hard power" of its military muscle. Yet from the very beginning of this American Century significant sections of the globe lay beyond the reach of American economic penetration, and in 1949 the Chinese Revolution dramatically expanded those regions. Hence the Cold War. This is not a *moral* judgment, and nor does it seek to prettify the undemocratic, national chauvinist, and police-state functioning of the Stalinist regimes in Moscow, Belgrade, Beijing, and Pyongyang. But it does recognize both the existence of conflicting social and economic systems and the fact that in China and Yugoslavia those systems were the product of popular social revolutions that unfolded *during* the long World War II.

The East–West tensions of the Cold War intersected with and reshaped relations between what would later be referred to as the global "North" (the "core" or "advanced" capitalist countries, most of them former imperial powers) and the "South" (the "periphery" of "developing" countries, mostly former colonies). This complex matrix gave former colonies room to maneuver between the competing superpowers and led in 1956 to the formation of the Non-Aligned Movement, in which leaders of former colonies in Egypt, Gold Coast, India, and Indonesia were joined by Yugoslavia, expelled from the Soviet bloc for its refusal to support Moscow's abandonment of the revolutionary movement in Greece.

In these complex and often contradictory ways, the American Century produced by Washington's qualified triumph in World War II structured world politics over the next decades. Today, after the overturn of the Stalinist regimes in Eastern Europe, the palpable weakening of American economic predominance, and the spectacular rise of state-capitalist China, this postwar order is unraveling with startling speed. World War II may have been a long war, but the American Century that it inaugurated turned out to be rather short.

Notes

1. de Grazia (2005).
2. Vine, D. (2015). *Base Nation: How U.S. Military Bases Abroad Harm America and the World*, 26–27. New York: Metropolitan Books.
3. Truman Doctrine, quoted in Offner, A.A. (2002). *Another Such Victory*, 207–208. Stanford: Stanford University Press.
4. Bayly and Harper (2007), 190.
5. OSS report quoted in Kolko, G. (1990). *The Politics of War: The World and United States Foreign Policy, 1943–1945*, 606. New York: Pantheon.
6. OSS political report, October 17, 1945, reprinted as an appendix to US Committee on Foreign Relations (1973). *Causes, Origins and Lessons of the Vietnam War*, 319. Washington: USGPO.
7. Heefner (2017), 51.

References

Bayly, C. and Harper, T. (2007). *Forgotten Wars: Freedom and Revolution in Southeast Asia*. Cambridge, MA: Harvard University Press.

de Grazia, V. (2005). *Irresistible Empire: America's Advance through 20th-Century Europe*. Cambridge, MA: Belknap.

Heefner, G. (2017). 'A slice of their sovereignty': negotiating the U.S. empire of bases, Wheelus Field, Libya, 1950–1954. *Diplomatic History* 41 (1): 50–77.

Further Reading

Buchanan, T. (2006). *Europe's Troubled Peace, 1945–2000*. Oxford: Blackwell.

Carruthers, S.L. (2016). *The Good Occupation: American Soldiers and the Hazards of Peace*. Cambridge, MA: Harvard University Press.

Cooper, F. (2002). *Africa Since 1940: The Past of the Present*. New York: Cambridge University Press.

Dower, J. (2000). *Embracing Defeat: Japan in the Wake of World War II*. New York: Norton.

Kim, D. (May 2010). Stalin and the Chinese Civil War. *Cold War History* 10 (2): 185–202.

Mazower, M., Reinisch, J., and Feldman, D. (eds.) (2011). Post-War Reconstruction in Europe: International Perspectives, 1945-1949. *Past & Present Supplement 6*. Oxford: Oxford University Press.

Laakkonen, S., Tucker, R., and Vuorisalo, T. (eds.) (2017). *The Long Shadows: A Global Environmental History of the Second World War*. Corvallis, OR: Oregon State University Press.

Little, D. (2002). *American Orientalism: The United States and the Middle East Since 1945*. Chapel Hill: University of North Carolina Press.

Mistry, K. (2014). *The United States, Italy and the Cold War: Waging Political Warfare, 1945–1950*. New York: Cambridge University Press.

O'Brien, P.P. (2015). *How the War was Won: Air-Sea Power and Allied Victory in World War II*. New York: Cambridge University Press.

Overy, R. (1997). *Why the Allies Won*. New York: W.W. Norton.

Vitalis, R. (1996). The 'New Deal' in Egypt: the rise of Anglo-American commercial competition in World War II and the fall of neocolonialism. *Diplomatic History* 20 (2): 211–240.

Epilogue

The trenches of the *Festungfront* Oder-Warthe-Bogen, built in summer 1944 to defend Germany from the onrushing Red Army, snake through the forests, lakes, and rivers of western Poland. Near the small village of Chycina, a stand of beech trees bears witness to the men who dug the trenches, some of whom used a few minutes of precious rest time to carve their initials into the bark. Many were Poles, and some added the name of Łódź, their hometown. Others, writing in Cyrillic, were Russians or Ukrainians. Some carved obscenities, which are joined by an enigmatic protestation of love carved in German, and also dated to August 1944. This bark text gives little away: we can only guess that the carvers were prisoners of war from one of several nearby camps, used under armed guard as forced laborers to dig trenches for the German army. Yet the bark text is also dense and complicated, carved – literally – into the landscape. It bears the initials of men who must have known that their chances of ever seeing Łódź again were slim. Yet they chose to make a mark that would last for decades, bearing witness to the fact that they had been there.

These men, and the Frenchmen and Italians who dug with them but did not carve their names, are but a handful of the vast legions of ghosts left by the global war that sprawled across the middle decades of the twentieth century. Many died unquiet deaths, and were buried in unmarked graves, or in communal pits, or at sea. They were buried without the prayers and funeral rituals appropriate to their faiths; interred, or simply "missing," far from home, they could not be properly mourned by their families and friends. There could be no tidy closure. It is surely not surprise, then, that their ghosts continue to haunt the living, imposing themselves on the texture of the postwar world, particularly in those

World War II in Global Perspective, 1931–1953: A Short History, First Edition. Andrew N. Buchanan.
© 2019 John Wiley & Sons, Inc. Published 2019 by John Wiley & Sons, Inc.

places where the killing was most intense. It is impossible to understand the postwar world without seeing these ghosts and thinking about the ways in which the living sought to redeem their suffering; it is impossible to understand the emotional significance of the Jewish settlement of Israel without listening to the ghosts of the *Shoah*, or to grasp the visceral depth of opposition to the partition of Korea without hearing the voices of those who fought for a unified, democratic, and independent nation-state occupying the entire peninsula.

Few of these ghosts speak with American accents. That is not because Americans didn't suffer and die in large numbers – they did – but because their deaths seemed to have been redeemed by victory and garlanded with moral certainty. The United States fought a war in which machines – whether crewed by Americans or supplied to their allies – played a decisive role. Theirs was primarily a war of seapower and of airplanes, a war of long-range power projection. It even *looked* different. When President Roosevelt spoke to the American people by radio on February 23, 1942, he asked them to have maps and globes ready so that they could *see* the points he was making. Roosevelt argued that in the modern age – the air age – the United States could not shirk its moral duty to provide global leadership by taking refuge behind vast oceans. Instead, he concluded, America had to fight "at distances which extend all the way around the globe."[1] In this new world, distance was measured in time, not in miles, and long-distance "airways" connected the United States – the "arsenal of democracy" – to its allies in Britain, China, and the Soviet Union.

President Roosevelt was famously photographed pondering a giant 750-pound globe given him as a Christmas present by US Army Chief of Staff George C. Marshall in 1942. American mapmakers and illustrators developed new cartographic representations to bring this heightened sense of globality to life. In images popularized through the pages of Henry Luce's *Fortune*, Richard Edes Harrison used azimuthal equidistant projections centered over the North Pole to highlight America's *closeness* to Asia and its *connection* to the entire world via a skein of "great circle" airways. These stunning maps gave graphic form to Luce's own vision, articulated in his prescient 1941 "American Century" editorial, of an interconnected, interdependent, and American-dominated world. This vision was widely shared by American elites who remade the global economic and political order in the years during and following World War II, and – as we have seen – it was backed by a military capable of unprecedented global power projection. It was not a new empire of territorial conquest, but one of bases, of global finance, and of worldwide trade; it made projects of imperial territoriality – whether the long-established colonial empires of Britain and France, or the upstart imperial-autarkic blocs projected by the Axis powers – look crudely brutal and hopelessly antiquated.

For all of this, America never had to propitiate the ghosts. They walked in different countries, from the bloodlands of Eastern Europe to the vast killing fields of Southeast Asia, and from the forced labor camps of Europe's African colonies to the famished fields of the Ganges delta. But their suffering, their slaughter, and their dashed hopes for a better world cannot, as I have tried to show, be disentangled from the more familiar – and more comfortable – narratives of "the war." They are two halves of the same walnut, and it is the enduring tension between them that gives the study of World War II its continued salience. Ghosts have long memories, and as signifiers of the end of the short American Century continue to accumulate, their voices will get louder.

Note

1. Franklin D. Roosevelt, "Fireside Chat," February 23, 1942, https://millercenter.org/the-presidency/presidential-speeches/february-23-1942-fireside-chat-20-progress-war.

Further Reading

Barney, T. (Fall, 2012). Richard Edes Harrison and the cartographic perspective of modern internationalism. *Rhetoric and Public Affairs* 15 (3): 397–433.

Black, M. (2015). The ghosts of war. In: *The Cambridge History of the Second World War*, vol. III (ed. M. Geyer and A. Tooze). New York: Cambridge University Press.

Farish, M. (2010). *The Contours of America's Cold War*. Minneapolis: University of Minnesota Press.

Kobialka, D., Frackowiak, M., and Kajda, K. (June 2015). Tree memories of the Second World War: a case study of common beeches from Chycina, Poland. *Antiquity* 89 (345): 683–696.

Index

World War II in Global Perspective, 1931–1953: A Short History, First Edition. Andrew N. Buchanan.
© 2019 John Wiley & Sons, Inc. Published 2019 by John Wiley & Sons, Inc.